A Well-Furnished Heart

Restoring the Spirit's Place in the Leadership Classroom

James T. Flynn
Wie L. Tjiong
Russell W. West

The Convergence Group
Virginia Beach, Virginia

A Well-Furnished Heart
by James T. Flynn, Wie L. Tjiong, Russell W. West
The Covergence Group, a division of Timely Word Teaching
Ministries

Printed in the United States of America

Library of Congress Control Number: 2002115555
ISBN 1-591602-86-6

Unless otherwise indicated, Bible quotations are taken from the
New American Standard Version. Copyright © 1995 by the
Lockman Foundation.

Xulon Press
11350 Random Hills Road
Suite 800
Fairfax, VA 22030
(703) 279-6511
XulonPress.com

To order additional copies, call 1-866-909-BOOK (2665).

The Convergence Group

The Convergence Group is a partnership formed to be a catalyst for change in ministry leadership education. Its focus is innovative, interdenominational and renewal-oriented theological training that meets the needs of today's emerging leaders, both nationally and internationally.

Meet the Authors

James T. Flynn, D.Min.

James Flynn has served in pastoral ministry for eighteen years. He is Administrative Dean in the School of Divinity at Regent University in Virginia Beach, Virginia. He is also President of Timely Word Teaching Ministries, which specializes in theological education and leadership development. He is married to Monica and they have four children – Stephen, Rachel, Heather, and Benjamin.

Wie L. Tjiong, D.Min.

Willie Tjiong has been involved in various capacities and levels in Christian higher education and theological education for more than 20 years in America. He is the Director of the Doctor of Ministry (D.Min.) Program in the School of Divinity, Regent University, in Virginia Beach, Virginia. Willie is married to Linda and they have two children, Joshua and Amanda.

Russell W. West, Ph.D.

Russell W. West is Associate Professor of Leadership Education at Asbury Seminary's E. Stanley Jones School of World Missions and Evangelism. He co-founded Leadership Training International, a non-profit ministry organization, dedicated to multiplying international ministry leaders in developing nations where evangelism has outpaced training. He lives in Lexington, Kentucky, with his wife, Jeri, and their son, Joshua.

Preface

In the twentieth century, the world experienced the greatest revival it has ever seen as hundreds of millions of people from every country on the face of the earth were swept into God's Kingdom by the power of the Holy Spirit. The twentieth century renewal movement, a truly international phenomena, has created churches of over 100,000 people, changed the face of whole cities and countries, as well as created a new thirst and hunger for the things of God. But, will this renewal continue? What will it take to sustain the fire that burns so brightly as we cross into a new millennium?

History clearly illustrates that if any renewal that God brings to His Church is to be sustained, it will be sustained by the effective training of a new generation of leaders to carry it forward. Each of the major renewals in America's church were sustained by raising up a new generation of leaders who knew the times and understood how to lead the church. History also demonstrates that the way Church leaders were trained has changed with each successive renewal to meet the unique needs and purposes of God for that time. Yet, theological training as it exists today is in turmoil. Many consider it to be irrelevant or unnecessary. Others have no access to the very training they need to lead the millions of new converts produced over the last few decades. What can be done to meet the needs of this generation for effective, relevant, and accessible theological training in order sustain the renewal flames that burn so brightly today? How will the harvests be preserved?

A Well-Furnished Heart: Restoring the Spirit's Place in the Leadership Classroom is a welcomed proposal for relevant ministry training for today's emerging leaders. It traces the historical role theological training has played in the great renewals of the last three centuries, illustrating the critical role it has played in sustaining renewal in the church. The book examines the root causes of the current crisis that exists in theological training as a foundation for change in the way that leaders are formed. These changes are sweeping - the hour is late and the stakes are high. Millions of souls are in desperate need of effective leadership. Radical change is needed in how we train our leaders in the Church if renewal is to continue.

In the book, authors James T. Flynn, Wie L. Tjiong, and Russell W. West bring their combined experience to bear on the current crisis in theological training to provide a prescription for change. Change must come at the level of values rather than methods. Significant paradigm shifts are needed in the way training is delivered rather than incremental modifications. Spiritual formation must become central to the whole effort of training once again, displacing the supremacy of conceptual and propositional academics in the process. Renewal distinctives must be central to theological training if it is to be relevant to the more than 530 Million Charismatic and Pentecostal or "renewal movement" oriented Christians that currently make up the fastest growing part of the visible Body of Christ.

God has already produced the fire. History is clear that the Church and its leaders play a large part in determining what will happen to renewal from here. Effective training for the Church's leaders is essential for the flames of renewal to continue to burn brightly. When critical changes to the training process are made, these changes and the leaders that are produced will act to "fan the flames" of renewal to sustain the greatest renewal the world has known to date.

James T. Flynn
Wie L. Tjiong
Russell W. West

June, 2002

Foreword

by

Vinson Synan

There are key times in history when people collectively realize a new era has emerged, displacing the former. Although remnants of the older order may remain for generations, it becomes clear their time on the stage has passed and that newer and more vital movements have become the cutting edge forces of the future. I believe it is becoming increasingly clear that Christianity, in the new millennium, will be far different from the past with vigorous new movements exploding all over the earth. Most of these will be of the Pentecostal/Charismatic variety.

I was so sure of this that I named my new book published in 2001, *The Century of the Holy Spirit: 100 Years of Pentecostal and Charismatic Renewal*. I chose this name because the Twentieth Century witnessed the most revolutionary changes in Christianity since the Protestant Reformation. In the center of this spiritual revolution was the Person and work of the Holy Spirit, who some had said was "the forgotten member of the Holy Trinity." Beginning in 1901, with one female student praying through her biblical studies homework in a Bible college, the movement ended the century with no less than 530,000,000 members and participants. The Spirit was recognized as the headmaster of that leadership classroom, and it made all the difference in the world.

The results have been astounding. The fastest-growing movements and local churches in the world are of the Pentecostal/ Charismatic variety. Mega churches that number in the tens and even hundreds of thousands of members are springing up almost everywhere. Places like Korea, Brazil, Chile, Ghana, Former Soviet Union were once mission fields; now they are sending mature and emerging missions forces throughout the world. The largest evangelistic mass crusades in history are breaking all records for attendance and mass conversions. Television and other types of mass media bring Pentecostal-style worship into the homes of masses around the world. Theme of intercessory prayer and spiritual engagement, once thought to be domain of fringe Pentecostals and Charismatics are taught in evangelical seminaries and missionary training centers as the most sought-after areas of skill and formational development.

In light of this enormously important and potent spiritual force, it is not surprising theological education will be drastically affected in the twenty-first century. Throughout this Century of the Holy Spirit, wherever fresh winds of revival blew, Pentecostals and Charismatic people established high-energy Bible institutes and ministry training schools to preserve and accelerate the revivals. The term "Topeka" now enters the lexicon because what has become the largest renewal movement to ever occur in the history of the Christian Church began in a Bible school in this small city in Kansas. What was discovered in Topeka in the context of a professor's Biblical study homework assignment has changed the world.

The results of the current renewal movement and the need to train renewal-oriented leaders in the Church have produced a convergence where renewal streams and educational streams meet to suggest a new way of doing the work of theological training. New types of seminaries and Bible Schools are being created to train leaders for this vast new ocean of Spirit-filled of believers. Older seminary paradigms will not be able to face the challenges of training pastors, missionaries, and teachers for these new churches. Indeed, with over 1,000,000 churches created by the Pentecostal/ Charismatic renewal, there must be, of necessity, a new type of educational effort to train the huge number of pastors to fill these pulpits. Since most of them are outside the Western world, they will need a totally fresh and new approach to Biblical, theological and ministry training.

This book, *A Well-Furnished Heart: Restoring the Spirit's Place in the Leadership Classroom* is written by three emerging leadership educators produced by this movement. James Flynn, Willie Tjiong, and Russell W. West have formed a team to produce this prophetic book while working in the trenches to make good on its arguments—pastoring renewal churches, planting bible institutes, mentoring doctoral ministry practitioners in leadership and renewal. They are hands-on leaders with incredible passion, vision and energy for emerging leaders of God's Church.

In this era, such schools as Regent University and its excellent School of Divinity will serve as models for a new generation of "convergence" schools that will teach the timeless truths of the Scriptures with the power and anointing of the Holy Spirit. No other model will meet the challenges of the future.

Vinson Synan, Ph.D.
Dean of the School of Divinity
Regent University
Virginia Beach, VA

Contents

CHAPTER ONE

Renewal Flames:
The Renewal Movement in
the Twentieth Century

A group of ten Christians began to meet in a living room together to seek the Lord. They all share a common experience — all have been shunned in their different denominational settings because of an experience called "the Baptism in the Holy Spirit." They bear the pain of leaving behind many longstanding friendships at the churches they come from. Some have also left family at these churches, straining their relationships with the ones they love. Other family members think their loved ones to be involved in some sort of cult . After all, who meets in living rooms for church? What goes on in these strange meetings? Why isn't church the way it has been done for decades "good enough" for them any longer?

The meetings in the living room are going well. One who can play the guitar steps up to become the group's new "worship leader." Another, who is currently a carpet salesman, agrees to lead the group and teach the Bible. There is a sense of freshness. There is also a sense of blessing and the feeling that God's presence is close at hand. The times of worship go on sometimes for two or three hours, yet time seems to stand still. The message given may not be "sermon quality," but all are hungry for more. Individual prayer after the message brings a new freedom to all who are present in the living room. The group is beginning to feel like family.

"Can we come to the living room to see what is going on?" By all means, feel free to come. At first there are ten people meeting. Then there are twenty. Within a few weeks there are thirty and then forty people attending this meeting in the living room. The obvious presence of God fills the room when the group meets. People that are addicted to drugs, alcohol, and immorality are brought to the living room and are miraculously transformed, dedicating their life to God. What is happening in this living room? Can we come and see? The floor beams are beginning to sway during worship. It is no longer safe to meet in the living room? What should we do? Should we turn them away and say we can take no more? Perhaps this is called to be something more than a living room Bible study. Could God be calling us to start a church?

We rent a temporary hall several miles from the living room. More are able to join us. At first, fifty come. Then 150 and finally 250 arrive each Sunday morning. The group in the living room has become a church. Once again, more want to come, but there is no more room. The church buys land and builds. Finally, we have a place that we can call our own. There is no more need to haul all of the set up equipment each week to the rented hall. We have room for 500 people. We start a Christian day school for our children. But, within three years we are out of room again. The solution - we will go to two services on Sunday mornings. Could this be happening? We don't have any formal training as pastors. We didn't ask for a church, we just wanted to meet in a living room where we could worship freely and not offend others with the joy of our experience with the Holy Spirit.

The fix does not last long. By 1985 there are over 1,000 people wanting to join us each morning for worship services. We can't adequately move that many people in and out of the parking lot quickly enough. Should we turn them away and say we can take no more? Can this really be happening? The church begins to build a 2,500 seat sanctuary and a massive expansion for its growing Christian school. It adds space for a benevolence ministry as an outreach to the community. Within a decade there are about 1,200 people meeting each Sunday Morning to worship together as a church. A living room with ten people has multiplied in a short time to a congregation of over 1,000 people, but this church is not alone. There are at least six other churches in the city that are experiencing the same growth and blessing. The climate of the city begins to change. Other churches take notice. Who are these people? Tell us about this experience you call "the Baptism in the Holy Spirit" — not that we will embrace it, but we are "holding the door open" to learn about what has happened in our city.

The Century of the Holy Spirit

The story related above is one that has been repeated many times over around the world. It is the personal experience of one of the authors of this book as the Charismatic renewal movement swept through his city in the late 1960s and early 1970s. This story is typical of one of the greatest renewals the modern church has ever experienced, but as Hollenweger points out, "… Pentecostals have failed to understand themselves, their history, and their experience" (Anderson and Hollenweger 1999, 20-21). Vinson Synan, a noted Pentecostal and Charismatic historian, has called the twentieth century the "Century of the Holy Spirit" (Synan 2001, ix). In just one century over 500 million people have been involved in a massive global revival that is still continuing at this time, with most of them coming to faith in just the last twenty years. The renewal has taken on such staggering proportions on an international scale that even people within the movement are not aware of the impact the renewal movement has had.

The origins of this great renewal sweeping the world lie in the Holiness and the Pentecostal renewal movements of the last half of the nineteenth century and the first half of the twentieth century. The Holiness-Pentecostal renewal movement and the Charismatic renewal movement that followed have had a profound effect on the worldwide Church. David Barrett estimates the number of Pentecostal and Charismatic Christians to be more than 523 million, making them the second largest religious block in Christianity behind the Roman Catholic Church (Barrett 2001, 4). As with previous revivals, the Holiness-Pentecostal renewal significantly changed the Church. The charismatic renewal that is currently underway promises to reshape many facets of the church in the twenty-first century as well. The Holiness-Pentecostal renewal movements together with the Charismatic renewal movement and the expanding renewal movement worldwide currently underway are known collectively as "the Renewal Movement."

Origins of the Renewal Movement

The Holiness-Pentecostal renewal movement had its origins in at least three British and charismatic movements over the last two centuries. These movements include John Wesley's Methodist holiness movement, Edward Irving's Catholic Apostolic movement, and the Keswick "Higher Life" conferences that were conducted in England and spread to America (Synan 2001, 2). The Holiness movement that originated in Methodist revivals of the eighteenth century led by John Wesley was the most decisive factor in the birth of the Holiness-Pentecostal Renewal Movement.

John Wesley was an ordained Anglican priest but experienced an evangelical conversion in 1738 that transformed his life and ministry. At his conversion, he said that his "heart felt strangely warmed" and coined the term "new birth" to describe his experience (Synan 2001, 2). From there, Wesley is noted for the pursuit of holiness in his Christian life. He and his brother are responsible for the Methodist movement that was noted for its evangelistic zeal. He birthed the idea of a "second blessing" after salvation. This experience was also known as the "entire sanctification", "perfect love", "Christian perfection", and "heart purity." It was John Fletcher, a colleague of Wesley, who was the first to call this experience "the baptism in the Holy Spirit." This experience grew to mean an unction of spiritual power accompanied by an inner cleansing, patterned after the Acts 2 experience of the baptism in the Holy Spirit and fire (Synan 2001, 2). The "second blessing" or baptism in the Holy Spirit became a cornerstone of the later holiness movement and the precursor of the defining distinctive of the Pentecostal and charismatic renewal movements of the twentieth century.

In early nineteenth century England, there was a pronounced interest in the renewal of the *charismata* (spiritual gifts) in the church. The French Revolution at the end of the eighteenth century had set off a plethora of speculation of an apocalyptic nature. Protestant scholars developed a sense of the imminent return of Jesus Christ, along with an expectation of the beginning of the millennial kingdom and a fresh outpouring of the *charismata* as on the day of Pentecost (Synan 2001, 21, 22). Edward Irving, pastor of the prestigious Presbyterian church in London's Regent Square, championed efforts to investigate supposed manifestations of the *charismata* in the form of healings and *glossolalia* (speaking in tongues). An experience that Irving had with three individuals who spoke and interpreted tongues in Port Glasgow, Scotland, convinced him of the reality of the *charismata*. From that time on Irving adopted tongues as the "outward and visible sign of that inward and invisible grace which the baptism in the Holy Ghost conferreth…" (Synan 2001, 23). In 1831, a manifestation of *glossolalia* occurred in Irving's church service and it severely divided the congregation, resulting in charges by the presbytery of London against Irving for heresy. Irving left the Presbyterian church because of these charges and founded the Catholic Apostolic Church, which emphasized the *charismata* and their function in the church as well as the restoration of the office of apostle (Synan 2001, 24). Though the Catholic Apostolic Church died out by the beginning of the twentieth century, the association of the baptism in the Holy Spirit and the manifestation of *glossolalia* were linked together by Irving's movement and became a cornerstone of the Holiness-Pentecostal Movement in the twentieth century.

In 1875, a series of conferences began in England known as the Keswick "Higher Life" Conferences. These conferences advanced a formal doctrine within the holiness movement concerning the "second blessing" or baptism in the Holy Spirit. The teaching of the Keswick Conferences displaced the holiness movement's idea of the "eradication" of one's sinful nature through the second blessing or baptism in the Holy Spirit. It instead formally reconceptualized the second blessing or baptism in the Holy Spirit experience as an "enduement of power for service", moving the emphasis from a cleansing experience to one of an anointing with power (Synan 2001, 29). The Keswick perception of the meaning of the baptism in the Holy Spirit came to define the concept embraced within the Holiness-Pentecostal and Charismatic renewal movements.

The British holiness and charismatic movements and Keswick conception of the baptism in the Holy Spirit made inroads into America in the late nineteenth century through several prominent figures. D. L. Moody was at first skeptical about any new spiritual experiences beyond salvation. In 1871, at a prayer meeting, Moody reported receiving the baptism in the Holy Spirit in a dramatic way and thereafter embraced the Keswick conception of the Spirit's baptism (Synan 2001, 30). Shortly thereafter, Moody began conducting "Higher Life" conferences in Northfield, Massachusetts, with an emphasis on individuals receiving their "personal Pentecost" (Synan 2001, 30). Through Moody and the first president of Moody Bible Institute, R. A. Torrey, the personal experience of the baptism in the Holy Spirit became a well-known evangelical belief. The work of Adoniran Judson Gordon (Gordon College) and A. B. Simpson (Christian and Missionary Alliance; Missionary Training Institute/Nyack College) also helped to mainstream the concept of the baptism in the Holy Spirit (Synan 2001, 29). For later reference in this book, it is noteworthy that all of these figures were associated with theological education and helped to champion a new movement centering on Bible institutes and colleges. This change in theological education paradigms is directly linked with revival and renewal.

The Pentecostal Movement

On January 01, 1901, at Bethel Bible School and Healing Home, in Topeka, Kansas, Agnes Osman was baptized in the Holy Spirit with evidence of speaking in tongues in a meeting conducted by Charles Parham (Synan 2001, 43, 44). She was the first of over 500 million individuals to have that experience in the twentieth century. Parham later moved his school to Houston, Texas, and had about twenty-five students, one of which was William J. Seymour.

William Seymour was born in Louisiana as the son of former slaves. He was converted in a Methodist church and was later ordained through the Church of God (Anderson, Ind.), and preached in several churches of that denomination (Synan 2001, 46). In 1905, while he was pastor at an independent holiness mission near Houston, he was exposed to the teaching of Charles Parham. Shortly thereafter, he accepted a call to minister in Los Angeles and took the message of the baptism in the Holy Spirit with him, though he had not yet received the experience himself (Synan 2001, 47). He was subsequently locked out of the Santa Fe Holiness Mission for preaching a Keswickian interpretation of the second blessing. He began holding meetings in a personal residence on Bonnie Brae Street. By April, 1906, people began being baptized with the Holy Spirit with the accompanying evidence of speaking in tongues (Synan 2001, 48, 49).

The meetings became so demonstrative that local neighbors began to come to see what was happening and the local newspaper reported on the story. After the crowds became so dense that the front porch collapsed, the meetings were moved to a warehouse in the African-American ghetto on Azusa Street. These meetings quickly grew into a global phenomena that crossed racial, ethnic, educational, class, and denominational lines with the baptism of the Holy Spirit. These meetings were charged with dynamic worship and eventually included people visiting from many different states and foreign countries in the two notable revivals that took place between 1906-1909 and 1911-1912. These visitors took the message of the baptism in the Holy Spirit and their own personal experience with them when they left, rapidly disseminating the message and experience on an international scale (Synan 2001, 56-93). Various denominations such as the Assemblies of God, The Church of God, Pentecostal Holiness denominations, and the Four Square denominations were formed to capture the momentum of the movement. The movement has grown to the point in the non-Western world that 75% of all non-Western indigenous denominations are Pentecostal (Land 2001, 21). Despite its international impact, for six decades (1901-1960), Pentecostalism was seen to be outside the bounds of respectable Christianity until it sparked the modern Charismatic Renewal Movement in the 1960s that has since impacted the entire spectrum of Christianity (Barrett 2001, 19).

The Charismatic and Neo-Pentecostal Renewal Movements

In the 1960s, an unprecedented move of the Holy Spirit began that has resulted in worldwide revival on a scale never before seen in the Christian faith. This movement began in 1960 with spontaneous outpourings of the Holy Spirit within denominational church settings that had been typically resistant to the Baptism in the Holy Spirit. The movement has been called the Charismatic movement and was originally associated more with the Roman Catholic Church, but has spread on a global scale to all 150 non-Pentecostal traditions, within 9,000 ethno-linguistic cultures, representing 8,000 languages, and covering 95% of the world's total population (Barrett 2001, 19). Pentecostal, Charismatic, and neo-Pentecostals now represent 27.7% of all Christians globally in 740 Pentecostal denominations, 6,530 non-Pentecostal denominations, and 18,810 independent denominations and networks (Barrett 2001, 19).

The Holiness-Pentecostal revival that began in the early 1900s has continued to the present day but took a decidedly different direction beginning in 1960. In November, 1959, Anglican priest Dennis Bennett was baptized in the Holy Spirit and exhibited the evidence of speaking in tongues. At that time he was the rector of St. Mark's Episcopal Church in Van Nuys, California. Many in his congregation subsequently received the same experience, but as a result of controversy, Bennett was asked by the bishop overseeing him to leave his church (Synan 2001, 151-155). He then received a call to St. Luke's Episcopal Church in Seattle, Washington, which became a center for renewal in the Episcopal church. Bennett's experience with the baptism in the Holy Spirit was the beginning of a distinct phase in American church history in which the emphasis seemed to switch to renewal within established mainline denominations, in particular those with a sacramental orientation. Bennett's experience marks the beginning of what has come to be known as the Charismatic Movement. The movement has spread within the Anglican church to the point where in 1994, 400 out of 7,200 parishes were involved with Charismatic renewal (Synan 2001, 158).

The Charismatic movement did not stay confined to the Anglican Church. Harold Bredesen, a Lutheran pastor, had some years earlier received the baptism in the Holy Spirit while working in New York. Through the 1960s, he led many into an experience with the baptism in the Holy Spirit including Pat Boone, Pat Robertson, and many others within his own Lutheran denomination (Synan 2001, 159). By 1980, between 1 and 1.7 million Lutherans were involved in Charismatic renewal (Synan 2001, 165).

Charismatic renewal continued to spread within mainline denominations throughout the 1960s and 70s. The Presbyterian, Nazarene, Southern Baptist, and United Church of Christ and Methodist churches are just some of the mainline denominational churches that experienced Charismatic renewal (Synan 2001, 166-203). The Presbyterian church was historically associated with the First and Second Great Awakenings. Edward Irving and A. B. Simpson, both Presbyterian, contributed to the modern Holiness-Pentecostal renewal movement in its earliest phase. The Charismatic renewal swept through the Presbyterian denomination in the 1960s. By 1985 there were nearly 250,000 Charismatics in the Presbyterian and Reformed Presbyterian churches in America (Synan 2001, 173).

The events most often associated with the Charismatic Movement are its effects on the Catholic church. On February 18, 1967, at the Ark and the Dove Catholic Retreat House just north of Pittsburgh, Pennsylvania, twenty-five Catholic students from Duquesne University were baptized in the Holy Spirit (Synan 2001, 209). Two Catholic faculty members at Duquesne University, Ralph Keifer and Bill Storey, had previously been baptized with the Holy Spirit after being prayed for at a Presbyterian Bible study at the home of Flo Dodge near Pittsburgh (Synan 2001, 211). The baptism in the Holy Spirit that occurred in the retreat setting, later known as the "Duquesne Weekend," quickly spread throughout the Catholic Church, especially through the route of Catholic universities such as Notre Dame (Synan 2001, 212, 215). The Catholic Charismatic renewal movement went on to be officially recognized at the highest levels of the church. This recognition includes a positive statement by United States bishops in 1969 and a Catholic Charismatic renewal conference held at St. Peter's Basilica in Rome in 1975 with more than 10,000 in attendance (Synan 2001, 216). Phases of the Catholic Charismatic renewal movement include a rapid growth phase in the United States (1970-1980), an integration into the Catholic church (1980-1990), and an international expansion of the movement (1990-2000) (Synan 2001, 218-230).

Since 1970, the Charismatic renewal has taken on a decidedly global nature. Many mainline denominational Christians were not prepared to leave the state churches in Western Europe and Asia to become Pentecostal in the early 1900s. Since 1970, the mainline denominational churches in both Europe and Asia have become massively pentecostalized with the members remaining within their mainline denominational churches (Barrett 2001, 19). As of the year 2000, there were over thirty-seven million renewal-oriented Christians in Europe and 137 million in Asia. This is compared with over 79 million in North America (Barrett 2001, 20). In some circles, the global nature that the Charismatic movement has taken on since 1970 has been described by the term "neo-Pentecostal" to tie it to the Pentecostal movement that began in the early 1900s. Another interesting distinctive of neo-Pentecostal churches is that many do not place an emphasis on the evidence of speaking with other tongues that accompanies the baptism in the Holy Spirit as has been common in the Holiness-Pentecostal and Charismatic Movements. In all, the combine renewal movement today has touched every continent, 236 different countries, and compose the majority of the world's "mega-churches" (50,000 or more members) (Barrett 2001, 19).

Questions about Theological Training

With over 530 million people within the renewal-oriented block of Christianity, many having been converted in just the last ten to fifteen years, it is not surprising that theological education is undergoing a transformation to meet the needs of the Body of Christ. Beginning in 1980, older forms of theological education have been called into question because they do not seem to meet the multicultural, interdenominational, and contextual needs of the massive number of non-Western believers that have been born into the Kingdom of God. The exuberant worship, anti-liturgical mindset, and passion of the Pentecostal renewal movement seems especially appealing in these non-Western settings, making converts in the non-Western World now estimated now to number over 154 million in number (Johns 1993, 63; Solivan 1998, 31-32). Renewal has swept through the African and Asian continents, with the world's largest church now existing in South Korea (Anderson and Hollenweger 1999, 20-21). This is also true in Latin and South American settings where renewal-oriented churches have become "… the largest church of the poor in the world" and the gospel message has fueled a vital movement to address social issues

(Solivan 1998, 30). The movement to address social, political, economic, and issues of injustice within these renewal settings has been termed "conscientization" and caused some to reexamine the whole pedagogy of theological education (Johns 1993, 11). Hollenger has noted that Pentecostal theology is revolutionary in these settings because it offers a truly viable alternative to Liberation Theology (a theology that promotes radical social redemption with Marxist presuppositions). At the same time "defrosts frozen theology" for those in a theological training context (Johns 1993, 19). In some cases, standard models of theological training have been dismissed as excessively expensive and irrelevant. In other cases, new forms and delivery models are emerging to contextualize theological education for the new task at hand. These models tend to be praxis-oriented, rather than information centered. The knowledge of God in these types of settings is not measured by how much information is transferred to the student, but rather by how one is living in response to God (Johns 1993, 35).

The Charismatic and neo-Pentecostal renewal and some of the paradigm changes that it has created have helped to catalyze a mounting crisis in theological education on a worldwide basis. Stephen J. Land points out that the "Full Gospel" message of justification by faith, physical healing provided in Christ's atonement, and an emphasis on the pre-millennial return of Jesus Christ that are trained in renewal theology have challenged standard paradigms for theological training (Land 2001, 18, 89). Through the 1980s and 90s, a debate has intensified in theological education circles as to how to address the changing situation in the body of Christ and prepare its emerging leaders for ministry. The renewal movement in the twentieth century has also progressively blurred the distinction between clergy and laity as distinct classes, continuing the trend started by Luther that recognized the "priesthood of all believers." This has led to increased demand for theological education that equips both clergy and laity for the work of the ministry, envisioning leaders as part of the church body rather than a separate elite group (Kinsler n.d., 4- 5). The rapid expansion of Christianity on a global basis has also produced the need for rapid preparation and deployment models for theological education that are economical and do not require individuals to leave their context of ministry

(Kinsler n.d., 6). Logistical and economic constraints simply do not permit the investment in relocation, travel, or formal seminary training over a period of seven years that are common in Western theological education. The economics will also not support investment in large stand-alone seminaries with expensive buildings and tenured faculty. Many of the emerging leaders do not have access to the undergraduate education required for graduate level theological education also common in the West. These economic and logistical constraints have birthed a trend toward theological extension education that originated in Latin America during the 1960s. Cheryl Bridges Johns, in her book *Pentecostal Formation,* points out the powerful impact that discipleship and the personal formation process within the renewal movement has had on millions of individuals in Central and South America. Many have literally come to "own and articulate the Christian story," yet our attempts to capture these same strengths in more formal Christian education have been less successful (Johns 1993, 7).

A survey of literature over the past two decades clearly illustrates that key individuals in theological education realize that something is drastically wrong and that something must be done to change theological education. The literature is filled with suggestions for how to fix things, but most often the perspective on how to fix things comes from those from evangelical circles where individuals do not understand what is happening with the renewal movement or who flatly reject the movement and its distinctives. In proposing their solutions, they do so while ignoring the largest block of Christians in the Body of Christ outside the Roman Catholic Church. It is time that those with a renewal perspective embrace the problem of how to adequately train leaders in the Body of Christ and begin to offer solutions that will meet the unique needs of emerging leaders in the renewal setting.

Theological training has changed with each successive renewal that God has sent to the Body of Christ. Lessons learned from past history illustrate that unless a generation of leaders arise to meet the challenge of capturing the essence of the renewal through systematically training and equipping a new generation of leaders, the renewal fires will die out. The renewal flames are burning brightly at this time. Now is the time to train a new generation of leaders to capture the essence of what God is doing and to pass the renewal on to further generations of people waiting to be born into the Kingdom of God. As this new generation of leaders is trained, the act of training will literally be one of "fanning the flames" of renewal for future generations.

CHAPTER TWO

"But They Put New Wine Into Fresh Wineskins..." The Role of Theological Training in Renewal

The church continues to grow and there are nearly 1,200 people attending on any given Sunday morning. What had begun as a living room Bible study only eight years before had mushroomed into one of the largest churches in the city. How could this have happened in such a short amount of time? What is the secret to such growth? Can we visit your church and have you explain to us how we can have a church and Christian school like yours?

You can come and visit, but we don't really understand all that has happened to us either! We did not ask for a church. We were content to meet in the living room or the hall. We loved the intimate times in the living room and the sense of awe and wonder at what God was doing. Now, this whole thing has begun to overwhelm us. Should we hire multiple staff to lead a church of this size? Where should this staff be trained? How does one manage a budget of over $1,000,000 annually? How should we structure the leadership of the church - elders, deacons, and boards? What about the by-laws, board meetings, financial controls, audits, 501(c) 3 non-profit issues? What about bond-issues and conventional financing for our sanctuary expansion? Should we hire a general contractor? How can we have an effective evangelism outreach to the community and missions outreach to the world? What makes a small group effective? All of a sudden, this doesn't seem like the living room church that began a few years back!

Where can we go to learn these things? We don't have time for Hebrew, Greek, or Systematic Theology right now - we have to run a church! What do you mean we can't attend your seminary without an undergraduate degree? We are years away from an undergraduate degree right now and we need answers to our questions. From the looks of things, your courses don't seem to address the questions and issues we have anyway. It looks like we will just have to make do with what we have learned from our experiences to date and fly by "the seat of our pants." God, we sure hope you are going to continue to walk through this time with us. We seem to be way beyond our knowledge and skills but have gone to far to turn back now!

Such were the high and low points of riding the crest of the wave of renewal that swept through the American church in the 1980s and 1990s. It was a time of great elation at the growth and evangelism that was taking place. It seemed that every week brought with it a new challenge or obstacle, but God was ready to meet that obstacle with a miracle or fresh word of direction. Without a doubt this same scenario repeated itself many times and in many places. Renewal created tremendous opportunities as well as tremendous challenges. This same scenario is being repeated many times over on a global basis today as renewal is occurring at a pace that has no end in sight.

The questions being asked by leaders in the renewal movement today are the same as those asked several years ago by one of the authors of this book as related above. Where can I go to get the answers I need to make this whole thing work? Who can offer me the much needed relevant knowledge and skill-base I need to capture the renewal that my church is experiencing? The answer should be found within theological education circles, but theological education is also in a crisis of its own as it seeks to come to grips with what God is doing through the renewal movement today. Many in theological education circles realize that how this crisis is resolved will determine whether theological education, as it exists today, survives or crashes or is discarded as irrelevant. Most are at least apprehensive, if not downright fearful, of the changes that must take place in order to make the whole enterprise of theological education relevant. Nearly all are grappling with hard questions as to how to change.

Change is not new to theological education, nor is the reason for change new. A study of American church history and renewal in the Church clearly show that as renewal has taken place, American theological education has had to make some major adjustments to capture what God was doing in the renewal. Many of these changes have been difficult and imperfect. Nearly all started out as an innovative solution to the new problems that renewal in the church has created. These changes were strongly resisted by established institutions offering theological education. Still, those pioneering the needed changes in theological training for a church in renewal learned some valuable lessons in making that training relevant and accessible to the emerging leaders of their time. They stand as an example for this generation as it seeks to fan the flames of the current renewal. The understanding of how theological training has adapted to past renewal serves as a platform for how it must change for this generation.

The First Great Awakening and Theological Education

The late 1600s and early 1700s saw considerable controversy develop in the New World over orthodox belief. Many of these controversies centered on the depth of Calvinism to be embraced and church polity. Other more serious controversies, as in the case of the Unitarian Church, revolved around basic orthodox beliefs concerning the Trinity and nature of God. Developments in theological education were in many cases driven by these controversies. Harvard College had a history of escalating theological liberalism, which in part lead to the establishment of Yale College in 1701 in order to preserve a more conservative form of Calvinism. The liberal trend at Harvard continued and in 1805 it embraced a Unitarian tradition (Gambrell 1967, 57). Both Yale and Harvard reacted against the "revivalist" movements spawned by the Great Awakening that occurred between 1735 and 1740 (Gambrell 1967, 21, 60).

The Great Awakening in the Colonies in the first half of the 1700s transformed the shape of colonial religion and its religious institutions. The preaching of Jonathan Edwards and George Whitefield introduced a whole new revivalistic paradigm to American religion. In 1720, German Pietist T. J. Frelinghuysen arrived in the Dutch Reformed churches in New Jersey and began preaching a revivalistic message. He was responsible for reaching out to the Irish and Scottish in Philadelphia and New Jersey with the gospel and theological training. He mentored Gilbert Tennant, an Irish Presbyterian minister and evangelist, and others in the paradigm of revivalistic preaching and evangelism (Synan 2001, 420). This form of revivalistic preaching and evangelism spread to the frontiers of the colonies and was championed by Jonathan Edwards. The period of the Great Awakening lasted from 1725-1770. The emphasis on conversion, move toward a more Arminian view of salvation, a tendency toward progressive millennialism, and a call to "concerts of prayer" for national and world-wide evangelism were some of the distinctives that marked this movement (Synan 2001, 421; Gambrell 1967, 21).

The Great Awakening seems to have been God's response to the Age of Enlightenment that was coming upon Europe and making its way into America (Gambrell 1967, 21). The Enlightenment's emphasis on reason as the way to acquire knowledge was laying the groundwork for a very rational form of Christianity to take hold in this country. The First Great Awakening produced a different paradigm of Christian faith that was more dependent upon relationship with God than reason and the emphasis on a personal experience with God rather than a corporate experience in a church setting through the sacraments. The distinctives of the First Great Awakening were largely rejected by the conservative Presbyterian and more liberal Congregationalist and Unitarian denominations, producing a number of different splits and sects.

The Great Awakening brought traditional doctrine into question in the American colonies and also served to accentuate controversies that were already in place. The Congregationalist practice of admitting the unconverted that were baptized as infants to church membership and sacraments under the "half-way covenant" produced fertile ground for asserting salvation through conversion. Churches in New England became filled with people who were baptized as infants but who had not experienced religious conversion (Gambrell 1967, 29, 30). The churches became ripe for a more Arminian view of salvation that required evidence of actual behavior and a conversion process apart from election that demonstrated salvation. Revivalistic preachers began preaching religious conversion as opposed to infant or adult baptism for salvation. The targets of many revivalistic sermons were the unconverted in the churches of New England, which naturally angered many of the traditional churches. The preaching also reacted against the deism and Arianism that was gaining acceptance in the denominational churches and schools of that time (Gambrell 1967, 30). Before long, there was a cry for a renewal in theological education that would support the new revival that was occurring in the colonies and for additional clergy to pastor the large numbers of new converts the First Great Awakening produced.

In his sermon entitled "The Danger of an Unconverted Ministry" (1740), Gilbert Tennant called for a new way of educating pastors that would sustain the flames of revival sweeping through the Colonies:

> The most likely method to stock the church with a faithful ministry, in the present situation of things, the public academies being so much corrupted and abused generally, is to encourage private schools, or seminaries of learning , which are under the care of skillful and experienced Christians...(Frasier 1988, 3),

This call for a new kind of minister was, by definition, a call for renewal in theological education and a reaction against the liberal movement in some of the established schools of the era. Many new sects were born from the evangelistic style of preaching common to the First Great Awakening. Jonathan Edwards was responsible for reaching Massachusetts and the Connecticut River valley with revival. Jonathan Dickerson and Aaron Burr were responsible for similar revival in New York and New Jersey. George Whitefield's preaching tours from Maine to Georgia further propagated the revival and served to unify the awakening throughout the colonies. The Presbyterian church itself was split into pro-revival (New Side) and anti-revival (Old Side) factions, being deeply divided over the Great Awakening and its results (Frasier 1988, 4). Additional controversy developed when ministers were raised up to pastor new congregations on the frontier composed largely of converts from the revivals. They began to pastor without "proper education" as was dictated by the standards that existed at that time. Some were denounced and censured. Others were recalled from successful pastorates with orders to acquire a "proper education." The events surrounding the Great Awakening called into question what was necessary to constitute a quality theological education that prepared the minister for his calling (Frasier 1988, 4, 5).

One of the most important developments in theological education as a result of the Great Awakening was the "Log Cabin College" movement. The Log College movement began with Gilbert Tennant, whose controversial sermon calling for change in theological education was quoted earlier.

Tennant was educated at the University of Edinburgh before coming to the New World in 1706 (Fraser 1988, 6). He served as a pastor in New York and Pennsylvania and developed an educational program for his sons patterned after the education received in Scotland. After settling in Neshaminy, Pennsylvania, in 1727, he included others in the educational program he had developed for his sons. He purchased additional land in 1735 and began using the log cabin attached to his home for college level instruction, educating two or three ministers a year until his retirement in 1742 (Fraser 1988, 6). George Whitefield himself commented on the effectiveness of the operation stating that it was "…bringing up gracious youths, and sending them out from time to time into the Lord's vineyard" and going on to state:

> The place where the young Men study now is in Contempt call'd *The [Log] College.* It is a Log-House, about Twenty Feet long, and near as many broad; and to me it seemed to resemble the Schools of the Prophets - For that their habitations were mean, and that they sought not great Things

for themselves, is plain from that Passage of Scripture, wherein we are told, that at the Feast of the Sons of the Prophets, one of them put on the Pot whilst others went to fetch some Herbs out of the Field. ...From this despised Place Seven or Eight worthy Ministers of Jesus have lately been sent forth; more are ready to be sent, and a Foundation is now laying for the instruction of many others [*sic*]. (Fraser 1988, 6; Gambrell 1967, 102)

Whitefield predicted that "The devil will certainly rage against them...", and such was the case, especially from the Old Side Presbyterian who railed against their product as "unqualified" (Fraser 1988, 7). Despite the criticism, the Neshiminy Log Cabin School produced a list of famous graduates who, in turn, became college and academy presidents themselves, as well as a good number of revival-oriented preachers to make the Great Awakening movement a viable force. By 1758, ten of the ninety-eight Presbyterian ministers in the local synod were graduates of this one college (Fraser 1988, 6).

Samuel Blair started Faggs Manor Academy in Faggs Manor, Pennsylvania, in 1740. He introduced the study of "moral and physical sciences, as well as the languages and theology" to the curriculum, an important development to the curriculum of log cabin schools (Fraser 1988, 8). His graduates include Robert Smith, who founded Pequea Academy in Pennsylvania and Samuel Davies, who went on to become the president of Princeton College some years later. By the end of the eighteenth century, sixty-five Presbyterian log cabin academies had come into existence, helping to spread the gospel into the Western frontier of the colonies and training a new breed of minister to be pastors in the frontier churches (Fraser 1988, 8).

Whitefield's comparison of the "school of the prophets" in the Old Testament with the frontier log college was appropriate for more reasons than one. There was an obvious similarity in simple accommodations at the log colleges when compared with the Old Testament school of the prophets. The more significant similarity lies in teaching method. The log cabin colleges were based on an apprenticeship between an experienced pastor (often nicknamed an "Elijah") and his students. The students would learn by "reading divinity" under the direction of the pastor, and then put what he was learning into immediate practice as they accompanied the pastor in his everyday pastoral duties. This was in sharp contrast to traditional colleges that were already beginning to drift toward liberal and secular philosophies in their curriculum and often lacked any practical application of what was learned (Gambrell 1988, 102, 103). The task of "reading divinity" that was done by the students in a log college and the student's attachment to a skilled practitioner in the educational process was very similar to the method for preparing physicians and lawyers for their professional roles in that time. The curriculum had a base of Latin, Greek classics, and biblical languages for its superstructure. It seems that even in the midst of revival, there was no move to subtract from the curriculum the Latin and Greek classics that were held in European educational models to be the mark of an "educated gentleman" (Fraser 1988, 20, 21). The pattern of "reading divinity" and the classics under the direction of an educated and skilled mentor was ideal for a frontier environment. Multiple faculty members with specialization in training were impractical (Fletcher 1983, 7).

The log cabin college method of instruction had a profound direction on the establishment of the Presbyterian churches on the frontier at that time — Pittsburgh, Pennsylvania. Education and the establishment of the church on the "Western frontier" were due in large part to the establishment of Log Cabin colleges in the Pittsburgh area, which spawned the area's first churches and institutions of formal education. John McMillan was involved in founding Canonsburg Academy, Washington Academy, Jefferson College, and Western Theological Seminary in the Pittsburgh area from humble beginnings in a log cabin setting (Fraser 1988, 14, 15). All of these schools, both secular and sacred, flourished in the 1780s and led to several schools, including Pittsburgh Theological Seminary, which have their descendants in the Pittsburgh area today.

The Great Awakening not only spurred the Log Cabin College Movement, but also gave birth to a proliferation of colleges along denominational lines and along lines of division within individual denominations, such as Old Side and New Side Presbyterian schools. During the period that followed the First Great Awakening, colleges such as Princeton (1746), Brown, Rutgers, and Dartmouth (1746) call came into existence. Kings College and the College of

Philadelphia both came into existence through opponents of the Great Awakening. Many colleges on the Western and Southern frontiers patterned themselves after revivalist tradition and the log cabin format (Fraser 1988, 10, 11).

During the last half of the eighteenth century, curriculum in these colleges eventually changed along denominational and philosophical lines. The larger colleges, such as Harvard and Yale, transitioned into more liberal and secular universities but retained their divinity components. Study in classical languages (Latin, Greek, and Hebrew) continued but other specialized oriental languages were added to the curriculum such as Chaldean and Syriac. Harvard and Yale began offering Bachelor of Arts degrees in the tradition of the European university. Theological education in the larger schools developed into a three year course of study of directed reading under the direction of a professor, culminating in a thesis by the student and the awarding of a Master of Arts degree (Gambrell 1967, 84-91). The Revolutionary War and the drive toward independence in the colonies in 1776 occupied much of the attention and energy of the new country and all but stopped further development in the United States of the schools delivering theological education in all of their forms (Fraser 1988, 22, 23). The country was ready for a new religious awakening in both the church and theological education.

The Second Great Awakening and the Rise of Theological Seminaries

At the beginning of the nineteenth century, another round of worldwide revivals occurred known as the Second Great Awakening, or simply the "Second Awakening", which lasted from 1800-1840 (Synan 2001, 237, 422). The beginnings of the Second Awakening can be traced to Cane Ridge, Kentucky. Three Presbyterian ministers at the Red River Presbyterian Church in Cane Ridge, James McGready, William Hodges, and John Rankin, led meetings that had as many as 25,000 people in attendance, which were eventually moved into the surrounding forest for lack of space (Synan 2001, 167). This revival quickly spread to the frontier between the years of 1810-1840. The revival movement was accompanied by a renewed religious passion in the church, spiritual manifestations that were also common to the First Great Awakening, and a large number of converts. The sheer number of converts forced ministers who had not been formally trained to enter pastoral ministry, creating a fresh controversy in the Presbyterian church over educational requirements for ordination and ministry (Synan 2001, 167). The Second Awakening once again resulted in new sects being formed within denominational churches (i.e., the Cumberland Presbyterian denomination that embraced the awakening) and formed the basis of the holiness revivals in the later half of the nineteenth century. These changes in the American church also produced a corresponding change in the way theological education was delivered in America as well.

The Second Awakening brought with it once again a call for reform in theological education. One of the forces calling for reform was Charles Finney, a former Presbyterian, who became one of the most outstanding revivalists of his day and one of America's first professional evangelists (Synan 201, 167, 168). When Finney was converted, he was convinced he was called to preach. He wanted to begin his preaching and forego the formal training required in his day, impatient to get to work in ministry (Fraser 1988, 57). His attitude can be seen in the remarks he made about his presbytery's call for him to get formal theological training:

> Some of the ministers urged me to go the Princeton to study theology, but I declined… and when urged to give them my reasons, I plainly told them that I would not put myself under such an influence as they had been under; that I was confident that they had been wrongly educated, and they were not ministers that meet my ideal of what a minister of Christ should be (Fraser 1988, 57).

This attitude was typical of many during the Second Awakening that grew to distrust formal theological education.

In the realm of formal theological education of the early nineteenth century, lines of division were also being drawn. In 1805, Harvard called a known Unitarian minister to be its college president, making a statement about the liberal direction the school was taking. In 1801, Yale College, under the direction of Timothy Dwight, experienced revival (Fraser 1988, 29). The resulting conversion of many of those studying for ministry helped to supply the preachers of the Second Awakening. Dwight and those that directly followed him felt that America had moved away from an orthodox faith toward deism and Enlightenment-based rationalism after the Revolutionary War (Fraser 1988, 30). He viewed the Second Awakening as a means to return America "to its true faith" and hopefully avoid the results of deism prevalent in revolutionary France and stem the tide of barbarism so common on the American frontier (Fraser 1988, 30). Dwight saw education as an important means to address the deist and frontier issues as well as the anti-Calvinist Unitarian views prominent in New England.

One of the developments in the upheaval caused by division in the theological education community and church was the advent of a new means of training ministers — the theological seminary. The theological seminary began with the founding of Andover Theological Seminary in 1808. The idea of a stand-alone theological seminary was conceived to address the problem of what was perceived to be increasing liberal tendencies in the established colleges of the day. University models for theological education became increasingly influenced by German ideals originating at the University of Berlin in 1810 that modeled a professional ideal for ministry. The stand-alone seminary allowed theological training to be specifically adapted for denomination distinctives and even more finely tuned for philosophical views such as pro or anti-revival views. When Harvard College installed a Unitarian president in 1805, Eliphalet Pearson resigned in protest from the faculty. He and several other supporters drafted plans for a stand-alone seminary in Andover to counterbalance the perceived heresy at nearby Harvard. Andover Theological Seminary opened on September 28, 1808, with nineteen students waiting for admission and thirty-six the following year (Fraser 1988, 31-35).

Andover Theological Seminary laid down a pattern for theological education in America that exists to this day. Andover affirmed the need for a classic undergraduate education that to this point in history was viewed as an end unto itself in preparing an individual to function in life. Andover championed the view that a classical undergraduate education was a better form of preparation for further studies and not necessarily complete in and of itself (Fraser 1988, 38). Andover became a model for professional education at a graduate level in theology. This view caught on as well in law and medicine in the following years (Fraser 1988, 38). Andover had a rigid format for studies as opposed to the theological reading done in earlier times at a university level under the guidance of a professor. The first year concentrated on sacred literature (Bible), followed by a second year of Christian and Natural Theology. The third year was devoted to Sacred Rhetoric (preaching) and Ecclesiastical History (Fletcher 1983, 9). The goal was to use the undergraduate exposure to Hebrew and Greek to build a basis for biblical exegesis. This same pattern for seminary education exists to a large degree in seminaries to this day.

The seminary movement resulted in a proliferation of theological seminaries that were founded along denominational and idealistic lines. By 1831, there were a total of twenty-two seminaries registered with the American Education Society (Fletcher 1983, 10). Two major Protestant seminaries in Pittsburgh had their origins in this time period. The Reformed Presbyterian Theological Seminary had its origins in 1810, shortly after Andover. Pittsburgh Theological Seminary's antecedent, Western Theological Seminary, was also founded in this time period. Pittsburgh Theological Seminary in particular has had a profound effect on the city. Both seminaries continue to this day.

In addition to the seminary movement, the Second Awakening also spawned several other means of theological education. The Methodist Episcopal Church in particular reacted strongly against the idea of formal theological education and the establishment of theological seminaries. The negative reaction was based on the grounds that these formal stand-alone seminaries, separated from the rest of the church, would cause ministers to "… lose their spontaneous dependence on the Holy Spirit" (Fraser 1988, 83). The Methodists instituted a system of informal apprenticeships between aspiring ministers and experienced pastors within the setting of local congregations (Fraser 1988, 84). The Disciples of Christ, under Alexander Campbell, launched a new effort called the "School of the Preachers" which consisted of preacher's institutes where Disciples preachers could spend an entire week with their peers in theological reflection (Fraser 1988, 85-87). Methodism also pioneered methods of informal theological education through its renowned system of circuit riders. A two to four-year period was spent in apprenticeship with a circuit rider before the candidate for ministry was examined. Having passed the examination, he was then given his own circuit to pastor (Fraser 1988, 89-90).

All of these systems of theological education, including the theological seminary, illustrate the profound need for theological education to be contextualized to meet the needs of the church and ministerial preparation of a certain time. Once again with the Second Awakening as with the First Great Awakening, revivalism played a major role in redefining the way theological education was delivered. This would not be the last time that this happened, as can be seen with the changes that accompanied the Holiness-Pentecostal revivals of the late nineteenth and twentieth centuries.

The Effects of the Holiness-Pentecostal Movements on Theological Education

As noted in the first chapter, the experience of John Wesley is at the heart of the Holiness-Pentecostal experience. It was he who coined the term "new birth" and the idea of a "second blessing" after salvation (Synan 2001, 2). Wesley's friend, John Fletcher, was the first to call this experience "the baptism in the Holy Spirit, patterned after the experience described in Acts 2 (Synan 2001, 2). This experience was to later become one of the defining distinctives of the Renewal Movement in the twentieth century.

It was at the Keswick "Higher Life" Conferences beginning in England in 1875 that the idea of the baptism in the Holy Spirit was popularized. Here, the idea of the baptism in the Holy Spirit was reconceptualized from earlier ideas that involved the "eradication" of one's sin nature to an experience that provided an "enduement of power for service" (Synan 2001, 29). When D.L. Moody received this experience at a prayer meeting in 1871, he became a strong advocate for the idea of the baptism in the Holy Spirit as an unction of power for service. He exported this idea to America in conferences held in Northampton, Massachusetts, encouraging individuals to receive their own "personal Pentecost" (Synan 2001, 30).

When Agnes Osman received the baptism in the Holy Spirit at Bethel Bible School and Healing Home, in Topeka, Kansas, on January 01, 1901, she was the first of over 500 million individuals to have that experience in the twentieth century. Charles Parham, the school's founder, later moved his school to Houston, Texas, and had about twenty-five students. William J. Seymour was strongly influenced by these meetings and eventually began holding meetings in a personal residence on Bonnie Brae Street in Los Angeles, California. By April, 1906, people began being baptized with the Holy Spirit with the accompanying evidence of speaking in tongues (Synan 2001, 48, 49). This became known as the famous "Azusa Street Revival" that led to the propagation of the message of the baptism in the Holy Spirit around the world in the twentieth century. It is interesting to note that this phenomena originated in a theological training setting.

As was the case with the First and Second Awakenings, conservative Christianity began to react in the last half of the nineteenth century against what it perceived to be a liberal slide in the nation's churches and centers of theological education. Many of the nation's top universities and some of its seminaries had come under the increasing influence of German higher criticism and thought. At the same time an intense missionary zeal was building as a result of the holiness movement in America and Europe. Traditional university and seminary models for the training and deployment of clergy and missionaries were not considered relevant for the task of training the emerging leaders of that time. In the 1880s, outstanding leaders such as Simpson, Gordon, and Moody turned their attention to founding schools targeted directly at training lay people in basic Bible knowledge and evangelistic methods (Brereton 1990, 55). The result was the beginning of the founding of separate Bible schools and institutes.

The Bible schools and institutes that were founded beginning in the 1880s had several common characteristics (Brereton 1990, 39-48). Most were started by small groups of individuals in an informal and spontaneous manner, "outside the supervision of educational officialdom" (Brereton 1990, 39). Many of the founders were reformers and highly critical of the coldness of mainline Protestant churches. There was a prominent zeal for missionary work among these reformers drew them toward models of theological education that were practical and skills-based in nature and that could equip the lay people to do evangelistic work at home and abroad (Brereton 1990, 40-45).

These Bible schools were purposely designed to provide less technical theological education and often functioned at what was basically a high school level of education (Brereton 1990, vii, 55). The curriculum often involved saturation in the Bible itself along with mentored practical work in missions, hospitals, and churches (Brereton 1990, viii). Most schools that developed during this time have an evangelical tradition in common, which emphasized conversion and a life of holiness through sanctification. Similar conservative views on culture, morality, and education were common, as well as an emphasis on the verbal-plenary inspiration of the Scriptures. Many groups also shared an interest in Bible prophecy and the imminent return of Jesus Christ in the framework of dispensationalist and pre-millennialist theology. The Pentecostal branches also emphasized the baptism and gifts of the Holy Spirit as well as divine healing (Brereton 1990, 1-13). From the list of common characteristics, it is easy to see why many traditional seminary and university based programs of theological education would not fit or be considered relevant.

The first schools to originate in America from this movement were patterned after European Bible schools that specialized in fast, effective, and practical training and were often missions-oriented (Brereton 1990, 55). These European schools were originally developed to train deaconesses and caught the attention of American missionaries in their travels through Europe. These and several other Bible colleges in Europe were founded to specifically address the shortage of workers in the mission field, who would otherwise be denied access to theological education (Brereton 1990, 57, 58). These European schools in most cases abandon the classical aspects of education that were language-oriented and instead concentrated on intense Bible study and practical skills such as preaching, evangelism, and discipleship (Brereton 1990, 58). Leaders such as D. L. Moody and A. B. Simpson were exposed to these types of European schools through the holiness movement and their travels in Europe.

The American Bible schools and institutes that began to spring up in America in the 1880s closely followed the pattern established by informal European Bible schools. The East London Institute for Home and Foreign Missions (1872), founded by H. Grattan Guiness, had a profound effect on A. B. Simpson (Witmer 1962, 33). The American schools also arose in an American environment of revivalism and the conviction that the laity should be mobilized for evangelistic work. They were primarily mission-specific schools designed to grant access to lay people so they could obtain training to carry on a specific role of service. Their programs emphasized

"...practical skills that could be used by missionaries, evangelists, pastors, Sunday school teachers, and Christian workers of other kinds" (Brereton 1990, xvii). They have accurately been compared to the log cabin colleges set up by revivalists in the eighteenth century after the First Great Awakening (Brereton 1990, 35). Leaders in the Bible school and institute movement, such as D. L. Moody the founder of Moody Bible Institute, rightly pointed out that this new form of theological education eliminated the removal of the student from their context of ministry (Brereton 1990, 63). It is not that he and others who founded the Bible schools and institutes over the next sixty years were all opposed to traditional education. They simply wanted to provide a shorter means of preparation and rapid deployment for the work of service in the Church. They also increased access to theological education for many who could not access traditional theological education such as women and those not able to economically or intellectually meet the challenges of a four-year classical-based undergraduate and three-year graduate course of study (Brereton 1990, 64).

The first such institution for theological training was founded in New York City in 1882 by Albert B. Simpson, who also founded the Christian and Missionary Alliance denomination (Brereton 1990, xvii). The school was called by various names throughout its existence, such as "Missionary Training College for Home and Foreign Missionaries and Evangelists" (1882), "The Training College" (1890), "New York Training Institute" (1894) and later after its move to Nyack, New York, "Nyack Missionary College" (1897) (Witmer 1962, 35). Simpson described the training offered there as "Distinct Bible training...practical training in Christian lines of work...Holy Ghost missionaries...simplicity and economy...actual results" (Witmer 1962, 35). After leaving the Presbyterian church and the comfort of successful pastoral work behind, Simpson started out with one congregation in New York and from there developed a network of organizations to propagate the gospel. From there he developed a network of "alliances" that was composed of additional churches, a newspaper and publishing house, and a number of Bible schools both in the United States and in the foreign mission field (Brereton 1990, 41). The beginnings of the school in the back of a theater on twenty-third street in New York City were quite humble. Twelve students and two faculty members studied a curriculum based on literary (English, logic, philosophy, natural science, ancient and modern history and geography), theological (apologetics, Bible, New Testament Greek, systematic theology, church history, and pastoral theology), and practical skills (homiletics, evangelism, Sunday school, and vocal music) (Witmer 1962, 35). Simpson specifically founded the school to grant access for training to the laity (Brereton 1990, 48). His school served as a standard for curriculum, passion for world evangelism, academics and spiritual emphasis (Witmer 1962, 35). In its first sixteen years, Simpson's school graduated more than 500 individuals who successfully completed the entire program of studies (Witmer 1962, 33).

Moody Bible Institute, founded by D. L. Moody and his associates in 1886, became the largest of the Bible Institutes founded at this time. Objectives for the school were formulated in 1887:

> ...to educate and direct and maintain Christian workers as Bible readers, teachers and evangelists, who shall teach the gospel in Chicago, and its suburbs, especially in neglected fields (Witmer 1962, 36).

When Reuben Archer Torrey, a Yale scholar, agreed to come and direct the institute, the school was poised for growth. Over the next ten years more than 3,000 people were educated at the school. The school later expanded to offer a wide array of correspondence courses and to do radio broadcasts (Witmer 1962, 37). Moody Bible Institute is a classic example of a three-year Bible institute that issues diplomas for course completion. Nyack Missionary College is an example of a degree-granting Bible college. Both have become accredited as they have continued to develop over the last several decades (Witmer 1962, 37).

There were several other notable institutes and Bible colleges that were founded in the nineteenth and twentieth century. Boston Bible School was founded by the Adventist denomination in 1897, later to become Berkshire Christian College. Boston Missionary Training School, later to become Gordon College, was founded in 1889 by the Baptist denomination. Azusa College, founded in 1899 eventually became Azusa-Pacific College. The movement picked up speed in the early twentieth century and other Bible institutes and colleges were founded including The Bible Institute of Los Angeles (Biola - 1908) and Central Bible Institute (1922) in Springfield, Missouri, which became Central Bible College, the headquarters school of the Assemblies of God. Individual districts within the Assemblies of God sponsored regional schools such as Northwestern Bible College, Bethany Bible College, Southwestern, North Central Bible College, Northeast Bible College (Valley Forge Christian College) and Southeastern Bible College. In all, Brereton publishes a "partial list" of schools and institutes naming 106 different ones that came into existence between 1882-1945 (Brereton 1990, 71-77).

The Bible school movement went through three distinct stages (Brereton 1990, 79-86). The initial stage (1882-1915) saw a proliferation of Bible schools and institutes that had a typical curriculum that was Bible-centered and lasted for two years. The Bible school movement entered an expansion phase (1915-1930) that was dominated by the acquisition of buildings and the availability of more resources. Beginning in 1940, these schools reached out for greater academic respectability through accreditation, offering undergraduate degrees, and acquiring advanced degreed teaching staff. Some Bible colleges expanded their curriculum to become liberal arts colleges and Christian universities. These moves were made in part to provide a sense of stability and permanence to the institutions and to codify their beliefs and teaching to pass on to future generations (Brereton 1990, 14, 32). Some expanded the role of the institution in order to meet the broader educational needs of their constituency.

From the foundational stages of the Bible school movement, the curriculum in the schools was dominated by a detailed study of the Scriptures in English. Study was not Hebrew or Greek based, but majored in a holistic understanding of the Scriptures to counter what was perceived to be a "fragmented exegesis" presented in formal theological education (Brereton 1990, 88). Approaches to the study of the Scriptures tended to be doctrinally based. A five-fold division of study consisting of general Bible, pastoral classes, Christian education, missionary studies, and music was common (Brereton 1990, 105). Practical work assignments were often connected with studies that involved diverse settings such as asylums, old people's homes, work with vagrants on the street, and street witnessing (Brereton 1990, 115).

Many of the original Bible institutes and colleges exist today and continue to provide a rapid deployment means of preparation for ministry to thousands of people in lay and professional ministry. In 1940, the American Association of Bible Colleges (AABC) was founded to extend accreditation to undergraduate Bible colleges and institutes and is growing yearly in member schools. The impact of the Holiness-Pentecostal renewal movement and the Bible school and institute movement have impacted world Christianity for the past century and continue to do so in the twenty-first century. Both have also helped to pave the way for the current Charismatic/Neo-Pentecostal renewal movement in the last part of the twentieth century that has resulted in world evangelism and conversions on a scale never before seen in the history of Christianity.

Virginia Brereton, in her book *Training God's Army: The American Bible College, 1880-1940* (1990), provides valuable insights into what happened in theological education in reaction to the revival of conservative Christianity during the Holiness Pentecostal renewal movements. As was the case with the First and Second Awakenings, conservative Christianity began to react in the last half of the nineteenth century against what it perceived to be a liberal slide in the nation's churches and centers of theological education. Many of the nation's top universities and some of its seminaries had come under the increasing influence of German higher criticism and thought. At the same time an intense missionary zeal was building as a result of the holiness movement in America and Europe. Traditional university and seminary models for the training and deployment of clergy and missionaries were not considered relevant for the task of training the emerging leaders of that time. In the 1880s, outstanding leaders such as Simpson, Gordon, and Moody turned their attention to founding schools targeted directly at training lay people in basic Bible knowledge and evangelistic methods (Brereton 1990, 55). The result was the beginning of the founding of separate Bible schools and institutes.

These Bible schools and institutes were purposely designed to provide less technical theological education and often functioned at what was basically a high school level of education (Brereton 1990, vii, 55). The curriculum often involved saturation in the Bible itself along with mentored practical work in missions, hospitals, and churches (Brereton 1990, viii). Most schools that developed during this time have in common an evangelical tradition that emphasized conversion and a life of holiness through sanctification. Similar conservative views on culture, morality, and education were common, as well as an emphasis on the verbal-plenary inspiration of the Scriptures (Brereton 1990, 55). Many of the original Bible institutes and colleges exist today and continue to provide a rapid deployment means of preparation for ministry to thousands of people in lay and professional ministry.

The Effects of the Charismatic and Neo-Pentecostal Movements on Theological Education

As was mentioned earlier, in the 1960s, an unprecedented move of the Holy Spirit began that has resulted in worldwide revival on a scale never before seen in the Christian faith. This movement began in 1960 with spontaneous outpourings of the Holy Spirit within denominational church settings that had been typically resistant to the baptism in the Holy Spirit. The movement has been called the Charismatic movement and was originally associated more with the Catholic church, but has spread on a global scale to all 150 non-Pentecostal traditions, within 9,000 ethno-linguistic cultures, representing 8,000 languages, and covering 95% of the world's total population (Barrett 2001, 19). Since 1970, the Charismatic renewal has taken on a decidedly global nature. Many mainline denominational Christians were not prepared to leave the state churches in Western Europe and Asia to become Pentecostal in the early 1900s. Since 1970, the mainline denominational churches in both Europe and Asia have become massively pentecostalized with the members remaining within their mainline denominational churches (Barrett 2001, 19).

In his book, *The Extension Movement in Theological Education* (n. d.), F. Ross Kinsler outlines one of the trends that has resulted in theological education due in part to the explosive international growth from the renewal movements of the twentieth century. The Charismatic and neo-Pentecostal renewal and some of the paradigm changes that it has created have helped to catalyze a mounting crisis in theological education on a worldwide basis. Through the 1980s and 90s, a debate has intensified in theological education circles as to how to address the changing situation in the body of Christ and prepare its emerging leaders for ministry. The renewal movement in the twentieth century has progressively blurred the distinction between clergy and laity as distinct classes, continuing the trend started by Luther that recognized the "priesthood of all believers." This has led to increased demand for theological education that equips both clergy and laity for the work of the ministry, envisioning leaders as part of the church body rather than a separate elite group (Kinsler n.d., 4, 5). The rapid expansion of Christianity on a global basis has also produced the need for rapid preparation and deployment models for theological education that are economical and do not require individuals to leave their context of ministry (Kinsler n.d., 6). Logistical and economic constraints simply do not permit the investment in relocation, travel, or formal seminary training over a period of seven years that are common in Western theological education. The economics will also not support investment in large stand-alone seminaries with expensive buildings and tenured faculty. Many of the emerging leaders do not have access to the undergraduate education required for graduate level theological education also common in the West. These economic and logistical constraints have birthed a trend toward theological extension education that originated in Latin America during the 1960s.

Theological education by extension (TEE) refers to a decentralized training program in which theological training is delivered in decentralized centers extended out from a centralized center. It makes it possible for the student to partake of a formal program offered by a centralized college or seminary while the student remains resident in their home, job, and ministry context (Clinton 1984, 165). The TEE movement began in the 1960s to extend theological education to functioning and developing leaders in congregations in Latin America (Kinsler n.d., 30). The essential elements of extension site study included sets of self-study materials on particular subjects including textbooks and workbooks to be studied through the course of the week. Once per week, a corporate meeting of students was held to encourage discussion and encourage spiritual encounters. The study was also tied into practical work in one's own congregation to ensure that the new knowledge that was gained could be applied immediately (Kinsler n.d., 34-35).

Lessons for Past Renewal

By examining American church history, its historical revivals, and the changes they have produced in theological education over the last three centuries, several conclusions can be drawn. The American church and its history are strongly associated with several historical religious revivals that have been instrumental in producing revival in the church every 80-100 years. Each of the historical revivals is linked to a corresponding renewal in theological education to equip ministers and laity to serve the Body of Christ along the lines of the new paradigms the revival has produced. The unprecedented Pentecostal, Charismatic, and neo-Pentecostal renewal movements of the latter twentieth century have produced over 530 million new renewal-oriented believers calling for theological education uniquely adapted for these distinctives. If history provides a glimpse at what to expect in the future, the changes in the nature and delivery of theological education that occur to contextualize it to meet the needs of the new generation of emerging leaders will be substantial.

The Log Cabin College movement was a result of the First Great Awakening in America. It illustrates the ability of theological education to adapt to changing needs and circumstances. The people that needed training were on the frontier, far away from the traditional sources of theological training such as Harvard, Yale, or Princeton. The renewal on the frontier produced tens of thousands of converts that needed pastors and teachers to lead them. These leaders needed practical hands-on instruction for immediate application in ministry under less than ideal conditions. Theological training on the frontier left its ivory tower mindset behind and became imminently practical in its orientation and was delivered in a mentor-apprentice format rather than exclusively a classroom-lecture format. This type of theological training produced a hearty robust type of minister that was well suited for ministry on the frontier with all of its hardships. It raised the ire of traditional institutions of theological education, but the work and results of these frontier ministers spoke for themselves, and within a generation, many of these log cabin college trained ministers had become the presidents of new Bible colleges themselves.

The names D. L. Moody, Adoniran J. Gordon, A. B. Simpson, and Charles Parham that have been mentioned in this chapter all have something in common - they were all involved in theological education. As was the case with the previous revivals in America, it seems that significant reform in theological education was once again linked with revival. By no means was the Holiness-Pentecostal renewal movement the only force behind the reforms that occurred in theological education in the early 1900s. The renewal was a result of a complex blending of fundamentalist, holiness, Methodist, Pentecostal, and revivalist forces at work in America and Europe (Brereton 1990, 1-13). Renewal and theological education seem to go hand in hand and innovative theological education always seems to result because of the strains and challenges that renewal forces in the church bring to bear on the training needs.

As was the case with the First and Second Awakenings, conservative Christianity began to react in the last half of the nineteenth century against what it perceived to be a liberal slide in the nation's churches and centers of theological education. Many of the nation's top universities and some of its seminaries had come under the increasing influence of German higher criticism and thought. At the same time an intense missionary zeal was building as a result of the holiness movement in America and Europe. Traditional university and seminary models for the training and deployment of clergy and missionaries were not considered relevant for the task of training the emerging leaders of that time. In the 1880s, outstanding leaders such as Simpson, Gordon, and Moody turned their attention to founding schools targeted directly at training lay people in basic Bible knowledge and evangelistic methods (Brereton 1990, 55). The result was the beginning of the founding of separate Bible schools and institutes. The same cry can be heard today within the renewal movement — the need for a conservative theology, but in the context of renewal distinctives, with room for the Holy Spirit.

The Bible schools and institutes that were founded beginning in the 1880s had several common characteristics (Brereton 1990, 39-48). Most were started by small groups of individuals in an infor mal and spontaneous manner, "outside the supervision of educational officialdom" (Brereton 1990, 39). Many of the founders were reformers and highly critical of the coldness of mainline Protestant churches. There was a prominent zeal for missionary work among these reformers that drew them toward models of theological education that were practical and skills-based in nature and that could equip the lay people to do evangelistic work at home and abroad (Brereton 1990, 40-45). The same cry can be heard within the renewal movement today from people who in the past would have been considered "laity." The renewal movement has blurred any artificial distinction between laity and clergy in the church, literally fulfilling the cry of the reformation nearly six centuries ago - "the priesthood of the Believer."

Frustration is building in both the church community and theological schools. The church is frustrated that the leaders produced in theological schools are academically-oriented with insufficient real-life skills to do the work of the ministry in the twenty-first century. It is the same cry that was heard during the First and Second Great Awakening - a cry for practical, application-oriented theological training. Institutions offering theological education are frustrated because the old ways are not working and attendance, revenue, and qualified individuals are lacking to get the job done. Access issues are once again on the table as they were in prior revivals. Many do not have the undergraduate training necessary to access education at a graduate level. Others are not interested in graduate level education because they are already active in ministry and want skills based training and solutions. Some renewal churches have come to the place where they are developing their own training systems to develop emerging leaders rather than wait on traditional theological education to change. What is the answer to this problem?

Theological education must once again change with the renewal that is taking place. New systems of training must be developed that "equip the saints for the work of the ministry" (Eph 4:12) in a practical, application-oriented manner. A new emphasis must be placed on conservative and renewal-oriented distinctives in that training if it is to be relevant the vast majority of the Body of Christ today. Access issues must be addressed that allow individuals to be trained at an undergraduate level, especially in developing parts of the world where graduate level education is only a dream. A new partnership between church and theological education must be initiated to repair the growing gulf that now exists. The shape of theological education and its institutions must change and new curriculum must be developed for those experiencing renewal who are asking the same kind of questions asked twenty years ago in the introduction of this chapter. These questions are highly practical and application-oriented rather than academic and knowledge-based. History shows that leaders have risen to the task of redesigning theological training suitable for the renewal of their day and adapted for the needs of the emerging leaders of their time. The question remains, will this generation of renewal-oriented leaders do the same?

CHAPTER THREE

Why Shepherds Can't Shepherd: The Current Crisis in Theological Training

The church begins a major building process in order to accommodate all of the new people that are coming. We settle on a new 2500 seat sanctuary - after all, we have grown from 10 to 1200 over the past nine years - isn't it logical to think that we will hit the 2500 member mark in the next nine years? We have trusted in the Holy Spirit and His leading to this point. We have had to trust - none of us has ever done this before. None of us has any formal theological training. We are into new territory.

The old ways of doing things at the church no longer seem adequate — we will need to make some changes. We need a children's pastor for the 200 children that now come on Sunday mornings. We also need a youth pastor for the 150 youth that attend. The Christian school needs a principal for the growing staff of teachers The lead pastor needs an adult ministry specialist to help with the counseling load as well as all of the weddings, funerals, and teaching. How does one manage multiple staff? What is team ministry and how does it work? What essentials should one know for effective leadership in the church?

The giving by church members is at record levels —

between the church and school there is over 1.5 million dollars that flow through the ministry. What kinds of financial structures should we put in place to handle the finances? How should we finance the money needed to build the new sanctuary? How should we structure compensation and benefits for all of our employees?

As the church begins to get bigger, we notice a definite change in the relationships - they seem cooler and more distant. We started as a small group in a living room. Many miss that kind of intimacy. How can we rebuild the small group structure in the church to give it that intimate feel again? What constitutes a healthy small group? How do we know when and how to multiply these groups?

As time goes on we realize that we are clearly out of answers - we are at the limits of our knowledge and training. Being led by the Spirit has been fine to this point, but it looks like it's time to "study to show ourselves approved...." We are shocked when we look into the theological training that is available in our city. We cannot even get into seminary because we do not have the undergraduate degree that will grant us access. Even if we could get into seminary, the classes there seem highly academic in nature. Hebrew and Greek are great, but what about church staff, budget, and administration? Systematic Theology and Church History would be beneficial in the long run, but what about our small groups and evangelistic outreach into the city? Should we get our training from piecemeal seminars? Should we develop our own training systems? We have the money, the time and the questions. Who has the training and the answers we need?

This scenario is being repeated over and over again in both the national and international church. The cry from developing nations for theological training is deafening as millions of converts come to Christ and need trained qualified leaders to move them to maturity. At a time when we should be sharing our expertise in theological education with developing leaders in other nations, the West finds itself in the midst of deep soul searching over how best to train emerging leaders to function in the church.

Much can be learned from examining the debate in theological education circles over the last twenty years. The issues and solutions that have been offered in this debate have advanced theological education in the West, but most would still agree that the training that is offered in many cases today is neither adequate nor relevant to the needs of emerging leaders. This is especially true because most of the emerging leaders, especially on the international scene, have a renewal orientation and need training that builds on interdenominational and renewal-oriented distinctives. The future of the Western Church and the Church in developing nations literally depends on the Church's ability to effectively train its emerging leaders. Will we rise to the challenge? Will we be willing to make the kinds of changes necessary to accomplish this task?

THE THEOLOGICAL EDUCATION DEBATE

The amount of change that has occurred in society since the beginning of the twentieth century is unparalleled in human history. This environment of rapid change has produced a context for church ministry that demands a different approach to theological education. The way that theological education is delivered has been called into question, as well as the content, setting, and targets of that education. A vigorous debate has developed, especially over the last twenty years, concerning the best way to deliver theological education to those preparing for ministry.

In the twentieth century, there has been an unprecedented shift in global demographics. Whereas in 1900, 85-90% of the Christians lived in the Western world, in the year 2000, 58% of the Christian population is in non-Western countries (Messer 1995, 55). Over the period from 1900-2000 the percentage of population that are Christian in Africa went from 3% to 50%. The Christian population in Latin America went from 62 million to 400 million. Likewise, in Asia, it rose from 19 million to over 225 million (Messer 1995, 55,56). The fruit of many years of missions work was finally being realized in staggering proportions.

With change on a global basis such as was described above, there is no way that theological education could escape the "growth pains" that the Body of Christ is experiencing on a global basis. As Tim Dearborn observed, theological education is at the front lines of the battle. Ideas are the major force behind actions. It is really ideas that are the battleground in any conflict. As ideas are worked out into reality and behavior in the real world, the events we later record as history transpire. Indeed, ideas are more "powerful than bullets" (Dearborn 1990, 3). Theological education, as the delivery vehicle for truth, becomes the critical deciding factor in the effectiveness of God's army in the battle for souls.

In the same time period between 1900 and 2000, schools that deliver theological education found themselves in a battle of their own, precisely because the world was changing around them. Many schools found themselves focused on "good grades" and "academic degrees" rather than on forming ministers to operate in effective ministry. Other schools found themselves entrenched in a curriculum emphasizing cognitive scholarly pursuits while pastors were crying out for practical answers for how to minister effectively in their churches. Many schools that had adopted a "clerical paradigm" for ministry, in which the pastor does all of the work of the ministry in the local church, had no idea what to do with the large number of lay people that wanted to be trained. There were no training programs to equip them to be effective missionaries, evangelists, or more effective servants in their local church. A general cry went out for a more integrated and less scattered approach to theological education that not only prepared "heads" but more effectively formed the heart as well (Dearborn 1995a, 1-3). Many schools in the last century realized that they could no longer have as their mission the propagation of a certain method of theological education. Instead, these schools realized that they needed to be catalysts for community transformation in the world around them by forming their students in new ways (Dearborn 1995a, 17,18).

As Virginia Cetuk observes, it is the responsibility of schools that seek to deliver theological education to "wrestle with holy things" (Cetuk 1998, 30). When the world changes around it, theological education must refine and reform the way that it conducts its holy business. Since it is "in touch with the Source" by the very nature of its mission, theological education must become what God shapes it to be in any given time period (Cetuk 1998, 31-34). This should include the radical intent to reframe the entire enterprise, if necessary, to make it relevant to the needs of the Body of Christ in any given time period. Polycarp dealt with second-century Church problems. Luther, Calvin, and Wesley dealt with problems common to their day. Those desiring to minister in the twenty first century share many things in common with their predecessors but have their own unique needs that must be addressed in theological education if they are to be effective in ministry.

Tim Dearborn proposes that changes in the way that theological education is delivered have a five-fold dimension to them that involves the institution itself, curriculum, faculty, students, and the process in which theological education is delivered (Dearborn 1995a, 4-15). The ways that Dearborn proposes that theological education be transformed are largely a result of a debate in the theological education community that has been ongoing for the last century. That debate has intensified since the 1980s because the rapid change in the world and the global make up of the Body of Christ.

Debate in the Early Twentieth Century

The debate in the twentieth century about theological education began in the early 1930s with a study directed by William Adams Brown of Union Theological Seminary. The study, funded by John D. Rockefeller, charted the proliferation of subjects in the theological curricula of the day and concluded "…. that the curriculum must be dictated by the practice of ministry rather than the explosion of research interests" (Ferris 1990, 8). In the 1950s, the Carnegie Corporation provided funding to staff and finance a center to study theological education in both the United States and Canada. The study team was led by H. Richard Niebuhr and surveyed more than ninety Protestant seminaries affiliated with the American Association of Theological Schools, now known as the Association of Theological Schools (ATS). The study concluded that seminaries should seek to develop "pastoral directors" rather than operate along the classical lines of developing professional clergy. It also suggested that seminaries begin to think about how they could integrate theological education and the diverse content of the curricula more fully by means of "personal synthesis" on the part of a student. The study also recommended that faculty attain this personal synthesis for themselves and understand the curricula in light of "the unity of the church" (Ferris 1990, 8).

One can see that Niebuhr and his peers struggled with the changing roles of the ministers in the twentieth century church and how best to educate them. Basic paradigms of theological education that had existed since the early nineteenth century no longer seemed adequate to cope with the theological education needs of twentieth century ministers in the church. Niebuhr's two books, *The Purpose of the Church and Its Ministry: Reflection on the Aims of Theological Education* (1956) and *The Advancement of Theological Education* (1957) wrestle with the need to somehow change the nature of theological education and the way that it is delivered. Despite the efforts of William Adams Brown in the 1930s and of H. Richard Niebuhr in the 1950s, there was no discernable difference in the way that theological education was perceived or delivered in the United States. Niebuhr's books and studies on theological education remain the one of the last bold voices to call for change in theological education before the debate was renewed in the early 1980's.

The Debate in the 1980s

Robert Banks, in his book *Reenvisioning Theological Education,* charts the course of the theological education debate over the last twenty years. In the early 1980s the debate over what theological education is and how it should be delivered resurfaced with a new vigor. Banks observed that the investigations into the nature and delivery of theological education in the early twentieth century seem to focus on the "means and the end" (Banks 1999, 9). These investigations looked at issues such as resources, the manner in which seminaries are governed, and faculty, staff, and trustee development. By the 1980s, the nature of the debate changed to new questions that centered upon the aims and purposes of theological education itself. Questions in this time frame seemed to center on whether the institution was attaining its primary goals in a manner that was relevant to its contemporary context and questioning what the goals of theological education should be. Barbara Wheeler notes that the biggest change in the debate that has surfaced over the last twenty years has a three-fold dimension. It is now the faculty members that are the chief participants in the debate rather than presidents and deans. The debate has also taken on a more scholarly approach rather than a mere matter of polemics. The recent debate has also focused more on the theological reasons for doing theological education a certain way rather than appealing to pragmatism or orthodoxy (Wheeler and Farley 1991, 9,10).

For more than twenty years after the Neuhaus study and books, the literature reveals no major study or debate on how to reform theological education in the United States. It is as if the theological education community decided to ignore the problems that existed until the last minute possible when the "dam was about to burst." During the period between 1960 and 1980, the United States and the Church experienced some of the most sweeping changes in its history.

With the advent of advances in communication, travel, and technology, the "size" of the world decreased. The paradigm of the "global village" emerged. Calls for theological education from remote parts of the world were heard. Western paradigms for theological education which are based on Greek thought or German method seemed foreign and inadequate to address the needs of people from non-Western cultures (Banks 1999, 10,11). By the end of the twentieth century, more than half of the world's Christian population no longer lived in the Western world (Messner 1995, 55). This has produced a crisis in theological education as the Christian community struggles with the change or scrapping of standard paradigms of theological education that are well entrenched in the West.

During the last twenty years in the United States, the context for theological education was also rapidly changing. The number of full-time students has rapidly declined over the last century, especially over the last twenty years. Most students are now above the age of thirty-five, live off campus, have a part or full time job, and are married with children (Banks 1999, 4-6). As such, they retained a full-time job during their studies and most often were engaged in theological education on a part-time basis. What was a nearly homogeneous male student body is now two-thirds male and one-third female in population (Banks 1999, 5). What was once largely a white male enterprise was rapidly changing because of the removal of racial and ethnic barriers toward education during the last twenty years. These changes have produced tremendous stress on the major educational paradigms that have been used to educate ministers over the last hundred years (Banks 1999, 4-6).

The religious revivalism that swept the country in the nineteenth and twentieth centuries has produced a new kind of student. Nearly five out of six seminaries in this country are denominationally or confessionally-based, while at the same time, many Christians were coming to saving faith with a Pentecostal, Charismatic, or renewal orientation (Banks 1999, 5). Vinson Synan, a noted renewal historian, makes this case dramatically by stating that the number of Christians with a renewal tradition has gone from "one on January 01, 1901 to 530 million by the year 2000" (Synan 2000, 1). Many within Charismatic and Pentecostal traditions have rejected standard paradigms for theological education as they exist within seminaries and universities. Leaders within these traditions founded Bible institutes and lay training centers to fill the vacuum they perceived to exist in theological education. Well over 100 AABC Accrediting Association of Bible College) accredited Bible institutes and lay training centers currently exist in this country that are increasingly renewal-oriented in their distinction and granting undergraduate as well as graduate degrees (Banks 1999, 5). The financial and numerical impact on traditional sources of theological education has caused many established schools to move away from a values-driven agenda for theological education to a more competitive and financially driven plan (Banks 1999, 4-6).

The above named factors focused the debate in the 1980s away from pragmatic issues of method toward core issues of values and philosophy. The trend in the debate of the 1980s was to focus on overtly theological questions that call into question the aims and the goals of the whole enterprise of theological education. At first, many at the start of the debate in the early 1980s tried to isolate the reasons that theological education seemed to be so fractured and fragmented. It no longer seemed to have a discernable and overriding "theme" that tied together the curriculum, goals, and ethos of the institutions delivering theological education. The early players in the debate began to offer their solution for reunifying the whole system of educating ministers. The debates seemed to center on defining the one "essence" that should define theological education in a broad sense. The other aspect of the debate was the manner in which theological education delivered, which, of course, takes the shape of its underlying educational philosophies. Banks identifies these two main educational philosophies as the classical model of theological education which focuses on a personal and sapiential knowledge of God and the vocational model which focuses on coming to know God by a reasoned process of investigation into the discrete knowledge of theology. The classical model is associated with Greek educational philosophies prevalent in early church history. The vocational model is closely associated with the movement toward Enlightenment philosophy embodied in the educational paradigms at work at the University of Berlin in the nineteenth century. Banks asserts that the manner in which theological education is delivered by individual schools in the United States falls somewhere on a continuum between these classic and vocational educational paradigms. The debate that has occurred since 1980 are largely the result of a tension in the theological education community over where on this continuum theological education should be.

What Should be the Focus of Theological Training?

A whole portion of the debate over theological education in the last twenty years has been what the focus of that training should be. This is perhaps more symptomatic of an identity crisis in theological education than all of the other debates about training emerging leaders to function in the Church. The answer to this question centers the whole endeavor and shapes the outcome. An understanding of the nature of the debate over the focus of theological education to date is essential to the reform of the whole enterprise.

The Centrality of *Theologia*

In the late 1970s and early 1980s, the theological education community began once again to engage in a vigorous debate that has not yet ceased since that time. Many began to see the fragmented nature of theological education as the effects of the Berlin model of education took their toll. Others began to validate the criticism from churches that said that the seminaries were no longer preparing graduates that could function well within the church when they graduated. Banks credits Edward Farley, at that time a Professor of Theology at Vanderbilt University, for beginning the debate process over theological education in the early 1980s. In his book, *Theologia*, Farley identified the fragmented nature of theological education. He noted the proliferation of subjects offered in a seminary and the inability of seminaries to prepare their students for ministry in the "real world" of the Church as it existed in the 1980s (Farley 1983, 3). He led what would be a series of serious proposals from theologians of his day to reunify theological education around a central core value or subject that would solve the problems being observed.

Farley asserted that theological wisdom or "*theologia*" should be the central unifying principle of all theological education (Farley 1983, ix). Farley defines *theologia* as a sapiential and personal knowledge of divine self-disclosure. He asserts that "…. Theology concerns the wisdom by which one brings the resources of a religious tradition to bear on the world" (Farley 1998, 113). By using the term "*theologia*," he is attempting to move away from the stereotypical "professional" feel implied by theology today toward a more Athens-like meaning of practical and experiential Christianity. In the early Christian church, theological education consisted of acquiring a "mystical knowledge of the One-God" (Farley 1983, 33-34). This ideal was also the driving force of the preparation of ministers through the Middle Ages. During the period of the Enlightenment, Western culture began to redefine reality and education according to a completely different and rational paradigm. The essential unity of the world and its associated realities, an essentially Hebrew and Greek paradigm, were exchanged for a paradigm of knowledge that broke reality into bite-sized pieces. Enlightenment wisdom takes these bite-size pieces and begins to systematically examine them to extract knowledge from them as a result of investigation. While sacrificing the organic unity of the whole, this paradigm for acquiring knowledge does allow for the development of detailed technical knowledge about creation. It worked very well when applied to natural creation. The results when applied to theological education have some negative consequences as Farley points out (Farley 1983, 33-91).

In the post-Enlightenment period of the eighteenth and nineteenth centuries, Enlightenment thinking began to permeate Western society and the church. Rather than theology being viewed as a quest for mystical knowledge of God and a means to know him more fully, the post-Enlightenment church began to view theology as a "science" or body of discrete knowledge. Theology began to be viewed apart from knowing God Himself, and began to focus on knowing about God (Farley 1983, 39). As a result, the emphasis of theological education began to shift to the practical know-how of pastoral work and away from the personal formation of a minister and his relationship with God. Theological education was disintegrated into an aggregation of specialties, each of which accumulated independent "theological encyclopedias" of knowledge in their own field (Farley 1983, 40,75).

The original institutions of higher learning in this country such as Harvard and Yale were founded specifically for the purpose of training ministers. They were modeled after the theological schools in England, Scotland, and Northern Europe and embodied a "pious learning" model of theological education (Farley 1983, 6,7). Renewal influences in the eighteenth and early nineteenth centuries, centered around revivals such as the Great Awakening, produced a "school of the prophets" type feel in the theological schools of that time period. The study of "Divinity," at that time, centered on a personal knowledge of God through salvation. Theology was clearly seen as "queen" of the sciences, and the rule by which they the other sciences were judged.

As institutions of formal theological education began to develop in this country in the nineteenth century, they increasingly adopted a more German model of education. As noted earlier, German schools were more highly influenced by post-Enlightenment thought. Enlightenment thought had vanquished theology within the country's universities as the "queen" of sciences. The question was whether it would be allowed to remain within the university system at all as a valid topic of study. The University of Berlin was founded in 1810 in order to deliver education in a new manner, and it certainly did. It flows from this paradigm that theological education is to be delivered as "professional education."

It is Farley's contention that Schleiermacher's legacy radically shaped the manner in which theological education was delivered from 1810 onward. Leith makes the point that Schleiermacher's original motives in arguing to include Theology in the curriculum of the University of Berlin was to challenge Enlightenment thinking to take Christianity seriously (Leith 1997, 40,41). While it is debatable as to whether this goal was ever accomplished, the model that was accepted at the University of Berlin, for theological education was gradually adopted over the next several decades as Enlightenment thought was generally integrated into higher education in the United States. This became obvious when the idea of "degrees" awarded for education came to include the German "Doctor of Philosophy" (Ph.D.) degree as the terminal degree for study in the time frame between 1861-1891 (Leith 1997, 58).

The legacy of German Enlightenment thought in theological education brought the idea of a "graduate school" of education for ministers with the goal of educating scholars who teach and do research. What was once an enterprise that had as its goal the preparation of ministers soon became, in many seminaries, an exercise in the preparation of scholars engaged in the "critical review of religion" (Leith 1997, 43). These scholars have participated in the accumulation of knowledge in increasingly specialized areas of theology that has led to further abstraction of theological education from reality and the actual practice of everyday ministry (Farley 1983, 139). The abstraction of theology has inadvertently led to the idea that "theology is for ministers (the leaders of a faith community), not for human beings, students, or laity" (Farley 1983, 134). It has also led to the proliferation of successive attempts to adapt new aspects of culture to the Enlightenment model of thinking, such as African-American Theology, Liberation Theology, Feminist Theology, Process Theology and other new "themes" for unifying theological education (Leith 1997, 53,54).

Farley contends that it is the transition in the manner in which we approach theological education that is responsible for the current fragmentation and disintegration that exists today. The switch ".... from one meaning of learning to another, from the study which deepens heartfelt knowledge of divine things to scholarly knowledge of relatively discrete things...." has changed the fundamental nature and product of theological education (Farley 1983, 10). Farley is responsible for initiating the debate to reform the current model of theological education that disperses the subject into independent sciences of study, and to move to a model that once again unifies the curriculum around theological wisdom or "theologia" as he calls it. He argues that the acquisition of knowledge is dependent upon a sapiential and personal encounter with God in the process of theological education and formation, rather than by human reason and the Wissenschaft (scholarship, reason, or research) of the Enlightenment model. His cry is obviously for theological education to move back toward a more "Athens-like" approach to theological education and a return to the development of the Christian paideia (training and discipline). Farley's debate is an attempt to pose solutions to correct the excesses that have developed by over application of the Berlin model to theological education over the last century. The results of the reintroduction of *theologia* as central to theological education, according to Farley, will be a reunification of the subject matter that makes up theological education and a superior product in the form of an excellently prepared minister.

The Centrality of Personal Formation

Richard John Neuhaus has been a powerful voice in the last fifteen years on refocusing theological education on personal formation. From studying the writings of the Church Fathers from the fourth century, it is clear that the value of spiritual and moral formation as a result of theological education in that time period was a high priority. Chrysostom, Gregory of Nazianzus, and Ambrose wrote at length about the building of moral character into church leaders of that day, which is typical of an "Athens" or Greek educational philosophy that dominated the early church (Neuhaus 1992, 22-59). Within the clerical paradigm that existed in the fourth century, ministry revolved around the character of the priest.

As recently as the nineteenth century, it was assumed that moral and spiritual formation were to accompany the academic training in theological education, as well as general secular education. When Enoch Pond joined the faculty of Congregationalist Theological Seminary in 1832, he gave a series of lectures to the student body on the "cultivation of character, piety, prudence, and gentility" (Neuhaus 1992, 57). Pond's ideal was to produce the "picture of a Christian gentleman" in the process of seminary education, which was often a mixture of Christian character traits with the cultural standards of the day.

Schools also regularly promoted "exercises in piety." When the Andover Theological Seminary was founded in 1808, it expected students to be present for morning prayer at sunrise, conduct daily devotions of their own, take up the "occasional duty" of fasting, as well as attend weekly conferences with faculty (Neuhaus 1992, 57). Many students also formed "moral societies" at their schools to hone debate and preaching skills, but also for moral accountability and development. The whole intention of these practices was to "cultivate religious and moral dispositions and habits" in the life of the students. This dimension is often missing in theological education as it has been delivered in the twentieth century.

With the advent of the "Berlin" model for education in the nine-teenth century, many of the classical "Athens-like" activities associ-ated with spiritual and moral formation were neglected. Neuhaus points out that when Schleiermacher argued for the inclusion of theology into the curriculum at the University of Berlin, he did so under the justification that it was a "professional" activity that was socially necessary for the good of society. This professional activity and the four-fold model for theological education that resulted (Bible, Dogmatics, Church History, and Pastoral Theology) essen-tially fragmented theological education into functionalist orienta-tion. The Berlin model of professional clergy strives to increase the expertise of a student in the functional areas necessary for ministry, defining the minister by what he does (Neuhaus 1992, 114,115). This line of thinking about theological education by definition took the focus from the making of a minister by spiritual and moral formation to formation by increasing professional expertise. It is Merle Strege's contention that theological education has been "chasing Scheiermacher's ghost" since that time the "Berlin" model for theological education took hold in the United states in the late nineteenth century (Neuhuas 1992, 114-118). Since that time, spiri-tual and moral formation in the life of the minister has been neglected at the expense of academic pursuit. It is as if theological education has traded its heart for a well-developed mind.

Banks credits Richard John Neuhaus with bringing the issues of spiritual and moral formation to the forefront of the theological education debate in recent years (Banks 1999, 24-28). Neuhaus serves as the editor for *Theological Education for Moral Formation* (1992) which contains a collection of works that bring the whole idea of a return to spiritual and moral formation of ministers to the forefront. The book argues against a "scholastic theology" where a "love for learning" has replaced a "desire for God." With the advent of credentials for professionals in ministry, the focus has too often been on the goal of a degree rather than a conversion of the heart that occurs when ministers are properly formed (Neuhaus 1992, 80,81). Neuhaus advocates that moral and spiritual formation be at the center of theological education once again, and that they be the primary values that are used to reunify the curriculum of theological education.

It has become even more critical today that spiritual and moral formation take place in the settings where theological education is delivered. Whereas the family once had the primary responsibility for the spiritual and moral formation of individuals before their adult life, more and more students arrive at seminary deficient in these characteristics (Farley 1998, 113). With the breakdown of the American family, and the increasing number of individuals growing up in agnostic or non-Christian homes, moral and spiritual formation can no longer be assumed, but must be built into the theological education experience (Kelsey 1998, 64-71). Where it was once assumed that moral and spiritual formation was a part of the church's responsibility before the student ever sought theological education, this can no longer be assumed. Many churches are not equipped to form the congregation spiritually or morally because their leaders themselves have never been formed in these ways.

Paradigms of post-Enlightenment American higher education have engrained themselves in the minds of potential Christian leaders infiltrating their way of viewing reality. These leaders actually need to be reprogrammed in the process of theological education with morals and spiritual values more consistent with Biblical standards than post-Enlightenment values. This moral formation must address the relativism programmed into their minds, which relentlessly asserts that truth is relative and can never be truly discovered. The spiritual formation involved in the theological education process must take to task a secular mindset, in which God is no longer viewed as relevant, and replace it with one where God is the center of each thought and action. It must also banish the materialist mindset fostered within American education, which asserts that the end result of education is more material gain and prosperity in the natural realm (Neuhaus 1992, 11). These changes must be intentionally built into theological education if the product it produces is to be adequate for ministry in the twenty- first century. The idea of "being" and proper spiritual formation for the theological student must once again be properly balanced with "doing" if theological education is to accomplish its job. As Bank's observes, this can only occur if curriculum changes to address these concerns and faculty is willing to set the standards and act as an example. The nature and cultural ethos of existing schools delivering the theological education will change once these end goals are embraced (Banks 1992, 27).

The Centrality of Contextualization

The best of programs for theological education, with all components balanced properly and well oiled, delivered by the most talented faculty, to the brightest of students is ultimately worthless unless it prepares them to function well in their intended task in the context of their culture. Tim Dearborn, in a comment he made of the current state of theological education in this country, observes:

> To state the problem in extreme terms, I am coming to the conclusion that there is no other professional organization in the world that allows its primary professional training institutions to produce graduates who are generally as functionally incompetent as the Church permits her seminaries. (Dearborn 1995b, 7).

The problem is as some in the recent debate have noted, that the modern "context" is become increasingly a global context as society pushes toward massive globalization (Schreiter 1994, 85-87). In the early 1980's several key voices in the theological education community began to raise the issue of the fragmentation of theological education and attribute it to a failure of the educational community to contextualize its education for the intended audience. John Cobbs, Jr. and Joseph Hough, Jr. in their book *Christian Identity and Theological Education* (1985), criticized the theological education community for failing to take into account the various sociopolitical realities present in twentieth century culture and a professionalized church setting (Banks 1999, 34-39). They began to argue that the task of theological education was to clarify the vocational identity of the minister and to help them contextualize their understanding of the Church from a world perspective. Their voice was a call for a global consciousness in the context of a multicultural student body in order to develop practical thinkers and reflective practitioners who could become effective problem solvers, pioneers, implementers, and teachers in the Body of Christ (Banks 1999, 36,37).

Their call is one of one of the first voices in the theological debate over the last twenty years to call the Berlin-oriented educational community back into the real world context around them. Their message was basically a call back to a more Athens-oriented style of reflection, thinking, and practical theology so that what a student studied actually related to real life and ministry practice. They hoped to deal with the fragmentation in theological education that they observed by building a new Christian identity in students that would reflect a more human, caring, and evangelistic model of Christianity (Cobbs, Jr. and Hough, Jr. 1985, 50). They argued that theological education should therefore be centered on forming a Christian identity within the ministry professional that is consistent with context and the need of the church.

In the late 1980s, Max L. Stackhouse, a Professor at Andover Newton Theological School, entered the contextualization debate in theological education with his book *Apologia: Contextualization, Globalization, and Mission in Theological Education.* Stackhouse asserted that the idea of witness (*Apologia*) should be the focus of theological education, and that it would once again be unified if it were to be given this proper focus. He makes the case that Christians should be able to "defend" themselves in the public discourse when challenged about the authority of the Bible, their Christian image of God, doctrinal essentials of the faith, and all in the context the global multicultural community in which we now live (Stackhouse 1988, xi,xii). This defense, or *"Apologia"* as he calls it using the Greek word, should be the center of theological education curriculum, and developed in the student by *Praxis* (reflective action), *Poesis* (imaginative representation), and *Theoria* (systematic reflection) (Banks 1999, 39-43). The overall curriculum and ethos of an institution delivering theological education, in the opinion of Stackhouse, should foster multicultural awareness and have an orientation toward practice rather than just theory. The goal of this type of ministerial preparation would be to produce a student who could articulate the central convictions of the Christian faith in a way that is contextualized to the target culture (Banks 1999, 41). As he observes:

> What we do in theological education is talk. We teach and we discuss; we preach and we analyze; we read and we write; we think and we criticize. Words are our medium; talk is our method; ideas are our *raison d'etre*. The question is whether any of them are worth something. (Stackhouse 1988, 3).

His point is that seminaries cannot afford to prepare ministers in a "cafeteria-like" manner that are so diffuse in their vision, purpose, identity, and center that they do not even understand the context in which they work, nor the practical purpose for which they are being trained (Stackhouse 1988, 4,15).

Stackhouse adds his voice to the lament of others over what the inclusion of theology in the university curriculum has done to theological education. Rather than theology being the force that shapes university curriculum as in the middle ages, theology is being shaped by anthropology, psychology, and all of the other secular disciplines that surround it in the university setting. As Stackhouse says, "so-long, *sola Scriptura*" (Stackhouse 1988, 50). In essence, he encourages us to forsake or balance the "Berlin" model of education with a more *praxis* oriented model that is centered in an action-reflection mode much more like the "Athens" model. This is not any easy job. As Stackhouse mentions, Plato and Aristotle themselves were constantly trying to balance both *theoria* and *praxis* but usually managed to get hung up on the theoretical things, which can easily become an end in and of themselves (Stackhouse 1988, 88). By moving into the practical realm and balancing the theoretical teaching it is so well known for, theological education can begin to make the case for "what it does every day", as Stackhouse notes, "it has seldom attempted" (Stackhouse 1986, 83).

It seems that Stackhouse began to successfully focus the theological education community on the abstract excesses engendered by the years of fixation it had given to theory rather than practice. Contemporary education and the increasing specialization that is going on in the various fields of study have brought those preparing for ministry to the place that "we are coming to know more and more, about less and less, until we know almost everything about practically nothing." It seems that "Schleiermacher's ghost" has stricken once again. In the natural sciences, abstraction is permissible and in many cases desirable. Many new discoveries begin with pure science and relate them to reality. This method works well in a secular setting when applied to inanimate objects and physical reality. It seems to be deadly in a theological setting when abstraction and theory become the major focus, to the point where reality is nowhere in sight. Such is the case in many areas of theological education today as Stackhouse has pointed out.

Besides a new awareness of the need for a *praxis* reorientation for theological education, Stackhouse is also responsible for the introducing the topic of contextualization into mainstream debate within the theological education community. Contextualization is the ability to make a message appropriate for an intended audience. The best of programs with the best of content are ultimately worthless if they do not connect with their intended audience. Any pastor will agree after delivering a few "well prepared" messages to a congregation who looked back with a glazed look in their eyes. The essence of communication is to convey intended concepts and ideas from the speaker to the listener and back again. If barriers exist that stop this process, they must be identified and removed, or at least worked around. These barriers may be cultural, but more often than not they are barriers that are constructed as sacred paradigms, expressed by institutional program, ethos, or curriculum. If theological education is to fulfill its intended purpose, it must become as skilled at exegesis of the surrounding culture as it is in exegesis of the Hebrew and Greek Scriptures.

The Centrality of Mission

Once the idea of *praxis* or practical orientation in theological education was revived, the ideal of unifying theological education along the lines of a particular mission came to the forefront of the debate. Charles M. Wood entered the debate on theological education in the late 1980s by centering theological education on the development of vision and discernment in the life of students in ministerial training. His approach was an attempt to synthesize the best of "Athens" with its emphasis on spiritual and moral formation and "Berlin" with its propensity to develop critical thinking and practical skills. The goal of Wood's position is to develop a synthesis of these models of in order to relate theological education to the whole of life, rather than merely emphasize the ecclesiastical world. This approach is a blend of the "Athens" concept of *Paideia* with the "Berlin" concept of *wissenschaftliche*. By taking this position, Wood was hoping to endorse a pluralism in theological education which allows the best of both worlds of educational thought, thus avoiding the "atomization of theology" by either philosophical school (Banks 1999, 46-57).

The way that Wood encourages an individual to develop as a

ministerial leader is by capacitating them to develop a sense of vision and discernment. He defines vision as an individual's capacity to generally understand the totality of the Christian. Discernment is defined as the ability of an individual to access proper insight into particular circumstances (Wood 1985, 73,74). In Wood's opinion, the aim of theological education must be to foster vision and discernment in a student by proper spiritual formation of the individual, proper transmission of the Christian tradition for perspective, and proper professional education to make the student proficient in the tasks of ministry (Wood 1985, 77-88).

Wood advocates proper spiritual formation along the lines of the classical or "Athens" approach to theological education. Spiritual formation takes place in the context of the transmission of tradition and the deepening of processes of normal spiritual disciplines and nurture. The key, asserts Wood, is a personal engagement with critical reflection (Wood 1985, 78-81). Proper spiritual vision and discernment can only take place in a well-formed person who has been dealt with by God personally and critically reflected on the matters encountered in the context of theological education.

Wood also urges a rethinking of how Christian tradition is transmitted. He reminds those engaged in theological education that tradition is meant to convey *habitus*, which he defines as a capacity or disposition toward something, rather than merely a mindless propensity to act in a set manner. Wood observes that most highly confessional and denominational branches of theological education are actively involved in the propagation of traditions, but have forgotten the witness that the tradition represents (Wood 1985, 82-86). If managed properly, the transmittal of denominational and confessional tradition can instill proper vision and discernment in a student toward proper doctrinal understanding so that they can act as "living witnesses" of the Christian traditions they represent. This occurs as the *habitus* theological education has instilled in their lives is worked out in their ministry (Wood 1985, 88).

Other voices began to enter the theological education debate that pushed a particular missional agenda for dealing with the problem of the abstraction and fragmentation of theological curriculum. Within the feminist community, groups in the late 1980s began to bring the issue of pluralism within theological education to the forefront of the debate. These voices began to criticize theological education for its failure to live up to the inherent pluralism resident in theological education, especially as it dealt with cultural relativism, specifically feminist issues. The Mud Flower Collective's *God's Fierce Whimsy* (1985) and work from the Network for the Study of Ministry embodied an early call for the theological education community to move away from its abstract, objective, and universal approach towards a more embodied, contextual, and experiential form of education (Banks 1999, 28-30). Rebecca Chopp, in her book *Saving Work* (1995), attributes the rise of this debate to the increasing presence of women within in the theological education community and having to deal with their unique issues (Chopp 1995, ix). She advocates a move toward a more "spiritual" emphasis within theological education in which the educational community becomes a vehicle for the insemination of ideas (Chopp 1995, 66,103). She is basically calling for theological education to move back toward a more Athens-like approach where spirituality is emphasized over *praxis* (Chopp 1995, 66).

Although much of his book is spent framing the issues of the debate over theological education over the last 20 years, Robert Banks, author of *Reenvisioning Theological Education,* also promotes a synthetic model of theological education centered on mission. He tends to fuse the ideas of *praxis* and contextualization introduced by Stackhouse with the introduction of practical theology, reflection, and thought for spiritual formation proposed by Cobbs and Hough (Banks 1999, 157). As with Wood, he advocates a synthesis of both the Athens and Berlin models into a third model of theological education that attempts to utilize the best of both worlds and minimize their weaknesses. To Banks, theological education would become a blend of action and reflection, theory and practice, the sharing of life and knowledge, and all delivered with contextualization in mind (Banks 1999, 157-181). The type of fusion of the Athens and Berlin models that Banks advocates is typical of the state of the debate over theological education as it exists at the end of the twentieth century. These types of changes sound good on paper, but strike at the very heart of how theological education is delivered in most American institutions today. To implement them would require a massive change in the curricula, types of teachers, values, and delivery systems that are currently in place.

Drawing Lessons from the Debate

Overall, the debate in theological education circles has been healthy and begun to address some of the important issues required to make theological training relevant to the needs of today's emerging leaders. The debate still suffers greatly from sectarian interests and a divisive call to choose one way or the other. It also suffers from the lack of ability to think "outside the box" as far as innovative solutions in theological training are concerned. What if the solution to the theological education dilemma is not one of these solutions, but several of them? What if the solution requires a radical reshaping of the endeavor altogether that will adversely affect vested interests currently delivering theological training? The solution could stretch educators to the breaking point because it would be easier, though more damaging in the long run, to let things go on as they are.

The debate has been healthy because it has revealed some of the deep problems that exist with theological education today. If theological training is not centered on *theologia* or coming to know God more fully, then what should it be based on? To not have this focus would be like medicine training doctors without a focus on patients or the human body. If theological training is not centered on personal formation, then is it any different than secular training that aims at the skill without developing the person? If theological education is not contextualized or mission oriented in nature, then is it not training people to deliver a product that has no specific market?

If the answer to more than one of these potential foci is "yes" then theological education as it exists today must develop a new foundation for delivering its product. This type of change is not done at surface levels by making adjustments. These types of changes involve significant paradigm shifting and values transformation to occur at the deepest levels of the training process. Such change is never easy, but the price must be paid for a generation of emerging leaders who desperately need the training and foundation to sustain the renewal God is sending to His Church today.

CHAPTER FOUR

The Heart of the Matter: Paradigm Shifting and Values Transformation in Theological Training

The question was not "if" we should get some further theological training to help guide us in the church, but "where?" We were long on questions and short on answers. People in the church began to sense that the leadership was stalled in its decision-making processes. This was perceived as a lack of sensitivity to the Holy Spirit and what He was saying to the church! We knew what He was saying - that we were at the end of our natural abilities and that we need to gain new knowledge and skills to take the church on to the next level. Graduate level education was not an option - none of us had completed our undergraduate education. Undergraduate level education would take a minimum of three years to complete. There were always seminars that we could attend - and we did - often spending several thousand dollars to travel and attend these sessions. Still, despite the excellent seminars, we could not tie all the information together and lacked the skill base to apply what we had learned.

Several of the pastoral staff did launch into under-graduate level training so that we could eventually access more focused education at the graduate level, though it was years away. In the mean time, the lead pastor became more and more burdened with the work of the ministry. He began to feel isolated and trapped by problems that seemed to defy solutions. The staff, leadership, and people of the church began to sense that there was "something wrong", but couldn't put there finger on it. People began to take matters into their own hands in a quest to discover the "real problems." Before long, there was obvious division on staff and in the congregation. People began to group around individuals that had "heard from God" about a problem and its solution. Things began to play themselves out like a bad dream.

First came the resignations on staff in protest. Then came the folks who began leaving the church because "the anointing was gone." The lead pastor began to isolate himself in frustration. His marriage began to suffer under the burden of the church and Christian school. Attendance and offerings began to go down just as the new building began to go up. It was just too much for the lead pastor to bear. He had had enough - how much could one man bear. Would this church survive a transition with the lead pastor leaving? Could the associate pastor who took his place lead the church through the transition. Where would this new lead pastor go for answers to the questions that were now on his platter? Relocating for seminary was not an option - the church and the new pastor's family were in this location. Focused education was years away after undergraduate work, and much of that didn't seem to apply anyway. The answers seemed distant but the mounting problems were all too close at hand.

How can emerging leaders access education at their location without having to relocate their families and leave their ministries? Is it possible to have relevant and application oriented instruction in ministry, even at the undergraduate level, rather than delaying it until graduate work can begin? Can the same high standards of degreed and accredited education now available through classical delivery systems in the college and seminary world be maintained if the system is changed? The answers to these questions make a strong point - the changes required to make theological training relevant for today does not amount to slight modifications. The changes that are required must occur at the most basic levels and assumptions about how to train emerging leaders theologically. These basic assumptions about theological education are called its values. The ideas that frame these basic values are called paradigms.

A basic understanding of paradigms and how to shift from existing paradigms is necessary if theological training is to be changed in a meaningful way. Paradigms often exist in the background quietly shaping the way reality plays itself out. They shape the enterprise because they are the basic units that human beings use to shape their conception of reality. Shifting of existing paradigms requires precision and skill and a basic understanding of how to make the shift happen.

So it is with values and values transformation. Values are the core assumptions that an individual, organization, or enterprise believes are true. Like the paradigms that drive them, values often exist at a subconscious level so that the very people who hold the values don't understand exactly what they believe is true or why they believe that way. Transforming values likewise takes time, great patience, and skill.

The changes needed to make theological training relevant and effective for emerging leaders today are not surface in nature. They require radical change at the level of paradigms and values. This shift in paradigms and core values in theological training often exact a high price on the existing structures and institutions which are based the old paradigms and values from past generations. By understanding the process of paradigm shifting and values transformation, those involved in theological training can count the cost of needed change. If they decide to pay the price that these changes demand, they can plot a course that leads to the much needed paradigm shifts and values transformation to make theological training relevant once again. A whole generation waits on our decision. Will we pay the price? Will we be willing to go to the very foundations of what we believe to be correct in theological training and rebuild them if necessary?

Paradigms and Paradigm Shifting

The debate over the last twenty years on what theological education is in its essence and for how to properly deliver it highlights the necessity for change. Many of the old paradigms for theological training are simply worn out and are no longer solving the problems that have arisen within the theological education community. Old paradigms for delivering theological training are often rigid and enhancement only brings incremental improvement.

Joel Arthur Barker, in his book *Paradigms: The Business of Discovering the Future* (1992), defined the process of exchanging old paradigms for new ones, or paradigm shifting as he calls it. He defined a paradigm as:

> ...a set of rules and regulations (written and unwritten) that does two things: it establishes or defines boundaries; and (2) it tells you how to behave inside the boundaries in order to be successful. (1992, 32)

Theological training, like any other human effort, has many written and unwritten rules and regulations (paradigms) that determine its essential nature and delivery. In some cases these paradigms are biblically based, and in other cases they are merely socio-cultural constructs based on cultural preference and tradition. In all cases, paradigms associated with the nature and delivery of theological training govern current training protocols. Some of the older paradigms that were adequate to address the problems of how to train individuals for ministry are now obsolete and do not solve current problems or needs. Many of these old protocols must give way to new paradigms for change in theological training so that it is relevant and effective in accomplishing its mission.

Robert Banks makes the general case for the irrelevance of current theological training paradigms on the basis of several astute observations that the authors have paraphrased with some italicized comments (1999, 4,5):

- **Five out of six accredited seminaries in this country are heavily tied to denominational or confessional standards**. *At the same time, renewal-oriented Christianity is expanding globally and is in many cases less oriented toward traditional*

*denominational or confessional standards. With the rapid
growth of interdenominational or renewal-oriented churches,
there is a growing gap in theological training specifically
designed to meet the needs of this target group.*

- **Two out of three of the students in the accredited seminaries in this country are over thirty years of age, have been out of college for a number of years, and are already involved in some form of ministry.** *The standard paradigms for theological training still center on paradigms that were effective centuries ago, such as the four-fold model for curriculum and classical education based on biblical and romantic languages. The current student population has a more practical orientation because it is already involved in ministry. These students are not academicians - they are practitioners who need to tie any knowledge gained directly to reflection and application. This is not possible in many seminary settings because these settings are highly pedagogical in nature, rather than andragogically centered on the education of adults.*

- **The population of the accredited theological seminaries in this country contains less than a 25% minority component, with African-American students comprising less than 9% of this component.** *The theological education, context of the training, ethos of the institutions, or curricula are either not appropriate for minority ministers or lay leaders in many cases. Even if they were, many in the renewal community do not have sufficient training at an undergraduate level to access theological training, which is primarily done at a graduate level, based on paradigms of training from the middle ages. This is especially true for the many of the minority students that are seeking training for ministry, but cannot find accredited and degreed theological training with a practical ministry focus that is accessible.*

Many of the changes just noted in the theological education community have been driven by the unprecedented rate of change in the world over the last century. Whereas in 1900, 85-90% of the Christians lived in Western nations, in the year 2000, 58% of the

Christians live outside the West. Likewise, during this same period, the fruit of many years of missions work has been realized within Africa, the Christian population went from 3% to 50% of the population. Christians in Latin America and Asia also increased many times over (Messer 1995, 55-56). The world is changing in extraordinary ways, but in many cases theological training continues on with the same paradigms that have existed for centuries, oblivious to the change around it. This has caused many in the church community to see existing theological training as ineffective as best and irrelevant or harmful to emerging leaders at its worst. A major shift in paradigms in theological training is necessary to remedy this problem. The old worn out paradigms for theological training will no longer do the job.

Barker also points out that paradigms exist on a continuum like a living organism, and follow a definite life and death cycle that can be graphically represented. He represents the life cycle of a paradigm as a sigmoid-shaped curve on a Cartesian plain. In this map of paradigm life and death, which he calls the paradigm cycle, the x-axis represents time and the y-axis represents a relative number of problems that the paradigm solves. This paradigm curve is represented in Figure 1.

Figure 1. The Paradigm Curve, representing the dynamics of paradigm effectiveness at solving problems over time (Barker 1992, 46).

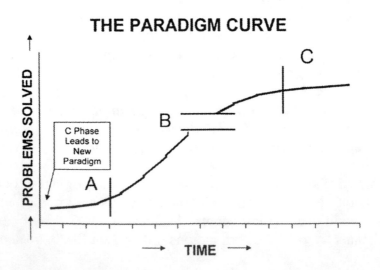

As can be seen graphically, each paradigm starts off at time zero and begins to be used to solve problems. A new mindset for how to solve a particular set of problems is developed by the individuals that Barker refers to as paradigm shifters (1992, 72). As many of the existing paradigms for theological training have aged, the theological education community has tried to enhance or repair them. It is time for individuals to begin the process of paradigm shifting in the theological education community to address today's problems from a new perspective.

Paradigm shifters act as a catalyst to produce change in thinking after the community begins to acknowledge that the old way of doing things will not solve all of the current problems it is encountering. Many times people who work with a particular paradigm and its mindset are blinded to other possibilities. They cannot see different methods that exist to solve problems "outside the box" they have placed themselves in with the mindset of their paradigm. This can be seen within theological education circles as people in this community try to enhance existing paradigms for theological training rather than develop new ones. This effect is what Barker calls paradigm paralysis (1992, 156). It often takes an outsider who is unfamiliar with the rules of the old paradigm to discover new ways to address problems that the current paradigm cannot address. Barker points out that those developing new paradigms to address a community's problems are often a new person hired to work in a particular field, or an older person shifting fields. In both cases, these people have significant operational naivete when it comes to the old paradigm, and are therefore not blinded by the effect of paradigm paralysis. They are free to think outside the box of the old way of doing things because they are not yet familiar with them (Barker 1992, 58-59).

Those existing within the old paradigms have vested interests in keeping the old ways of thinking. Oftentimes, a lot of financial, emotional, and time investment has been made to actualize the old paradigms. Many times, people who are part of the old paradigms have jobs and their well-being dependent on the old paradigm and its use. One of the authors comes from outside the theological education community. He sees things in that community from the standpoint of a pastor and practitioner. He is not blinded to the same ideas that exist "inside the box" as some may be who have lived in that box for all of their career. Many of the traditional assumptions that govern theological training today simply do not make sense to one of the authors because of his outside perspective.

Paradigm shifters begin to create and pioneer new ways of thinking about the problems and in the process, new paradigms are created. As can be seen in Figure 1, at first the new paradigm meets with resistance as the paradigm shifters initiate the use of the new set of ideas to solve a problem. Some individuals embrace the new paradigm and begin to apply them to problems, often taking the brunt of the criticism from those trying to hang on to the old paradigm. These individuals are referred to as paradigm pioneers, and they are the ones who experience the first successes with the new paradigm. These pioneers also begin to capture the attention of those embracing the old paradigm as their new way of looking at problems begins to generate tangible success. On the sigmoid paradigm curve (Figure 1), phase A represents the beginning of a paradigm's life. It is the time when paradigm shifters bring the new paradigm to life and when paradigm pioneers begin to use it.

At first, there are not many problems solved with the new paradigm as it encounters resistance and the paradigm pioneers incrementally change it to make it work in the real world. As these pioneers experience success, the paradigm is accepted more broadly and the number of problems that the paradigm solves dramatically increases as more people abandon old paradigms and adopt the new one. This results in a much greater number of problems solved over a shorter amount of time, and is represented graphically in Figure 1 as phase B, with a much higher slope.

As more people embrace the new paradigm, it eventually replaces the old paradigm and becomes an accepted set of rules, regulations, and boundaries. The people who adopt the new paradigm because of its success are called paradigm settlers because they begin to "put down stakes" and invest money in actualizing the new paradigm. At the same time, paradigm shifters begin to notice that the new paradigm does not hold all the answers for the problem that a particular community faces. It is at this point on the paradigm curve, in phase B, when the paradigm shifters begin to pioneer new ways to think about the problems that the old new paradigm cannot solve. The whole process of paradigm shifting enters a new generation at this point in phase B as new paradigm shifters begin to abandon the "new" old paradigm in favor of yet another way of thinking that solves problems that the current paradigm will not address.

As people abandon the "old" new paradigm in favor of the next generation paradigm, the current paradigm can be seen in to flatten out and enter into phase C (Figure 1). In this phase, those with time, resources and therefore vested interest in the current paradigm, dig in to resist change. The old paradigm has plateaued, however, and will become increasingly less useful for those who have actualized it. It will fossilize and become less and less useful as time goes by for solving problems. It rapidly becomes a relic of the past, and requires much time and energy to prop it up since it is no longer useful in solving problems. It is alarming to see how many people are willing to invest in their old paradigms once they have plateaued because of their paradigm paralysis or vested interests.

American church history and its theological training strongly evidenced paradigm shifting each time renewal has broken out in the church. With the current wave of renewal occurring on a global basis, theological training is ripe for further paradigm shifting. Many of the current paradigms for what theological training is and how it should be delivered have been developed over the last 150 years. Over the last forty years, the theological education community has been asking itself how best to change these paradigms to better deliver theological training. In the late 1950s and 1960s, changes that were focused on paradigm enhancement for existing paradigms of theological training rather than a complete paradigm shift to new ones. Enhancement of existing administration, efficiency, and streamlining curricula were the topics of that time period.

The urgency noted in the debate over the last twenty years is due to old paradigms and enhancements to them do not address the obvious problems that exist today with theological training. Many of these problems are so severe that further enhancement of existing paradigms will not work as a solution. In 1994, the Murdock Charitable Trust released its review of graduate theological education in the Pacific Northwest. This study, which went off like an alarm clock in the theological education community, shows how broken theological education is today. Tim Dearborne expounds on these same types of concerns addressed in the Murdock Report (1995b, 7,8). Current paradigms used in theological training are not solving problems as is evidenced in its fruit - the leaders of today's churches. Dearborn notes that many churches today are visionless, "…like Columbus: going to a destination he knew not where, seeking something he would not recognize once he found it, and doing it all on someone else's money" (1995b, 7). This is because the leaders of these churches are directionless themselves and not equipped to minister as leaders in the twenty-first century church effectively.

The nature of pastoral ministry and the role of pastors are being called into question. Clergy is not able to properly prioritize what should be done in and through the church. The Church itself sees how unprepared for real-life ministry seminary graduates are, and has begun to question the validity of seminary as a source of theological training. As Dearborn notes, many churches are deciding against sending students to seminaries at all, feeling that they can do a better job themselves in preparing their ministers for leadership in the local church (1995b, 8). All of these facts are compelling reasons that theological training must change drastically if it is to have a valuable contribution to Kingdom life in the twenty-first century.

The voices in the debate over theological training in the last twenty years are largely those of paradigm enhancers. A precious few are actually the voice of paradigm shifters. It would be much easier to continually attempt to enhance prevailing paradigms concerning theological training than to replace them. Current paradigms are highly entrenched in the everyday life of the institutions currently delivering theological training. Large endowments numbering in the billions of dollars exist to perpetuate current models of theological training. Huge structures have been built to house theological training endeavors. Complicated infrastructures have been developed and implemented to run these theological education machines so they can crank out pastors efficiently and in large numbers. Faculty has been hired according to certain standards and with certain backgrounds to teach within existing paradigm structures. Many thousands of jobs exist that depend upon how well the individuals who hold them conform to the current paradigms of theological training. Barker notes that most paradigms that age and become ineffective are discarded, unless there is some significant vested interest involved that invests time and energy to keep the old paradigm working. These individuals are at risk because of high financial and personal investment in the old paradigm, providing the time and energy to perpetuate old paradigms and reduce their personal risk of loss (Barker 1992, 69).

What happens to all the buildings that have been built if it proves more effective to deliver theological training in local church and ministry contexts? How does one educate the hundreds of millions of future leaders in third-world countries who have no endowments and little capital at all to invest in the process of theological training? What happens to tenured academicians if it is more effective to educate with professors that have practical experience in a subject area (i.e. pastors teaching pastoral theology) rather than just an intellectual understanding? What will happen if the answer to congruence in theological training is immediate application of the knowledge in the context of a student's current ministry rather than deferred application after graduation at the church an individual experiments with? The answer to all of these questions is that major paradigms that currently exist to define and deliver theological training will have to be greatly modified (if that is even possible) or exchanged altogether in favor of new paradigms. The cost will be enormous and the change monumental if this is to happen. The changes will have to be as basic as the values that govern current thinking for theological training and not merely a change in the structures that currently exist. The problem at its basic roots is a core values problem, not a problem of methodology or structure.

Values Transformation and Theological Training

Structures and forms in the natural world do not exist in a vacuum, nor do they come into existence by accident. There is always a cause for them. Outward forms come into being as an expression of thoughts and ideas. Each institution or system is a complex blending of paradigms that mix together to give a distinctive life or essence to it, formally referred to as an entelichy. The paradigms, whether written or assumed, are the engines that drive and shape the forms that a visible expression takes. If the paradigm that drives a system's shape can be discerned, then cause and effect roles can be followed within an institution to trace the source or a problem to its root paradigms so that new and more effective paradigms to address problems can be developed and implemented. If healthy paradigms can be isolated and identified, then new models for theological education, can be tailored so as to avoid the problems that exist in current models for theological education.

But what drives the paradigms? What are the underlying ideas that give shape and form to paradigms that exist in theological education today? The answer to this question, as with all institutions or systems, is the values that are its foundation. Paradigms exist as a means to an end. Values are the end. Paradigms are the ideas, boundaries, rules, and regulations for how to do something. Values are the reasons why something is done.

If theological education is to be changed significantly, it will not come by enhancing existing paradigms. Marginal improvement is not needed. Drastic change is needed. Even implementing new paradigms to replace the old ones, as painful as it may be, is not the answer. These new paradigms and the structures that would result would soon need to be replaced as well. The answer is to go to the root of the problem. The root is not in the means to the end or the "how to" of theological education. The root exists in the values that form the basic assumptions for what theological education is and how it should be delivered. When these values are identified and addressed, then changes in the paradigms that are built on them will change in accordance with forms that these values demand. The problems that must be solved in theological education are values problems firstly and paradigm problems secondly.

Aubrey Malphurs, in his book *Values-Driven Leadership* (1996), discusses the importance of change based on values rather than mere structure. He points out that values are not "vision", which answers the question of what an institution should do. Values are not "strategies", which answer the question of "how" an institution should accomplish tasks. Values are the "end" that an institution is striving for. They are also the basic reasons, sometimes written and many times assumed, for what an institution does (Malphurs 1996, 31-41). Values answer the question "why" an institution does what it does. They are the passionate, unchanging, and hopefully biblical assumptions that are made and held as core beliefs for an institution. All values exist based on principles (fundamental truths), and in the case of a Christian pursuit such as theological education, hopefully these principles are biblical in nature. Sadly, this is not always the case. In many cases the principles behind the actual values that exist as the foundations of the theological education paradigms in use today are a casual mixture of Christian and non-Christian principles. The process for "fixing" what is wrong with theological education today starts with identifying biblical principles. From there, biblical values must be developed that answer the deep "why" questions involved in the nature and delivery of theological education. Only then can a vision for how to do theological education in a particular context, such as the interdenominational renewal-oriented community, be developed. Once this vision is established, proper paradigms for strategy that answers the question "how" can be developed. The authors propose that any model for theological education that is developed must follow this stream of methodology in its development. This methodology for approaching theological education will change the way theological education is done and thereby bypass some of the current problems that the theological education is facing. The authors assert the need for this type of action in the greater theological community if it is to experience meaningful change that produces effective ministers for the twenty-first century.

The Heart of the Matter

The changes required to make theological training effective and relevant to today's emerging leaders must occur at the basic level of the values and paradigms at the heart of the enterprise. Paradigm shifting and values transformation at a core level require the identification of old paradigms and the values that drive them and the reengineering with new ones that will take their place. Once these new paradigms and values have taken root, they will ultimately reshape the whole nature of theological training and the educational system that delivers it. Surface changes and adjustments of what exist are far easier. The price for simply modifying the existing structures and systems appears much more palatable. The results of such "tweaks" to theological education will not sufficiently change the whole enterprise as is needed to render it effective in preparing leaders in the Body of Christ for ministry in the twenty-first century. The question is, will we pay the price now and do what it takes to change the paradigms and values, or we pay the price later, when it could be much more costly?

CHAPTER FIVE

When Athens Meets Berlin Meets Topeka: The Clash of Values in Theological Training

The first years as lead pastor at our struggling church seems like a roller coaster ride. Just when it looks like the church will go under, God provides miraculously. In between the sorrow, heartache, struggles, there are salvations. People's marriages are restored. Drug addicts are delivered and set free. There is door to door evangelism, missions work overseas, and a food bank to feed those in need. The Christian school begins to recover from the shock of transition and doubles in size over the next couple of years. We deal with issues of broken trust, new leadership, and the everyday grind of pastoral ministry. We are forced to learn finances and financial systems rather quickly after an internal audit uncovers systematic embezzlement by someone we thought was there to help. That also introduced us to the world of news media, private investigations, district attorneys, and corporate law. The learning curve is rather steep, but we are gaining ground as a church.

We still feel so inadequate to face the tasks at hand in church ministry. Is there anyone or any number of people who have walked these paths before? Is there anyone who can give us wise counsel and direction? These times can be the loneliest ones for an independent church. Undergraduate studies take less than two years to complete. Seminary and the M.Div. take about eight years. The journey is one of discovery yet confusion. I am a forty year old man in school with many twenty year olds. I have been in ministry for nearly sixteen years, since some of my class mates were eight years old when I was starting out. We struggle together with Greek, Systematic Theology, Church History, and Pastoral Theology. For many of them, Homiletics is a class. For me, it happens five times a week at the church. For some of the classes, I go through the motion keeping my eyes on the degree that will open new doors for me. Yet, there is one professor that constantly encourages me, challenges me, and urges me onward.

There seems to be such a gap between my peers and me. Everything seems so theoretical. I pass tests. I make "A's" and pass each of the 135 quarter hours of class with high marks. Still, the real tests are everyday at the church and in the board meetings. My peers "leave the door open" to the possibility that what I believe about the Holy Spirit is true, for which I am very thankful, but renewal issues are not addressed directly except for an occasional negative reference. I graduate with new friends and more knowledge than I had before. I have learned many new things, some of which I can apply to ministry. The experience has left me a more effective minister, yet many of my questions remain unanswered. Where do I go now to find the answers?

Seminary can be a confusing place. They exist to produce leaders in the Body of Christ who can function effectively in ministry. Their whole purpose for existence revolves around effective training to do the work of the ministry, yet their product so often seems inadequate for the task. Many seminaries are highly academic in nature, and modeled after medieval paradigms for theological education even though those times are long gone. There seems to be little emphasis on application and skill-based knowledge. Those teaching are experts in their narrow fields of knowledge but often have little or no experience in doing what they teach. Would these same conditions exist in a teaching hospital or a business? Would the professors in these schools be allowed to teach students without ever having seen a real patient or handled a balance sheet? If not, why is this the way it is done in many seminaries?

As said before, form exists because of deeply held assumptions that exist at the level of values. Many of these values exist at an unconscious level, but drive and shape the institutions we call Bible colleges and seminaries. Where did these values come from? Why are things the way they are? Which values are at work right now in our institutions of theological education? Should they be at work there or should they be replaced with new ones? The answers to these questions exist in other countries and cultures. They herald back to German and Greek cultures that have long since passed away, but still leave their mark on reality. Defining these values is essential for understanding why things are the way that they are today. Putting in place the right values is essential for shaping theological education as it should exist tomorrow.

Six Eras in the History of Theological Education

There are six distinct eras in the history of theological education adapted - John Gratian "Contextualization." Each era has a favored mode of delivery for the training. Each era also has prominent implications that result from the basic assumptions associated with it:

Six Eras in Theological Education

New Testament Era

- Mode: Church-based, master-apprentice model

- Example: Eph 4:11, 12 – Elders equip the saints for ministry

- Implications: Relational transfer of knowledge

Post-apostolic era

- Mode: One teacher in a small group that is isolated
- Example: Monastic orders and catechism classes
- Implications: Relational-skill based but isolated from people

Post-enlightenment Era

- Mode: Biblical languages, scientific process, rhetorical methods
- Example: University model
- Implications: Clerics ("one who reads") and laity

Colonial World Era

- Mode: Vocational-professional training in residence
- Examples: Log Colleges, Harvard, Yale, Princeton
- Implications: Theoretical basis, Degrees

Modern Era

- Mode: Mechanistic, progressive, efficiency, learning systems
- Example: Pastor making machines, minister making experts, degree mills, professors that are ministry making experts
- Implications: Self actualization, preparation for a role, rather than preparing the person

Post-modern Era

- Mode: Individualization, professionalization
- Example: On the job training, continuing education, D.Min.
- Implications: Real, practical, mentor-based

Each era has associated with it a specific mode of transmission for the theological training that occurs in its time period. It also has certain institutions or methods associated with it and implications that result from the prevailing assumptions of the time period.

The New Testament Era of theological education was characterized by church-based instruction where leadership in the church, most notably the eldership, trained the people of the church to do the work of the ministry in the pattern of Eph. 4:11, 12. The educational process was highly relational in process and had a high application content. By contrast, education in the Post-apostolic Era began to occur in isolation from the church and society in small groups by one notable teacher who specialized in such training. The primary mode in this era became the monastic orders and catechism classes. This was the primary method of training throughout medieval times.

The Post-enlightenment Era was marked by a noted shift in training toward classical education in a university environment. The use of biblical languages and scientific method figured prominently in this era. Greek rhetorical method was valued and taught. The university model was used and rapidly developed a class of clerics, who could "read" (the origin of the word, from *kleros*) and a laity who could not. A strong professional clergy paradigm resulted. In the colonial world, this was replaced by the Colonial Era in which the ministry was viewed as a vocation and the minister trained as a professional. The Log Cabin Colleges, Harvard, Yale, and Princeton, originally founded to train ministers, are examples of this era of training. The idea of degrees proliferated, especially in the German university model of education, where theology remained a part of the university curriculum because it was a "socially necessary profession."

The Modern Era of theological education reflects a mechanistic and industrial culture in the Western world. In a time of material progress, automation, efficiency, and empiricism, theological training took upon itself a mechanistic feel. Seminaries became pastor-factories that dispensed degrees. Professors became ministry-making experts and were far removed from the practice of much of the practical aspects of ministry. The goal of the education became more self-actualization in its orientation rather than personal formation oriented.

The current era is the Post-modern Era of theological training. In this era the ideals of individualization and professionalization are becoming more pronounced. Community is more highly valued and a trend back toward individual mentoring is taking place. There is a move to upgrade many of the degrees offered and the idea of continuing education is pronounced. A more practical orientation in learning is being reemphasized and character skills and personal formation are once again being emphasized. It is interesting to note that theological training is going back to the future in ways that are reminiscent of New Testament times.

Athens or Berlin?

David H. Kelsey, who was Professor of Theology at Yale Divinity School in the early 1990s, did much to advance the understanding of the impact of the philosophies that are foundational to theological education. His two books, *Between Athens and Berlin: The Theological Education Debate* (1993) and *To Understand God Truly: What's Theological About a Theological School* (1992) have become important reference points in the debate over how to fix what is wrong with theological education. They were defining works that brought the issue of the classical and vocational models for theological education to the forefront of the debate.

In *Between Athens and Berlin*, Kelsey attempts to classify the two most prominent philosophies that are the foundation for theological education. These philosophies drive the various institutions that are engaged in theological education, and they have practical implications for the way the institution conducts itself, the ethos and curriculum that is offered, as well as their beliefs about the very nature of what theological education is. He defines these two philosophies by their geographical and cultural origins - Athens and Berlin. The "Athens" philosophy or classical model of theological education is based upon Greek educational philosophy and dominated theological education in early church history. The "Berlin" philosophy or vocational model of theological education was developed in German post-Enlightenment culture and has been embodied in the education delivered at the University of Berlin since its founding in 1810.

Kelsey traces the Athens philosophy of education, called the "classical model" by Banks, through its origins in Greek thought.

Education in Greek culture centered around the concept of "παιδεία" (*paideia*) which embodies the Greek philosophy of education. It is roughly translated as the "culturing" of the soul as character formation occurs through the process of education (Kelsey 1993, 6,7). The concept comes from the ideas of Plato's *Republic* in which he discusses the philosophy of education. He contended that education should prepare a person for their responsibilities in life. The "Guardians" in Greek society should be schooled in understanding Greek civic tradition and virtue, while the "Philosopher-Kings" must be schooled so as to have the knowledge of good itself, and not just Greek tradition. Plato felt that education should be done through the "culturing" of the soul in such a way that the character is developed. In this way, the student is able to identify for himself the virtues needed to function as an adult in his role in society (Kelsey 1993, 6,7). The formation of *paideia* in the student involved both bodily disciplines as well as the formation of the soul through reflection on Greek classical literature such as the writings of Homer.

As Greek culture evolved from the time of Plato, so did the Greek idea of education. The clear purpose of education in the Greek mind was the cultivation of "αρετε" (*arete)* or "excellence" of the soul. The end result was "to know the Good." "Good" was thought to be the underlying principle of the universe itself. Education was therefore the religious pursuit of the "Good" through contemplation. The Greeks believed that the knowledge of good must come through contemplation, because it could not be directly taught - it was a "γνωσις" (*gnosis)* or intuitive insight that was developed or revealed in the student. The job of the teacher was to put the student in the appropriate context that would facilitate the flash of insight needed for the development of *paideia*. The proper environment would result in a "conversion" of the soul, as the soul turned from a preoccupation with appearances to a focus on true reality or "the Good." It is also important to note that the Greeks believed that this type of conversion could only be accomplished in the context of a community (Kelsey 1993, 10,11).

The influence of Greek thought and culture on early Christianity are obvious. Werner Jaeger, in his book *Early Christianity and Greek Paideia*, makes a strong case for the hellenization of Christian culture as is evidenced by the way early Christians categorized thought, the inherited Greek metaphors in literature, and subtle connotations that emerge in thoughts expressed in the Scriptures. In Eph 6:6, the "παιδεία κυριόυ" (*paideia kuriou* - discipline of God) is used to describe how Christians are to raise their children. In Heb 12:11 "παιδεία"(*paideia*) is used to speak of the discipline process that God puts His children under in order to develop them. These elements are also echoed in the writings of Clement, one of the earliest church fathers. He would use the phrase "*paideia* of God" and "*paideia* of Christ" routinely in his writings. Jaeger asserts that the use of these phrases by Clement are evidence of Greek educational philosophy at work in the minds of early Christians (Jaeger 1961, 25). The early Christians at Alexandria were more explicitly Greek in their thinking, including their ideas of education, as is recorded in their writings well into the third and fourth centuries (Jaegar 1961, 70-83). Clement of Alexandria thought of Christianity in terms of Greek educational philosophy. His writings record that Christianity is *paideia*. Instead of pursuing a knowledge of "good," the Christian is to pursue a knowledge of "God." The manner in which Clement advocates to pursue the knowledge of God is uniquely Greek — by forming the person's soul in such a way as allow the proper holiness to be resident and so produce a radical conversion that can only be produced by the Holy Spirit. As such, Clement affirmed the Greek ideal that this type of knowledge cannot be "taught" but must be "caught" through the instructor providing the right environment and expose to Scripture and other literature in order to facilitate conversion (Kelsey 1993, 11-14).

Kelsey's point is that the "Athens" or Greek philosophy of education dominated early Christianity and became the mode of education in the Christian community through the Middle Ages, in the universities where they began. The Athens model for theological education was normative until the impact of Enlightenment thought on theological education in the eighteenth and nineteenth centuries. Thomas Aquinas embodied this type of educational philosophy in his writings in the Middle Ages.

Hatch, in his book *The Influence of Greek Ideas on Early Christianity*, traces Greek educational philosophy through Christian education in the Middle Ages and in the universities as they first developed in medieval Europe. The main subjects of study in the medieval universities were Grammar (the study of literature) and

Rhetoric (the study of literature by studying literary expression and argument), just as it was with the Greeks in ancient times (Hatch 1957, 28-30). The idea of a "professor" in an educational setting comes from the Greek "sophist," who was skilled in "σοφος" (*sophos*) or the art of life. "Lectures" in the universities were modeled after the Greek teacher who made remarks on literature to help the student come to his moment of *gnosis*, leading to a flash of insight on the divine nature. Even the idea of a university "chair" (a teacher's office) and "faculty" (branch of knowledge that a professor taught) herald back to Greek educational philosophies (Hatch 1957, 43,44). There can be no doubt that Greek educational philosophies, or as Kelsey calls it, the "Athens" model for education had a great impact on the way that Christianity has approached education until recent times.

The second philosophical school of thought for delivering theological education is referred to by Kelsey as the "Berlin model." Banks refers to this as the "vocational model" for doing theological education. This model for theological education gained acceptance with the advent of the Enlightenment and its emphasis on the ability of human reason. This emphasis on human reason manifested itself in the educational community with the development of a movement toward scholasticism. This influence can be seen in the Reformation and in the writing of the reformers themselves. Indeed, the Reformation itself seems to have come about by a healthy blend of an "Athens" philosophy of character and spiritual development, mixed with healthy scholastic reflection on the true meaning of the Scriptures and what it means to know God.

In post-Enlightenment times, the exaltation of human reason has given way to the worship of human wisdom and a humanistic philosophy that has no room for God. Whereas theology was the "queen of sciences" that was the normative standard for judging truth in the period before the eighteenth century, humanistic elements within the European university system began to "turn on the queen." Theology was demoted to a lower place in study for the very reason that the Greeks had identified thousands of years earlier. It was not deducible by human intellect, but had to be understood as a result of reflection and revealed insight rather than empirical investigation. Theology was simply not a good candidate for the new rational paradigms of education and inquiry that resulted from the Enlightenment — God could not be seen and studied. The Enlightenment methodology of empirical inquiry and reason are not evil in and of themselves. Empirical investigation worked well in man's attempt to understand the physical world around him as he accumulated the knowledge about the underlying truths in God's natural creation. These methods do not, however, function as well when applied to some areas of knowledge that involve spiritual truths, specifically when it comes to knowing the person of God.

This conflict of competing epistemologies came to a head when the University of Berlin was established in 1810. A committee of scholars was given the task of designing a university that would shape education deliberately along the principles of Enlightenment thought. Friedrich Schleiermacher (1768-1834) was one of the individuals on this committee and was a theologian. The committee was ready to "excommunicate" theology from its intended curriculum because it had no place in a university setting in their opinion. Theology had been the "policeman" that restricted their prized *Lernfreiheit* (freedom to learn) and *Lehrfreiheit* (freedom to teach) with its "restrictive" truths. Theology was no longer wanted as the "ultimate censor" in a university environment, and it seems, was about to be censored itself (Kelsey 1993, 15).

Schleiermacher argued that theology should be viewed as a "socially necessary" discipline because it deals with concepts of bodily health, social order, and religious needs that are central to human sociology (Kelsey 1993,15). He argued that theology should be included in the university curriculum in order to hone the "professional" skills necessary to skillfully execute pastoral ministry, as a discipline of "specialized knowledge." He also argued that these skills are best honed by subjecting the various disciplines within the theological curriculum to the discipline of research or *wissenschaftlich* as it was called. Schleiermacher's arguments were accepted, theology was added to the new university's curriculum, and the concept of the pastoral ministry as a "profession" was born.

The key element in the education found in the University of Berlin was the Enlightenment principle of *wissenschaftliche* or the application of rigorous investigation to deduce wisdom and truth. *Wissenschaft* involved the use of disciplined scientific principles of investigation in the pursuit of truth. A renaissance was taking place in the natural sciences as these principles were being applied to various scientific fields of study and nature was yielding up God's entrained principles of truth. Could the *wissenschaftliche* be applied to theology as well and lead to a better understanding of God and theological truth? Schleiermacher argued that it could.

Kelsey best summarized this model for education that arose from the Enlightenment ideals employed at the University of Berlin:

> The model of excellent theological schooling [at the University of Berlin] symbolized by the inclusion of a faculty of theology in the University of Berlin tie "practical" education for a socially necessary profession (the clergy) to the "theoretical" education of a research university on the grounds that future clergy would be best equipped for their ministerial functions if they acquired capacities for rigorous critical research (Kelsey 1992, 227-228).

The result of Christian theology subjected to German Enlightenment thought by *Wissenschaftliche* has resulted in the proliferation of specialization within theology much as it has in the sciences. Farley, in his book *Theologia*, points to this specialization as the cause of a disintegration of theology into increasingly smaller disjointed "subjects" that are to be researched and learned by the student (Farley 1983, 8,9). Inadvertently, "Schleiermacher's ghost" now defined theology as being unified around the skills necessary to adequately equip a professional to function within society. This produced a whole new identity for the church and the minister — that of the professional and his organization. (Hough, Jr. and Cobb, Jr. 1985, 11-13).

The legacy of Scheiermacher, or as some would say "Scheiermacher's ghost," has been the division of theological education into a "four-fold" system of subject matter that includes Bible, Dogmatics (Systematic Theology), Church History, and Practical Theology. While one would hope that this division is a naturally planned outcome of values most necessary for properly formed ministers, Kelsey and others assert that it is more likely a haphazard outcome of the desire to include theology in university curriculum

(Kelsey and Wheeler 1994, 79-80). The result has been a division of theology into ever increasing specialties. This specialization of knowledge has required that the professors hired to deliver theological education be specialists in one of these fields, rather than actual practitioners. In order to fit into the world of the university, theological education was moved to the realm of "graduate study" and made attainable only to those who had obtained undergraduate education first. As the German university "degree" system, most notably the German "Doctor of Philosophy" (Ph.D.) degree, became accepted as standard in American education in the late nineteenth century, more and more professors at seminaries were required to obtain this degree as a prerequisite for being on staff. It can be seen how powerfully "Schleiermacher's ghost" has shaped modern theological education. While furthering the more concrete aspects of theological inquiry such as biblical archeology, textual criticism, and church history, some would argue that this model for theological education has fragmented theology to the point where it is no longer coherent. Some would also argue that the Berlin model has moved theology away from its intended purpose — the knowledge of God Himself in a sapiential and personal sense.

The Athens or Classical model emphasizes the appropriation of wisdom about God through a personal knowledge revealed in the context of a personal relationship with Him. The purpose of this model of education is to provide a person with the deep spiritual formation necessary to appropriate revealed wisdom directly from God, because by the nature of this wisdom, it cannot be "taught" and must be "caught." Because of the way that this knowledge of God is viewed, the teacher facilitates the immersion of the student into a context that facilitates self-knowledge and God-knowledge. The purpose of the student's study and the school's curriculum is to expose the student to texts, thoughts, and experiences that facilitate the revelation of the divine wisdom and knowledge of God. The student appropriates a knowledge of God directly for himself as he is formed spiritually in relationship with God and through exposure to the learning environment (Kelsey 1993, 21). As within Greek education, the idea of community is in the forefront of the educational process. The appropriation of wisdom in Greek thought is in the context of a community that strives together to acquire that knowledge. The end result is that the student is equipped to function in a public setting for the betterment of the greater community and skillfully within that community's language and culture. These values are usually embodied within educational institutions that function in a Classical or Athens-type theological philosophy.

The Berlin or vocational model of theological education holds to a rigorous application of *wissenschaftliche* to theology in order to gain the knowledge and wisdom of God. This rigorous method accumulates data, develops a theory concerning the meaning of the data, applies the theory to actual practice, and uses the results to test or modify the theory. Within this model, teaching is the direct communication of wisdom and knowledge concerning God. The student is taught the rigors of scientific method and research in order to discover the truths about the origins, effects, and essential nature of the "Christian phenomena" (Kelsey 1993, 24). The focus is a "professional education" that prepares the student for ministry by rigorous study of theory and practices of the professional minister in his vocation within society. The faculty must be specialists in individual branches of theology that have the demonstrated capacity to engage in scholarly research and application of scientific method. They do not need to have practical experience in real life situations as much as to be able to demonstrate their research abilities through original contribution to knowledge in their respective fields of expertise by publishing results of their critical inquiries.

It becomes clear as one reviews the literature concerning theological education in the last twenty years that most of the arguments, cures, and proposals come down to the tension that exists in theological circles between these two models of theological education and their individual nuances. Some of the debate centers on which way is most "biblical" or which way is "right." Each side of the debate seems to pick out the less desirable results of "Athens" or "Berlin" and use it to show that the one model or the other is seriously flawed. Neither side of the debate seems to realize that both models are not "biblical" as such in a very strict sense, but that each is a result of a cultural construct to accurately discern the truth about God and His Word.

When either side of the spectrum takes their educational philosophy to the extreme, bad things happen to theological education. When "Athens" gets extreme, people "listen for God" rather than rigorously studying the Word of God as it is written to discover the truth. When this classical model is carried to its extreme, people tend to "gaze at their navels" rather than engage in practical work to further the Kingdom of God. When the Athens model is used exclusively, there is a tendency to use the authority of "hearing God's voice" in a subjective manner to justify just about anything.

When "Berlin" gets extreme, there is a tendency to exalt reason and human understanding beyond their proper place in God's natural order, and to make them the only vehicle for knowing God. God cannot be apprehended exclusively by human reason. Scholastic men of the Middle Ages tried and failed. Ultimately, God cannot be understood by *wissenschaftliche* or any other rational pursuit, but must be revealed and understood by faith. To try and understand Him purely by application of research is to invite the travesty that has resulted as the authority of the Scriptures has been thrown away. "Higher" biblical criticism has dismissed the authority of God's written word and the ability of theology to act as the norm by which truth is measured. Many of the schools that have over-emphasized the Berlin philosophy have become dispensers of a godless and faithless gospel that has largely been rejected by the world as irrelevant.

The center of the debate as it revolves around "Athens" or "Berlin" should be to determine how best to implement both models within a theological education setting in a balanced way, thereby taking advantage of the best of both "worlds." The sapiential and personal revelation of divine wisdom and knowledge of God is the only biblically attested model for truly coming to know Him. "Athens" educational philosophy is best applied to theological education to obtain a curriculum that produces deep spiritual formation rather than just intellectual formation. The Athens approach to having a spiritual community that facilitates a search for the truth is a Biblical concept. It seems to provide the best hope of producing individuals that can be functionally literate within their individual cultures and church communities. Beyond this, theological education must deliver the practical aspects of ministry to its students. Students cannot be left to "gaze at their navel" and try to figure out how to apply their knowledge to real life after they leave school. The Berlin model must be used to train students to think critically concerning their ministry and relationships in order to apply the abstract knowledge they have gained to the real world.

It would seem that there is no "right" blend of these two models to come up with one "ideal" form of theological education. There must rather be a healthy dialectic tension of both models of education in each institution. One must keep vigilant watch for the symptoms of excess that so often display themselves when one model is applied to the extreme. The proper blend of Athens and Berlin is dependent on many factors within each individual institution such as culture, ethnicity, denominational distinctives, inherent weaknesses and strengths. Rather than wasting time and energy debating the merits and intrinsic correctness of either system, an effort should be made to realize the best way for them to work in each individual setting.

Values and Relevancy to Culture

Western society is currently in a classical phase shift between a materialistic, Enlightenment-based worldview and an emerging post-modern-based integral worldview. The context for church ministry and theological training are changing accordingly. The Scriptures clearly say that we are "in the world but not of the world," but where does the line get drawn? Is it Scriptural or even desirable to adapt theological training to its surrounding culture or should the church form a culture of its own? Does it matter if the message, content and product of theological education are relevant to its cultural context?

If these types of questions were being asked about foreign missions, the answer would be obvious. The problem is that all ministry is foreign missions at its core as the Gospel of Jesus Christ invades the foreign kingdom in which the Church exists. Why then does the pattern and product of theological education seem to be so irrelevant at times? The answer lies in the paradigms and values that exist at the core of the whole enterprise. Theological training must change along with the Church in order to effectively minister in this new cultural context. Identifying a clear and biblical theology of culture are central to the task at hand in theological education. Uncovering the values that will facilitate this task is essential to adequately equip emerging leaders to function well in their context of ministry.

A Theology of Culture

In the Old Testament, the men of Issachar are commended because they were people who "understood the times with a knowledge of what Israel should do" (1 Chr. 12:32). There were several sources that were essential to helping the authors develop a theology of culture and in understanding the nature of the cultural changes occurring in Western society at this present time. Leslie Newbign, in his book *Foolishness to the Greeks* (1986), was a valuable source for understanding the different roads the Church has taken as it has confronted culture and in helping the author develop a theology of culture. *The Twilight Labyrinth* (1997), by George Otis, Jr., was essential to our understanding of the realities that make up a culture. Charles Kraft's book, *Christianity with Power* (1989), was an excellent source for understanding the nuances of cultural epistemology, tracing how a culture comes to develop assumptions that are held as axioms of truth. H. Richard Niebuhr, and his classic work *Christ and Culture* (1951), was also consulted for understanding the nuances of the Western culture and a theology of culture. Jimmy Long, in his book *Generating Hope: A Strategy for Reaching The Post-Modern Generation* (1997) and Leonard Sweet in his books *Soul Tsunami* (1999) and *Aqua Church* (1999) were instrumental in understanding trends in the post-modern culture that is emerging today.

Cultures result based on the complex interaction of numbers of people over time in their unique geographical, economic, and historical context. Newbigin defines culture as "… the sum total of ways of living developed by a group of human beings and handed down from generation to generation" (Newbigin 1986, 3). George Otis, an expert in cross-cultural ministry, observes that as a group of people interact over a period of time, they begin to develop a set of shared experiences based on certain assumptions, values, and commitments underlying those people's perception of the nature of reality (Otis, Jr. 1997, 56). A society's collection of memes, consisting of its shared assumptions, values, and commitment to these values, are called its "worldview" (Otis, Jr. 1997, 56-57). A society's worldview determines what the group perceives to be real and what that group dismisses with euphemisms as being false (Kraft 1987, 32-33).

One view of how Christianity should relate to its cultural

context is to actively oppose the culture and to attempt to substitute a "Christian culture" in its place (Niebuhr 1956, 40, 50-54). This view represents a mindset that is counter-cultural or even anti-cultural in perspective. It broadly interprets the Greek word "κοσμος", often translated "world" or "world system" to be synonymous with culture (Niebuhr 1956, 40). The opposite extreme is the complete agreement and synthesis of Christianity with culture. Christ is seen as the "hero of human culture" and a great liberator of mankind in the context of its various cultures (Niebuhr 1956, 41). This mode of reconciling culture and Christ eliminates any tension between Christ and culture and instead accommodates it, many times without question (Niebuhr 1956, 83-85). Within the boundaries of these two extremes in reconciling Christianity and culture are three different ideals that have also been championed by great figures in historical Christianity. Aquinas viewed Jesus to be the "restorer of true society" (Niebuhr 1956, 42). In this view, Jesus was not completely opposed to society, nor was he in agreement with it. He is viewed as one who comes to offer a true sense of community back to the world with an ideal culture. Luther represents a duality in how culture is viewed as it relates to Christianity (Niebuhr 1956, 42). He represents a very healthy dialectic tension recognizing the authority of both Christianity and of culture in the lives of human beings. Calvin's view, a more conversionist one, saw culture as one of the primary vehicles for the transportation of sin, a position that aligns itself with Augustine in early Christianity (Niebuhr 1956, 43).

Long best describes a theology of culture that communicates the gospel message by contextualizing it for a certain worldview as "incarnational theology" (Long 1997, 55-79). He describes incarnational theology as the demonstration of the truths of Christianity as Christians live them out by "fully inhabiting our cultural space" and "joining people where they are" (Long 1997, 79). As Leonard Sweet notes, God is not anti-cultural or counter-cultural (Sweet 1999a, 76,79). Neither is He establishing one "Christian culture" or actively enculturating the Church with any given set of cultural assumptions. He is working within societies and their cultures by using a gospel message that need not change despite its cultural context (Heb. 13:8). A mindset that embraces an incarnational theology of Christianity and culture necessitate that the Church and theological education understand its surrounding culture and contextualize their message for the particular worldview in operation at any given time. This theology of culture is particularly important for the task confronting the modern Church and its institutions of theological education in America today as it is contextualized for a generation in transition from Enlightenment to a post-modern worldview. The authors most closely identify with this theology of culture as a valid way to approach culture when contextualizing theological education.

Western Culture and its Worldviews

The current cultural context of the American church is a hybrid of European and many different international cultures with its own unique set of assumptions about reality, shared experiences, and commitments to defined values. As cultures undergo transformation, they do not eliminate most of what has been, but add to what has been and emphasize new assumptions about the nature of reality. Western culture has profoundly shaped the way theological education has been delivered. By understanding how Western culture has shaped theological education, a strategy for reshaping it can be developed.

Walter Wink, in his book *The Powers that Be* (1998), provides a fivefold paradigm for understanding how Western culture has been formed. Five distinctive worldviews have shaped Western culture through its existence and given birth to the shape of the worldview emerging at the present time within Western culture and in particular, American Western culture (Wink 1998, 15-19). Western culture's ancient worldview is reflected in the Old and New Testament Scriptures (Wink 1998, 15-16). The ancient worldview has as its underlying assumption that everything earthly has its heavenly counterpart and therefore reality is a construct of the interaction of both dimensions of reality (Wink 1998, 15). The spiritualist worldview emerged within Western society after A. D. 100 and radically changed the underlying assumptions held about reality in the prevailing culture (Wink 1998, 16). It is a typically Greek dualistic view of material creation emerged in which spirit was "good" and material creation was "evil". Things associated with material creation were associated with "bad" and "evil" such as the human body, sexuality, and earthly life in general. The materialist worldview became prominent as the Enlightenment period of Western culture began in the nineteenth century (Wink 1998, 17). The assumptions that are foundational in the material worldview are in many ways a reaction against the spiritual oppression that the church of the Middle Ages inflicted upon society. It asserts that there is no heaven or spiritual world, no God or human soul, and that nothing exists except that which can be known through reason and the five senses (Wink 1998, 17). Human beings are viewed as accidents of material creation composed of chemicals and atoms, with no higher self or purpose.

Several themes have emerged that comprise a collective set of assumptions in the Western world's worldview that have endured through most of the twentieth century. These assumptions have had a profound impact on Western culture, its associated perception of reality, and the Christian church. An assumption that self-knowledge is the foundation of all true knowledge and that human reason is the only thing necessary to make sense of life emerged. From this self-centered assumption, the ideas of an autonomous self, the sovereign self of individualism, self-reliance, and self-sufficiency arose. With the advent the emphasis on human reason and its role in life, revelation became unnecessary. As Long observes, "God's revelation was no longer needed or desired because human beings, not God, were in control of the learning process" (Long 1997, 62). The new assumption was that man could best come to understand reality by trial and error and through cause and effect as it is observed in material creation. A deep distrust of supernatural things developed in the Western culture. The infatuation with self and individualism supported by a platform of human reason and a materialistic view of creation gave rise to Romanticism of the nineteenth century, and the idea that man could solve his problems by scientific means rather than religious means. These assumptions and the resulting worldview that they support have become synonymous with Western culture over the last four hundred years and have greatly influenced Western society and religion, including Christianity.

The failure of Western cultures' ideals of human potential met with reality in the twentieth century. Wars, atrocity on a global scale, and a longing for something more than materialism is leading to a change in culture and worldview once again. When these forces are coupled with the multicultural atmosphere that is now common in Western society, a syncretism of various Western and non-Western worldviews is occurring as the ideas from many world cultures mix in Western society. This mixture, facilitated by rapid ability to communicate ideas and their underlying assumptions, is bringing about the existence of what Wink calls an "integral world-view." The implications for change in our culture that this development brings are staggering. Wink postulates that the fusion of many Western and non-Western streams of thought are giving rise to a new integral view of reality that once again acknowledges the existence of an inner and outer dimension to physical reality (Wink 1998, 19). This view of reality is more reminiscent of pantheism than Christianity with the thought that the spirit world and the natural world are one. God is perceived as in all things and identical with all things. In a syncretistic fashion, these assumptions merge with the idea that the human being and the individual are preeminent to elevate the individual to equality with God. It is the marriage of materialism and pantheism to form a new pseudo-spirituality that allows for the exaltation of human reason and existence while making room for the supernatural and the unexplained.

Western Christianity, in some cases, has unconsciously adopted a highly naturalistic worldview and superimposed it onto the Scriptures by removing their authority to dictate truth and reinterpreting supernatural events described in the Scriptures as "myth" or "allegory." The result has been a form of "powerless Christianity" that has invaded many corners of the Western Church that downplays the supernatural, emphasizes reason over supernatural revelation. It also diminishes the role of personal experience with God in one's Christian life, and accentuates order and control at the expense of God's sovereignty (Kraft 1989, 41-47). The exaltation of human reason over revelation can also be seen as theological education began to emphasize a "professional" mindset, championed by the "Berlin" model of education developed at the University of Berlin by Schleiermacher in 1810. The result has been a rationalistic form of Christianity and theological education over the last two centuries that has denied the verbal-plenary authority of the Scriptures, minimized the supernatural and experiential aspects of Christianity, and in some cases, denied the most basic tenets of orthodox Christian faith. In many ways, the renewal movements of the twentieth century may be God's sovereign answer to Enlightenment Christianity. The return to an emphasis on the supernatural, the sovereignty of God, sapiential Christianity, and the authority of the Scriptures that are the distinctives of these movements are reorienting Christianity on a global basis at this present time.

Post-modern Culture and Theological Education

Western society is currently in a classical phase shift between a materialistic and Enlightenment-based worldview and an emerging post-modern-based integral worldview. The contexts for church ministry and theological education are changing accordingly. Theological education must change along with the Church in order to effectively minister in this new cultural context. Leonard Sweet and his two books *Soul Tsumani* (1999) and *Aqua Church* (1999) were instrumental in understanding post-modern culture and the changes needed to reach this generation. George Barna in his book *The Second Coming of the Church* (1998) provides statistical information that support many of Sweet's observations. As Leonard Sweet observes it is not that change is something new to Western culture or the Church, it is the rate of change that is profoundly different from anything Western culture has ever before experienced (Sweet 1999b, 73, 77). He notes that culture has literally become a "fluid, seeping surface" and that "change has changed" (Sweet 1999b, 77). In the past, the flow of information in society along with the communication infrastructures has allowed change to be incremental. Ideas and assumptions within Western culture traveled at the rate of horse, train, boat, or mail. As methods of communication such as telegraph, telephone, radio, television, and more recently the Internet have been introduced to culture, communication can now take place in seconds rather than days or weeks. Ideas can flow through our information culture at a pace that allows cultural constructs to change in months or years rather than decades or centuries. The "change in the way change" is occurring has been altered forever by the ability of people to communicate quickly and efficiently. Western culture is literally reinventing itself at the rate of once every three to five years (Barna 1998, 2). At this rate, change is more like a "churn or blur" rather than a gradual, incremental, manageable change over time that can be more easily assimilated. More information has been generated in the last three decades than in the past five thousand years combined (Sweet 1999b, 112).

Western culture is currently making a transition from an Enlightenment-based materialistic worldview to a post-modern-based integral worldview. The common values, commitments, and assumptions that were common to the worldview as it existed in the twentieth century are rapidly being supplanted by a whole new set of assumptions, values, and commitments that reshape the way that Western society perceives reality. The shift to a post-modern and integral worldview has a profound impact on the way that the Church must present the gospel. A sound theology of culture dictates that the Church contextualize its message for the sake of the culture that it exists within that they might understand and receive the gospel.

These considerations lead to several conclusions that would help to contextualize theological education to meet the needs of today's emerging leaders in the Body of Christ. Theological education must model for emerging leaders the ability to "exegete the times." It must avoid the extremes of an anti-cultural attitude as well as cultural syncretism that occurs when Christianity is absorbed by the surrounding culture. An incarnational theology of culture that seeks to demonstrate Christ to those in one's cultural context in a way they can relate to while being fully present in that culture must prevail. It must redouble its efforts to resist some of the most common worldly attitudes that Western culture has stamped on Christianity. These philosophies include materialism, rationalism, existentialism, and relativism to name a few. Theological education has the responsibility of reorienting emerging leaders to the supernatural. God's power and the resulting revival in the Church with hundreds of millions of souls being saved can no longer be denied. In past days, revivalism and renewal Christianity could safely be relegated to the "fringes" of Christianity. This is no longer the case. God's power and an experiential religion are being craved by this generation in its neediness. Theological education must lead emerging leaders toward renewal and a sapiential form of Christianity before these leaders can, in turn, give it away to those in the world. Perhaps most importantly, theological education must once again be intimately involved with the Church instead of standing alone in its mission. The Church and institutions delivering theological education must be in dynamic partnership with each other so that they can cooperate in the process of equipping emerging leaders.

Athens meets Berlin meets Topeka – Toward Relevance in Theological Education

The debate in theological education circles can no longer afford to be one of Athens or Berlin. Both systems of education, if left to themselves or their extremes, prove flawed and produce leaders that are lacking in academic excellence or in spiritual formation. Both systems also produce vital results in the individuals under their influence. An emerging leader in the Body of Christ cannot afford to be without the personal formation emphasized in the Athens model of theological training. The personal formation of the character and spiritual disciplines of a leader are vital to their success, as is a strong sapiential relationship with God. An emerging leader must also have a strong cognitive knowledge base for their life and ministry founded in an excellent understanding of theology and the Scriptures. To argue for either Athens or Berlin is like a bird arguing over which wing is most important – the bird needs them both to fly. It is not Athens or Berlin, but rather Athens *and* Berlin. The negotiation becomes the correct balance of each in a particular institution based on its tradition, calling, and mission.

The current renewal movement has added another dimension to the consideration of Athens and Berlin – the dimension of "Topeka," a city in Kansas where on January 01, 1901, Agnes Ozman received the infilling of the Holy Spirit, and became the first of over 500 million people in the twentieth century to have this experience. It is interesting to note that Ozman was studying at Bethel Bible School and Healing Home in Topeka when she was baptized in the Holy Spirit with evidence of speaking in tongues (Synan 2001, 43, 44). Her instructor, Charles Parham, instructed the thirty-four students to examine Acts 2 as a text and to search for the true evidence of the end-time outpouring" (Burgess and McGee 1988, 850). Outside the classroom door listening, and not yet welcome in because of the racial barriers in place, was William Seymour who was born in Louisiana as the son of former slaves. He would later go on to be the major catalyst of the Azusa Street revivals in Los Angeles. Parham later moved his school to Houston, Texas, and had about twenty-five students, one of which was William J. Seymour. From the very beginning of the movement, something new was being birthed in Topeka that has changed theological education and the face of the Body of Christ.

The "Topeka" philosophy of theological education is multicultural from its beginnings, inviting men, women, and people of color to join together in seeking God. It also began to actively tear down the artificial clergy-laity distinctions in the Body of Christ left over from medieval times, actualizing Luther's dream for the "priesthood of believers" as men and women were equipped to serve God. It also ushered in the renewal distinctives of the inspiration and authority of the Scriptures and effectively checked the rising tide of liberal theology rampant at the turn of the twentieth century. Topeka represents a fusion of Athens and Berlin and represents the best of both. It dictates a strong sapiential and formation-oriented approach to Christianity and theological education because of the experiential dimensions of the renewal experience. It also dictates a strong reverence and respect for the authority and inspiration of the Scriptures, driving the student toward cognitive excellence in the scriptural knowledge and theology.

The authors believe that it is the very forces of renewal prevailing on a global basis that are driving the current need for renewal in theological education. The authors also believe that dialogue on Athens and Berlin to date in the literature have missed the mark precisely because those outside the renewal movement have not understood the dynamics that the renewal movement has brought to bear on theological education. Those in the renewal movement also share the blame for this lack of perspective because they have not adequately thought through or understood the dynamics in operation in their own theological education. It is Topeka that is driving the changes needed in theological education today. Athens *and* Berlin must both be a part of these changes, with both wings present if the enterprise is to fly. Theological education can no longer afford to choose between Athens or Berlin. It cannot afford to train leaders that are either too reflective or too academic, but must equip them with the best of both worlds. Topeka demands excellence in both.

CHAPTER SIX

Aiming for the Heart:
The Place of Spiritual Formation
in Theological Training

At the request of John Wesley, George Whitefield set out to Georgia to help with the Savannah Orphan House set up for children of the colonists who had succumbed to the frontier's harsh environment. Most of the Anglican clergy were against him because he preached a gospel calling for the "new birth" and regeneration quite contrary to the Calvinist doctrines of the day. As J. C. Ryle states, "The plain truth is that the Church of England of that day was not ready for a man like Whitefield... to much asleep to understand him and vexed at a man who would not keep still and leave the devil alone" (Ryle 1978, 39).

With the ability to preach in churches rapidly closing to Whitefield, he resolved to take the gospel to those outside the church who desperately needed Christ. His first attempts were made in February, 1739, to several hundred coal miners near Bristol. He preached on Matthew 5:1-3. The crowd was "glad to hear of Jesus who was a friend to publicans and came not to call the righteous but sinners to repentance (Pratney 1983, 94). The scene was amazing:

> The first discovery of their being affected was
> the sight of the white gutters made by their
> tears which fell plentifully down their black
> cheeks as they came out of the coal pits...
> Sometime when twenty thousand people were
> before me, I had not in my own apprehension a
> word to say either to God or to them. But I was
> never totally deserted... The heavens opened
> above me, the prospect of adjacent fields with
> the sight of thousands, some in coaches, some
> on horseback, and some in trees and at all times
> afflicted with tears was almost too much for me
> (Pratney 1983, 94, quoting Whitefield).

The word about Whitefield's preaching spread and
the audiences began to grow. Soon he was preaching to
up to 30,000 people at one time. Thousands would come
to hear him at 6:00 a.m. in the morning in the snow.
During the span of his ministry from 1739-1770, whole
cities would turn out to hear Whitefield preach.

The conversions on the frontier at that time produced
an overwhelming number of converts, and an overwhelming need for clergy. Some responded to the call to pastor
without the usual formal training for ministry that was
expected from a school in Europe or one of the New
World's schools in the Northeast. Others began to set up
churches and school young men by "reading divinity" in
the morning and apprenticeship in actual ministry in the
afternoon, eventually sparking the name "log cabin
colleges". Whole denominations were thrown into disar-
ray as normal systems of training were called into question by the need of the moment. Should a man be
removed from his ministry on the frontier and taken to a
college in the Northeast and be educated with Hebrew,
Greek, and a classical theological education? How should
a denomination give credentials to such men, some of
which seem to have no aptitude for classical studies, but
in the legacy of Whitefield were pastoring successful
congregations of notable size on the Western frontier?

How does the system of "reading" with a practicing pastor and apprenticeship under his ministry work in a world of credits, degrees, and systematic theology? It seemed that renewal was forcing traditional modes of theological education to examine their methods, practices, and way of forming people for the work of the ministry.

Any human effort is guided by a complex matrix of assumptions and beliefs that exist at the root level of values. Values are the reason for our actions and behavior and the thought paradigms we have built based on these values govern the way we act and conduct our day-to-day business. Theological training is not different. Theological training and the way it is done is a unique expression of the visionaries and practitioners that administer that training. The core values and assumptions these individuals hold will ultimately shape the whole way the training is done and will determine its effectiveness. With this in mind, what should be the primary focus of theological training? What core values will help to focus the whole enterprise so as to produce an individual who is effective in the ministry work to which God has called them? Is knowledge the primary goal of training? Perhaps skills should be the emphasis. The authors assert that the primary focus of theological training must go much deeper than that. The focus must literally become once again a matter of the heart.

Formation and Theological Training *(Paideia)*

At its deepest level, theological training is actually the spiritual and moral formation of individuals in a manner that allows them to identify, sharpen, and effectively use their gift-mix to serve the Body of Christ and to fulfill God's plan and destiny for their life. There are many paradigms in Bible colleges and seminaries for how this formation should take place. In some cases, institutions question whether it is the job of theological training to address this area at all. What do the Scriptures say about spiritual and moral formation? How do they say it should be accomplished? How should spiritual and moral formation be involved in the process of theological training?

The Fear of the Lord

There are several key passages in the Scriptures that address the basis of spiritual and moral formation. A more detailed exegetical excursis on this topic that addresses the Hebrew and Greek roots can be found in Appendix A. The Scriptures, as the plenary-verbal inspired Word of God, are the ultimate source of truth and the standard by which truth is to be judged (2 Tm. 3:15,16; 2 Pet. 1:20,21). They must therefore be the source of and basis for understanding spiritual and moral formation as well. There are many verses that address the topic of spiritual and moral formation that can be found in the Book of Proverbs. The first is found in
Prv. 1:7 which in the English text states:

The **fear of the LORD** is the **beginning of knowledge**; Fools despise **wisdom** and **instruction** (Prv. 1:7, NAS, *emphasis added*).

This text contains several key phrases that establish some basic principles for spiritual and moral formation. They include:

- The "fear of the Lord" - The fear of the Lord is represented here to be a basic requirement to gain knowledge, wisdom, and understanding. It is presented as a prerequisite for acquiring this type of knowledge. The phrase "fear of the Lord" implies a reverence or awe for God in the context of relationship with Him, and is therefore impossible to gain outside this context.

- Knowledge, Wisdom, and Instruction *begin* with a relationship with God. Outside this relationship with Him, it is therefore impossible to acquire them.

Knowledge and Wisdom

Knowledge and wisdom are central to the Old Testament concept of spiritual formation. The root words in the Hebrew text for knowledge occur a total of 944 times in the Old Testament, expressing various shades of knowing. Some of its uses are (Harris,

Archer, and Waltke 1980, 366):

- God's knowledge of man (Gen. 18:19; Deut. 34:10).
- Man's knowledge (Isa. 1:3).
- Knowing of skills (Gen. 25:27; 2 Chr. 8:18; 1 Sam. 16:16).
- Learning in general (Isa. 29:11).
- To have acquaintance or relationship (Gen. 29:5; Exod. 1:8).
- To have sexual intercourse with (Gen. 4:1; 19:8).
- To know secular matters (Deut. 13:3, 7).

The word form used in Prv. 1:7, refers in particular to a personal, experimental kind of the knowledge. The verse reveals that all knowledge begins in the context of the knowledge of God. A true grasp of knowledge in its proper context and meaning is therefore only available to those who know God as their redeemer and creator (Banks 1999, 74).

There is also a deeper, more personal concept for wisdom and understanding in the Hebrew text. The word for wisdom in the Hebrew text covers the whole gamut of human experience. It can mean (Harris, Archer, and Waltke 1980, 282):

- Technical skill or craftsmanship (Exod. 28:3; 31:3, 6).
- Execution of strategy or tactics well (Isa. 10:13).
- Administration (Deut. 34:9; 2 Sam. 14:20).
- Leadership (Isa. 11:2).
- The exercise of prudence (Ps. 37:30; Prv. 10:31).

One striking feature of wisdom is that it is personified in the Scriptures in Proverbs 8, strongly connecting it with the nature and character of God. As such, it is no wonder that an understanding of wisdom is only possible in the context of a relationship with God and based on the truth in His inspired Word.

Spiritual Instruction *(paideia)*

In Prv. 1:7, the word "instruction" is also mentioned. It has a Hebrew root that conveys the meanings of discipline, chastening, and instruction. The Greek Old Testament translation (Septuagint) text gives another key to the understanding of this word when it uses the Greek word root *"paideia"* to translate the Hebrew word for understanding. The use of *paideia* in the Septuagint to translate the Hebrew word ties in the concept of *paideia* with the New Testament in 1 Tm. 3:16 where "instruction" is also mentioned (Harris, Archer, and Waltke 1980, 386-387).

One of the outcomes of the Scripture's inspiration is its ability to be used to "train" (*paideia*) people as 2 Tm. 3:16 notes. The word *paideia* denotes instruction that relates to the whole training and education of a child, including the cultivation of the mind, moral life, commands, admonitions, and cultivation of the soul. Linking the Scripture in 2 Tm. 3:16 and Prv. 1:7 together, an intimate and experiential knowledge of God is necessary for instruction, or as it would be called, "training," to take place properly. This training is dynamically linked with knowing and doing. Training in the context of relationship with God produces proper spiritual and moral formation (*paideia*). Training outside this context is either warped or impossible. A sapiential knowledge of God is indispensable for true instruction and formation to take place.

Robert Banks traces the methods of spiritual and moral formation in Jewish culture as are recorded in the Scriptures. There were several primary ways in which *paideia* occurred in a Jewish context, adapted from a discussion on this topic by Banks (1999, 83-90):

- The Home: The primary method of spiritual formation in Israel was the family, and in particular the mother (Deut. 4:9; 6:7; Exod. 12:26,27; 13:7-8; Prv. 6:20-23; 13:1; 23:22-25). The mother took the lead in general, religious, and informal training (Prv. 1:8; 6:20-23; 23:22-25).

- Capable Men: The Elders played a role in instruction (Num. 18:21). National leaders also had a role (Exod. 24:13; 33:11), as did those with specialized callings such as priests and prophets (1 Sam. 2:21,26; 2 Kgs. 12:3; Amos 7:15; 1 Kgs. 19:19-21).

- Rabbis: In later Jewish culture, the learner (*talmidh*) followed a particular teacher (*rabbi*) as their disciple (*mathetes*). In this model of instruction, the student was committed to the learning process through a particular person or school. The students accompanied the teacher and often lived with or near them. Learning took place in the context of service and in diverse settings. This was the manner of instruction for Jesus and His disciples in the New Testament.

Jesus modeled a definite pattern for spiritual and moral formation in the New Testament. The New Testament pattern for this type of formation is strongly linked with the idea of discipleship. His followers are referred to as "The Twelve" (Mk. 3:14; 9:10; 35; 10:32; 11:11). They are called His disciples and He their rabbi just as was normal in Jewish culture. Instruction occurred in the context of relationship with Him as they were called out from their usual surroundings to sit under Him (Mt. 10:2-4; Mk. 3:16-19; Lk. 6:14-16). As their teacher, Jesus imparted practical cognitive knowledge linked with an opportunity for application in diverse settings that they experienced in everyday life to serve as a background for understanding what He was teaching. The process included children, scenery, objects, people, and the circumstances of life (Banks 1999, 94-99). He also took advantage of practical experience and skill development by actually using the opportunity for on-the-job training to occur for the disciples in real life settings (*praxis* – Mt. 10:1-42).

G. B. Caird points out that this pattern for discipleship continued in the context of the New Testament community of believers following the time of Christ (1993, 73). The transmission of knowledge took place through teaching and preaching in the context of community (*koinonia*) in an effective way as all related to each other and to their new found Savior (Acts 2:42-48). This transmission of knowledge and wisdom through instruction in the context of community is the biblical model for training. The result of the learning experience is spiritual and moral formation evidences by discipleship and maturity. The transformation process in the life of a believer as a result of instruction and the resulting discipleship and maturity follows a clear path (Gangel and Wilhoit 1994, 15):

- Believers receive new cognitive knowledge into their life (knowing).
- Integrates the data into their life by applying it (doing).
- Processes the information to be part of their values systems

(being).
- Is transformed morally and spiritually (being).
- Changes their behavior based on the new values (doing).
- Begins to transmit the new knowledge to others (doing).

This process of spiritual and moral formation describes the biblical process of discipleship that is commanded by Jesus at the Great Commission (Mt 28:19,20). Several marks of discipleship are also described clearly in the Scriptures. These marks include (Gangel and Wilhoit 1994, 15-17):

- The willingness to follow Jesus (Lk. 9:23-24, 57-62).
- The willingness to be a living sacrifice (1 Cor. 15:31; Rom. 12:1).
- The willingness to die daily to self (Gal. 2:20).

The application of the work of the cross is critical in the discipleship process. The relationship that the cross purchases is essential to spiritual and moral formation (Prv. 1:7). Spiritual and moral formation are the results of training. All is predicated on the cross and the personal relationship with God that makes it possible to come to know and understand God (Rom. 1:16-17).

Spiritual and moral formation took on another dimension in the New Testament after the time of Jesus. Paul formed more of a partnership than a rabbinical relationship with his followers to impart instruction (2 Cor. 2:12,13). He often took companions with him, such as Silas and Timothy, for the purpose of training in the field. These individuals included men, women, married, widowed, and single people (Acts 18:1-3; Phil. 2:2-4; Rom. 16:7, 12). He had smaller circles of companions (2 Cor. 8:16-17) as well as larger circles. Paul acted as their teacher (Acts 20:21) in the context of community and fellowship (Banks 1999, 113-115).

Spiritual and Moral Formation

The passages of Scripture examined in this section yield several clear principles relating to spiritual and moral formation that can be related to the process of theological training. Some of the principles that emerge from the process of interpretation are:

- Transmission of knowledge and wisdom in the process of instruction can only take place properly in the context of a relationship with God. Knowing Him is a prerequisite for proper transmission of them without distortion.

- Instruction or training is identified in the Scriptures with the Greek word *paideia*. It is more than the transmission of knowledge, but rather involves the shaping of the spirit and moral faculties of the soul through the transmission and deliberate application of knowledge and wisdom.

- The Scriptures are the source of truth and are the only standard that the Bible itself empowers to act as the judge of what is true. They are therefore to be central to any instruction process as its foundation to judge what is true knowledge and wisdom.

- Discipleship results from a process in which knowledge is received, integrated into life, and is processed to become part of one's personal values system, resulting in a changed behavior. The process is complete when the individual can impart the knowledge to others. Discipleship is a direct result of the process of spiritual and moral formation (*paideia*).

- The training process and the resulting discipleship and maturity took place in the context of relationship, community, and varied real-life settings in the Scriptures. Life was used as an instruction tool for teaching. Those learning were given the immediate opportunity to apply what they learned to real life.

- The spiritual and moral formation and the resulting discipleship and maturing are dependent upon the cross as the means to link the disciple in relationship to God and to empower them daily in the process as they die to themselves and are transformed. This transformation into new creations was actualized through the process of spiritual and moral formation as it occurred in the discipleship cycle.

These biblical patterns for instruction and the associated spiritual and moral formation that results are paradigms that are vital to theological training. The fact that most theological training does not utilize or value these paradigms is, in part, the reason that, in many cases, it is not an effective means for preparing ministers for their work in the church.

Spiritual and moral formation as they relate to theological training lead to several conclusions:

- *Paideia* (spiritual and moral formation): The first task is to realize the importance of spiritual and moral formation to the whole enterprise of theological training. With the advent of the professional paradigm of the minister and ministry, the idea of preparing and forming a minister spiritually and morally has been forgotten in many cases. The focus instead has been on manufacturing ministers according to a more mechanistic paradigm with little regard to their spiritual and moral formation. With disregard for the plenary-verbal inspiration of the Scriptures, the standards for spiritual and moral formation are gone from the theological training process. Spiritual and moral formation in the context of the home and church can no longer be assumed as it was in the past. They must be planned for in the process of theological training and seen as a central purpose of the endeavor.

- *Sapientia* (personal relationship with and knowledge of God): It is sad to say, but God has become lost in the process of theological training in many cases. In the past, theological training placed a much higher emphasis on ministers coming to know God in a more intimate way so that they were empowered to teach, lead, and care for their congregations by His strength and wisdom. The professional paradigm has reduced ministry to a process to be done with a particular skill set like any other professional endeavor. Many times, little is done to value or encourage a personal relationship with God. Some students are not even saved. Since this sapiential knowledge of God is a prerequisite for true instruction and formation to take place, a sapiential relationship with God and an emphasis on knowing and understanding God emerge as a central mission of the whole endeavor.

- *Praxis* (practical application and real-life contexts): The Scriptures demonstrate that learning should take place in the context of relationship and community and that those learning should immediately be able and expected to apply what they have learned. This completes the triad of knowing, doing, and being that is exemplified in the Scriptures. On-the-job training is vital to theological training. Immediate application is also necessary rather than waiting until after the learning process is complete. The surroundings in which theological training takes place should not be a sterile building, but in the context of life so as to allow the walls to speak. The action of applying what has been given cognitively is the vital bridge that leads to transformation.

- *Koinonia* (fellowship in community): Instruction should take place in the context of relationship with the teacher and other students. This relationship provides the basis of knowledge and wisdom being "caught" rather than just verbally taught. Attention should also be given to the fellowship and community context at a Bible school and seminary to be sure that it enhances the educational process and encourages intimate relationship. Such an *ethos* does not occur by accident, but rather must be strategically planned for and preserved.

- Integrative Educational Philosophy: Since the advent of the professional paradigm for understanding ministers and ministry, spiritual and moral formation have been neglected in the process of theological training. The professional paradigm as it emerged at the University of Berlin did emphasize the need for practical skills to be taught to the minister. Even this emphasis has been lost in the fragmentation that has occurred in theological education due to specialization. A more Athens-like Greek philosophy emphasizing *paideia* once again must be employed to balance out the professional paradigm. The Berlin ideals of professional skills must be updated in order to keep theological training relevant. It is not a case or either-or, but all are necessary in their integrative and dynamic whole.

A biblical definition emerges from this study joining theological training and formation:

> Theological training is the process of spiritual and moral formation that takes place in the context of fellowship with God and the Christian community by which cognitive knowledge and wisdom are gained and their direct application facilitated, resulting in devoted discipleship and maturity.

This research confirms the fundamental importance of a sapiential relationship with God to the process of theological training. It also confirms the importance of a dynamic link between formation and the training, in the context of God's community — the Church. With a new emphasis on spiritual and moral formation, theological training is focused on a biblically centered outcome, and the product of it — the student — is more adequately prepared to function in his or her individual place of ministry in the Church. Theological training must be designed to focus on *paideia*, and as such, is a vital part of the discipleship process as students are formed spiritually and morally in the process of discipleship. This focus on *paideia* shifts the balance in training back toward a more biblical perspective. It also ensures that formation takes place as a result of the application of cognitive knowledge to real-life situations by focus on *praxis*. With this type of emphasis restored to theological training, it truly does become a "matter of the heart" and allows for proper formation of the heart of an emerging leader in addition to the intellect.

CHAPTER SEVEN

Making Room for the Spirit – Renewal Distinctives in Theological Training

In 1959, a young man and his family came to the Tidewater area of Virginia with $70 and a vision. His passion was to establish a television broadcasting ministry that would glorify God. The first two years were filled with immense personal struggle in both his personal life and that of the new ministry he was planting. The first television station was born after two years of effort. The second station was born after ten more years of intense effort and trials. This was the beginning of the Christian Broadcasting Network (CBN) television ministry founded by Pat Robertson, which is now global in its outreach (Robertson 1982, 142, 143).

Some years later, CBN found itself hopelessly over-crowded and renting multiple sites across the Tidewater area to try to support the growth they had experienced. Robertson began to investigate the possibility of buying five acres of land in Virginia Beach as a possible head-quarters site, but the owner of the land he was interested in refused to sell a portion of the 143 acre tract (1982, 195). Robertson was sitting in the coffee shop of the

Grand Hotel in Anaheim, California, after being invited
to a conference at the Melodyland Christian Center
(1982, 195). He had arrived late and was eating alone. As
Robertson recounts:

> When my meal of cantaloupe and cottage
> cheese arrived, I bowed my head to say grace –
> and the Lord began to speak to me about the
> site [of land] three thousand miles away. People
> around me in the shop must have thought I was
> terribly grateful for that cantaloupe, for I
> remained in the posture of prayer for a long
> time. 'I want you to build the land,' the Lord
> said. 'Buy it all,' He said. 'I want you to build a
> school there for My glory, as well as the head-
> quarters building you need (1982, 195).

CBN University, later to become Regent University,
was born that day over a simple prayer of grace in the
heart of a man who was sitting in a coffee shop giving
thanks for his lunch.

Upon his return to Virginia Beach, Robertson
approached the banker responsible for the major mort-
gage on the property and told him that he wanted to buy
the entire site and build a school on it. The banker
exclaimed "Praise the Lord!" It turns out that seven years
before the acquisition of the property, an Assembly of
God minister had shared with a mutual acquaintance of
Robertson a vision for an international center on that
same land. He had envisioned an international center
reaching out to the world with students and dormitories
that would serve missionaries from around the world
(1982, 196). He proceeded to buy the 143-acre site – at an
interstate site worth $2.9 million – with no money down,
no principle payment for two years, and the balance at
8% interest payable over the next twenty three years. An
adjoining piece of property was later purchased, adding
140 more acres to the complex (Robertson 1982, 196).
The school was born in 1977 with the School of

Communications.

Today, Regent University exists as a thriving education center that is world renowned for its renewal distinctives. In 2002, the university graduated over 600 students with undergraduate, graduate, and doctoral degrees. The university's law, government, and business schools produce graduates that are equipped with the skills and biblical wisdom to impact their disciplines and the workplace with the gospel. The schools of divinity, psychology & counseling, education, and leadership studies have a distinctly renewal orientation to their programs that equip their graduates to be leaders in the worldwide renewal occurring at this time. The university is currently expanding its communication and the arts program with a multi-million dollar state-of-the-art building program and graduates dozens of arts and communications students each year to be salt and light in the entertainment industry and beyond.

As mentioned earlier in this book, the global Church is experiencing renewal on a scope could only be imagined only two decades ago. The large number of new converts that have a renewal distinctive is producing a profound change in the Church and even in its surrounding culture, particularly in non-Western countries. This trend appears to have no immediate end in sight. As emerging leaders prepare to take their place in the Church they often find that theological training is years behind what is currently happening in the Church, operating on paradigms and values that were more a part of the medieval church than the twenty-first century Church. If the needs of the majority of the emerging leaders in the Church of the twenty-first century are to be properly formed and equipped to do the work that God has for them, it is imperative that theological education make room for the Holy Spirit.

Theological Training and Renewal Distinctives

Theological education, when it is reduced to its core purpose, is the training and equipping of members of the Body of Christ in each generation to serve the Church and effectively reach those in the surrounding culture. Institutions which have as their purpose the training and equipping of the Body of Christ exist to serve the Church. It is the Church that has a scriptural mandate for its existence (Mt. 16:18). While the process of theological education is a scriptural pursuit (Mt. 28:18,19), there is no direct mandate for theological educational institutions to exist apart from the Church. This simple fact makes the relationship of the Church to theological educational institutions a vital issue. Theological education must exist for the Church and by the Church's authority, operating in intimate partnership with the Church or its role will become distorted and the theological education it dispenses will become irrelevant to the very people it was designed to serve. Just as the body is dead without the spirit, so the enterprise of theological education is dead without the Church.

If this type of relationship between theological education and the Church exists, then it must be the job of theological education to be current with the needs of the Church. It also means that that theological education must be contextualized by the Church to reach the generation that exists at the time. Theological education cannot afford to become fossilized in one manner of format, content, or delivery. When this occurs, it becomes less relevant to the mission for which it was designed. The Review of Graduate Theological Education in the Pacific Northwest produced by The M. J. Murdock Charitable Trust in 1994 cites provides some tangible examples that show that theological education needs to have a major overhaul that reorients it toward its primary purpose (Murdock 1994, 2). One pastor in the study commented that "... seminary lacks a deep spiritual base." At a forum of seminary presidents and deans, some commented that "...there is distance and even hostility between seminary faculty and pastors." The study also notes that "... pastors believe that seminary professors do not understand their need for ministry skills or mentors" while "... seminaries often turn a deaf ear to the needs of the local church and arrogantly defend scholarly education" (Murdock 1994, 2-3).

As the Church of Jesus Christ adapts to reach the lost of each generation, theological education must change to conform to the church's needs. The message of the Church never changes (Heb 13:8). The context for that message — the cultural context of the Church — is always changing. In order to meet the needs of the Church in its current cultural context, a theology of culture must be developed that allows the Church and its theological education to adapt its message and training to be relevant to the surrounding culture. A theology of culture must be developed that allows this to occur. It must be the job of theological education to understand the cultural context in which the Church is expected to minister and adapt its programs, curriculum, and learning styles to keep relevant with those changes. No business school would dream of training its business professionals for professional work in the business world in the same manner today as it did in 1900. There are basic business truths that do not change to be sure, but the content, delivery, and curriculum have changed appreciably as have the institutions that deliver business education over the last one hundred years. This has not always been the case for theological educational institutions. Many are frozen in the same format, curriculum, and learning styles that were used at the turn of the century or earlier. For a business school, this would be suicidal. This is also true for schools in the "business" of imparting theological education to spiritually form, train, and equip people in the Body of Christ to serve in the Church.

An essential understanding of the cultural changes that are occurring in society and the needs of the church in our current time are also essential for delivering effective theological education. It is important to understand why theological education is delivered in the current manner that it is, and what changes are needed in order to meet the current needs of the church and this generation of potential students. For the Western church and its theological educational institutions, that means that an understanding of Western culture is vital for contextualizing the gospel message. With Western culture in a state of flux at this present time, it is also important to understand the current cultural constructs that exist in Western culture and how they are changing in a post-modern cultural environment. Understanding these cultural changes and the implications they have for effective theological education in the twenty-first century are vital for the health and success of the Church in this generation in fulfilling its God-given mission (Mt. 28:18-20). Making these changes in the way that the Church and institutions of theological education conduct their "business" in the twenty-first century is literally a matter of life and death for the many that are looking for the truth, but are lost in darkness.

Renewal Distinctives and the Church

In the Body of Christ, Christians constantly use the word "church" to mean a variety of things. These meanings are a result of tradition, cultural constructs, and the Scriptures being mixed together to form people's concept of church. For the purpose of theological training, the meaning of the term is of utmost importance. The church, whatever it may be, is central to theological training. The church is the context in which the product of theological training will function. Theological training exists to train Christians to function effectively within the church. To leave the context undefined would be similar to training physicians to function in their context without knowing what a hospital is. The results of that training would not be very effective, as is the case with the product of theological training many times today. Research to define these parameters was essential to the design of the model for theological training presented in this book. A more detailed and exegetical excursis on the topic of the Church can be found in Appendix B.

The most frequently used Hebrew and Greek words used in the Scriptures to define the Church yield a meaning of "assembly" (Old Testament) and "called out ones" (New Testament). This assembly of God's people is called out and apart from the world as a distinct kingdom of people that exists both in a fixed geographical location and universally in a way that transcends distance. It is organic and living in nature, rather than merely an organization. The Scriptures make it clear that the Church is the living representation of Christ on the earth to the world, by calling the Church His "body" in one sense and His "bride" in another sense.

At conversion, a new believer is baptized into the Body of Christ and becomes a part of the organic whole called the Church. The resulting fusion of a new believer's life to the Body of Christ, His Church, results in a kind of glue called fellowship or *koinonia* that hold the Body of Christ together as one. Believers are held together through this fellowship with Christ and one another. The result is an organic living Body that represents Christ's love, nature, and authority to the world. This holy assembly of called out ones, bound together with the glue of fellowship, are Christ's witness to the world. These considerations lead to several vital conclusions about the Church that locate the place of theological training in its relationship with the Church:

- The Church is a living organism: The Church is clearly a living organism rather than an organization. The metaphors that describe the church are pregnant with life and demand that the Church be thought of in this way. Theological training must likewise be a living, organic endeavor that is alive in its ability to change and adapt to the needs of the Church since it exists to serve Her.

- The Church is universal: The Body of Christ exists in all parts of the world and crosses the ages of time from the Old Testament through the New Testament to the present day. Local assemblies are merely an expression of this universal assembly. The Church is composed of multicultural and multiethnic peoples but it transcends these differences in the unity of fellowship. Theological education must likewise be multicultural and multiethnic in its design considerations, without prejudice to one culture's ideal outlook on training.

- The Church is local: The local gathering of believers is an expression of the universal church of Christ and meets in a certain geographical location, which in the New Testament times was in homes. Theological training must take the local church into account in the process of training or risk becoming an island unto itself and irrelevant as it loses touch with the Body of Christ. Once again, if this training takes place outside the local church, it must be involved with the local church or risk becoming unfit to train the very leaders it is preparing to serve it.

- The Church is a community: Fellowship or κοινωνία is the key glue that holds the church together in unity. This fellowship is an extension of the Old Testament concept of community that existed from the creation of mankind, was developed in the people of Israel, and expanded upon in Jesus Christ and His church. It is this sense of community that was the context for teaching, maturity, and growth in Christ. The bond of community also fused diverse peoples together across racial and cultural divides. As such, community or *koinonia* should be a central value in theological training.

- The Church is one with Christ: The metaphors involving Christ's body, His bride, and His sons show the intimacy that He has with the church. The church is God's family by birth. Can institutions delivering theological education afford to be less intimate with the Church since it His Body and physical representative on the earth? What can be the Scriptural connection of a parachurch organization delivering theological education to Christ if not through His Body in an intimate way?

- The Church is precious to God: The metaphors of His beloved and His bride show the precious nature of the Church to Her Savior. The Church must be precious and central to the process of theological education if it is to mirror the heart of God.

All of these principles that are defined by the Scriptures lead to a proper understanding of what the Church is. The Church is a community of witnesses to the good news of Christ and His resurrection, empowered by the Holy Spirit to share that good news, and to live in obedience to Christ as its Lord and Savior (Hays 1996, 194-196). They also help define central responsibilities of any endeavor of theological education if it is to remain on Scriptural footing.

Implications for Theological Training

Since the Church is the recipient of the ministers who are trained by theological education, it should have several implications for the way that the training must be delivered if it is to be effective:

- *Praxis* (practical application): Theological training must be designed to meet the needs of the church since the church is the context for theological training. Abstract training and concepts will not prepare a minister to meet the needs of the living Church. What is taught must be as imminently practical and directly applicable to the reality of everyday church life.

- *Apologia* (contextualization): Theological training must be delivered in a manner that is relevant to the Church as it exists at a particular point in time. There is no such thing as a universal way to do theological training right — it varies with the people that make up the Church and their place in space and time.

- *Ekklesia* (organization and organism): The church is a living entity. While it does have organizational aspects prescribed in the Scriptures, it is in essence something that is alive. It should be no surprise that it changes with time as all living things do. It should also be no surprise that its needs change over time as well. The professional paradigm for preparing ministers can only be used to a certain point in light of what the church is until the role of the minister becomes distorted.

- *Koinonia* (community): Theological training should not take place in a vacuum or apart from the church. To isolate the theological school from the Church is to make it a disembodied soul. Partnership with the local church is essential for the delivery of theological training because it is the church that is empowered by Christ. The theological school exists to serve the church. The *ethos* of the school is very important to theological training since the sense of community will facilitate or hinder the process.

The nature and process of theological training, if it is to be delivered in an effective manner, must take into account the biblical nature and definition of what the church is. Based on this study, the Church can be defined as follows:

> The Church is the beloved living and universal community of God's children who, being knit together by the bonds of fellowship and expressed in local assemblies, are the visible expression of Jesus Christ on the earth.

This definition has many implications for how to train ministers to function in ministry since the church is their context of ministry. The church is not a building or an organizational system. All of these things are constructs of man and are negotiable and subject to change if it will facilitate God's purposes. Community and fellowship (*koinonia*) are at the heart of what the Church should be and must somehow be modeled in the process of theological training rather than delivering sterile facts in a sterile setting and calling this theological training. Theological training must be designed to exist in partnership with the local church.

Proper training should also impart reverence for the Church to the student since the Church is the beloved bride of Christ. This type of reverence has little to do with professionalism and more to do with an ability to form a love relationship with the Body of Christ so that the motive for ministry will be right. The universal nature of the Church and its many local expressions must also translate into respect for diverse expressions of the Church and a sense that a local church is knit to the greater whole as theological training is delivered and contextualized for a specific location. Based on these findings, partnership with the local church in providing theological training is an essential element to effective theological training. This posture will avoid the problems introduced by the stand-alone seminary concept that isolates theological training from the very context it trains leaders to function in.

Renewal Distinctives of Minister and Ministry

What is "the ministry" and who are "the ministers"? Obviously these questions are central to any endeavor in theological training. In order to effectively train an individual for an activity or place in life, the position and the profile for who should be involved in the training must be defined. Many of the current ideas for what ministers are and what ministers should do are a product of tradition rather than biblical in their origins. Before any enterprise in theological training is designed, it is therefore essential that a biblical understanding of what a minister is and how his or her function should be understood. This concept is vital to the design of effective theological training.

This section deserves more attention than others because theological training is essentially a function of "equipping the saints" for a particular work of service that is called the ministry. While Eph. 4:11-13 makes it clear that the work of the five-fold ministry offices are to equip all saints for the work of the ministry, a segment of those saints will also have experienced a divine calling to function in one of the five-fold ministry offices. Because of the calling to one of these offices, some individuals in the Body of Christ will therefore need a special type of equipping. One of the goals of theological education is to provide such training. It seems, however, that a means of theological training should not limit itself to merely equipping those with a calling to one of the five-fold ministry if all of the saints are to be equipped for ministry according to their individual gift-mix. The key to understanding how to equip and who should be equipped can be found in Eph. 4:7-16, especially 4:11-15.

When Jesus was on the earth, He was literally "all things to all men." The Scriptures say that He is the "Apostle and High Priest of our confession," as the founding Apostle of the New Testament Church (Heb. 3:1). He functioned as a Prophet (Mt. 24:1-31; Jn. 4:19) and an Evangelist (Lk. 4:18-21), with an excellence that cannot be equaled. He was the model Pastor and Teacher as well (Jn. 10:1-18; Mt. 5:1-7:29, especially 7:29). Jesus was all these things when he was on the earth, and remains these things as He is seated at the right hand of the Father in Heaven (Heb. 13:8). The Church, especially at its inception, was still in need of the function of all of these ministry offices, though Christ would no longer physically be with them.

The context of Eph. 4:11-15 reveals Christ's solution to the dilemma of His departure, and the ongoing needs of the Church. In Eph. 4:7,8, Paul speaks of grace that was given to us, according to the measure of Christ's gift. In verse eight, the Psalms are quoted. The context for Ps. 68:18 is David's victories over his enemies, and the giving of gifts from the spoils of war. Such are the grace gifts that Christ now distributes to us as the spoils of His conquest and victorious ascension.

In the passage that follows, Paul describes some of these gifts, their purpose, and the results of them functioning properly. There is some debate as to which of the gifts, or ministry offices, described in Eph. 4:11, are still in operation or necessary for today. There is also debate over what the precise purpose of these offices are, based on the exegesis of Eph. 4:12. There is, however, no debate as to the need of the results described in Eph. 4:13-15. An examination of the Scripture passage found Eph. 4:11-15 can shed some light on the nature of these debates, and yield greater understanding of offices, purposes for those offices, and the anticipated results of their function in the Body of Christ.

The Five-fold Ministry

Traditionally, theological training was almost exclusively offered to individuals who were training to become full time pastoral professionals in church ministry. There was a strong division between the clergy and laity, partially enforced by the availability of theological training. Is this division biblical? Should theological training be restricted to preparing full-time ministers for professional positions in the church? Should theological training be limited to those who are determined to fill the place of one of the five-fold ministry offices in the church? These questions are essential to theological training since their answers determine who should have the training.

The city of Ephesus was known as a center of learning and religion (Goodwin 1958, 2). It was known for its devotion to the goddess Diana, and converts burned their demonic literature after they were saved (Acts 19:19). The city was known also for its excess, as is noted in a manuscript found on "The Banishment of Hermodorus." In the manuscript, it says, " Let no man be frugal and temporal among us; let no one excel in a virtue, or if he do, let him be gone from us forever" (Goodwin 1958, 11). Many believe Ephesians to be a canonical work of Paul the Apostle. Westcott notes that Ephesians occurs in all of the primary uncial manuscripts (Codecies Sin., Alex., Vatic.), as well the Old Latin, Latin, and Vulgate texts (Westcott 1950, xix-xxi). The Epistle also is attested to by early patristic evidence, with Clement of Rome referring to the Epistle (c. 64 – Eph. 1:4), as well as the Didache (Two Ways, c. 36 – Eph. 1:18), and the writings of Ignatius (Abbott 1964, xiii, ix).

It is against this backdrop that the Epistle to the Ephesians was written - Christ was Victor (Eph. 4:8), and gave the gifts/spoils of war to men (Ps 68:18). In verse Eph. 4:11, Paul lists some of those gifts (NAS - *emphasis mine*):

> And He gave some *as* **apostles**, and some *as* **prophets**, and some *as* **evangelists**, and some *as* **pastors and teachers**,

In this passage, Paul enumerates what some have called the five-fold ministry gifts or offices of the church. They are His ministry gifts to the church. Eadie points out that the Greek grammatical construction of the passage lends itself to the interpretation that the men occupying the offices, as well as the offices themselves should be considered gifts from God (1979, 297). The verb in the phrase "And He gave..." is in the aorist tense, signifying that the offices themselves were given by divine institution of God, according to His timeless plan, to be a blessing to the Body of Christ. As Calvin points out, these gifts are distributed sovereignly, according to God's wishes, and not dispersed equally, but according to God's order (1975, 361). When Paul starts to describe the individual offices, the construction "...some as apostles" is meant to point toward the man who would also occupy the office, in Eadie's opinion, to signify that the man in the office is also the gift to the Body of Christ. Theological training is therefore aimed at some individuals called to a particular office in the church and its purpose is to identify, sharpen, and deploy the gifts to serve the Body of Christ.

The first gift or ministry office mentioned by Paul is that of an apostle. The word "apostles" is constructed of two obvious words in Greek, meaning "to send," and the preposition "out from." Putting these meanings together, it would seem that an apostle is one who is sent out from the church, to minister. The context of Scripture provides much more definition to the nature and function of apostles.

One position commonly held is the position that interprets this gift or ministry office to be that of the plenary apostle, limiting the office to the Twelve Apostles and Paul, all of whom were directly appointed by Jesus Christ. These Apostles occupied a special place in God's plan, and are unique in their apostleships, as the word plenary, meaning fullness, implies (Hendrikson 1967, 196). The dialogue in Acts 1:21-26, where the early disciples talked about replacing Judas with another Apostle, gives clear insight on what they believed was required to fill the place of a plenary apostle, or as Lightfoot calls them, an "Apostle of Christ" (Abbott 1964, 117). In order to qualify to be an Apostle of Christ, one must receive the commission directly from Christ (Acts 1:21; Gal 1:1), have seen the Lord Jesus Christ, risen from the dead (Acts 1:8,21-23; 1 Cor. 9:1,2), and exhibit the "signs of a true apostle" (Acts 2:43; 2 Cor.

12:12). If these definitions are applied to the office in Eph. 4:11, it obviously limits the office to a few select group of men, and cannot be duplicated today.

The Scriptures are clear, however, that others functioned in the ministry office described in this passage as "apostle." Barnabas is clearly referred to as an apostle along with Paul (Acts 14:4, 14). James, the brother of Jesus, is referred to also as an apostle (2 Cor. 15:7; Gal 1:19). Silvanus is also called an apostle (1 Thes. 2:6). Irenaeus (ii, 21.1) and Tertullian (Adv. Marc. 4:24) also plainly refer to Andronicas and Junia, mentioned in Rom 16:7, as being apostles (Abbott 1964, 117). There seems, therefore, to be a general sense in which the office of apostle can be applied to individuals who do not meet the requirements for a plenary apostle, or Apostle of Christ. In any case, an apostle was a "sent one," who took the witness of Christ's resurrection to the world, with the signs of an apostle in operation. Some understand the position to be that of a missionary or church planter. If these convictions are held, theological training must be designed to equip individuals with this calling to function in this gifting.

The ministry office of prophet was also well known in the early church. Hendrikson describes those occupying this office as "occasional organs of inspiration" (1967, 196). In the early church, Chrysostom described them as those that "utter from the spirit", while, in contrast, teachers "sometimes discourse from their understanding" (Abbott 1964, 117,118). From the prefix "pro" the inference is that they are speaking for God, under His divine influence of revelation, to make predictions (Acts 11:28), and to presumably bring "edification, exhortation, and consolation" (1 Cor 14:3) to the Body of Christ.

The ministry of the apostles and prophets are considered foundational to the Church (Acts 2:20; 3:5; 13:1; 15:32; 21:9). The four virgin daughters of Phillip the evangelist were prophetesses (Acts 21:9). The prophets and teachers in Jerusalem are referred to in Acts 13:1, and Judas and Silas are also called prophets (Acts 15:32). The offices of evangelist, pastor and teacher are also mentioned in this text. These offices are more generally accepted in the Body of Christ as valid gift expressions for today. Theological training must take into account all of the possible offices with focused training if it is to properly equip the saints that have one of the five-fold ministry gifts resident in their life. Merely training pastors is not enough.

Understanding Ephesians 4:11-16

The text for Eph 4:11-16 deserves some special comment in order to uncover the biblical meaning for "minister" and "ministry." An exegetical excursis of the Greek nuances of this passage can be found in Appendix C that support a renewal distinctive – that the "work of the ministry" belong to the "saints" (laity) who are meant to be equipped by the five-fold offices of the Church to do the work of the ministry.

Renewal distinctives differ from other traditions in what the actual function of the five-fold ministry is within the Church. One philosophy of ministry, enforced by the King James Version, asserts that the function of the five-fold ministry is to actually *do* the work of the ministry described in Eph 4:12 (KJV):

> 11 And he gave some, apostles; and some, prophets; and some, evangelists; and some, pastors and teachers;
> 12 For the perfecting of the saints, for the work of the ministry, for the edifying of the Body of Christ:

With the comma inserted after "saints" in verse twelve for the King James Version, the clause seems to indicate that the five-fold ministry is responsible for the perfecting of the saints *and* for the work of the ministry, *and* for the edifying of the Body of Christ. Calvin echoed this in his comments on this passage, with his emphasis on the role of the ministry offices (1975, 373-375). He felt that it was the role of the pastor-teacher to preach the word, and thereby perfect the saints, do the work of the ministry, and edify the body. In his thirteenth sermon on Ephesians 4, he states that the "preaching of the Word brings the body to soundness," thereby assigning the "work of the ministry" to the pastor-teacher. There is no emphasis on "equipping the saints *for* the work of the ministry," and the interpretation of Calvin seems to agree with the translation found later in the King James Version and its insertion of commas to divide the clauses in this passage.

There is also a revival in some Reformed circles today of an emphasis on preaching, and preaching alone to accomplish the work of the ministry, such as evangelism and ministry to the body. This model pictures ordained clergy as the ones appointed by this passage to do all the work of the ministry, because they are called to do so. This paradigm is existent in many church settings today, and limits the potential of the Body of Christ to effectively distribute the work of ministry to those who are not called to one of the five-fold ministry. This paradigm is perpetuated in many realms of theological training as a result of a faulty exegesis of this passage of Scripture.

Renewal distinctives as to the relationship of the believer to the work of the ministry differ radically from prevailing views that emphasize a strong clergy and laity division. Renewal distinctives also view the role of those in one of the five-fold ministry offices differently that the prevailing view in the traditional church. Both differences center on the interpretation of the passage in Eph. 4:11-16. While it is proper to translate the original Greek text in Eph. 4:12, "for the perfecting of the saints," the proper translation of the next phrase should be "into" the work of the ministry and "into" the building up of the Body of Christ. The meaning should be understood to direct the responsibility of the "equipping or perfecting" toward the saints, not the professionals holding ministry office in Eph. 4:11. The meaning of the passage in light of this interpretation would be that the five-fold ministry offices have the responsibility to equip the saints *for* (into) the work of the ministry, and *for* (into) the edifying of the Body of Christ. The job of the fivefold ministry becomes one of equipping the saints to serve in ministry, according to their God-given gifts, under the authority of the pastor-teacher (Westcott 1950, 62). Thus, every believer is charged with a personal service toward God, rather than just those that fill the five-fold ministry offices. Westcott holds that the purposes described in Eph. 4:12 are the spiritual ministry of all the saints, not just those ordained to ministry (1950, 62,63). As Abbott points out, Chysostom treated the interpretation of this passage the same way (1964, 119). The dearly held idea of a professional clergy doing the "work of the ministry" is not new, but the interpretation of this passage as related above seems to negate this fact. This view of the role of those holding one of the five-fold ministry and view of the responsibility of "the saints" frames two key renewal distinctives and has great implications for the way theological education takes place, even to the point of defining who should be trained.

The original Greek word used for "equipping" used in this passage is found nowhere else in the Scriptures. It refers to the perfecting or equipping of the saints, in harmonious power for the work of the ministry to the Body of Christ. Gingrich relates the word to medical literature, where it is used to describe the setting of a bone (1957, 419). It refers to the ultimate purpose of the five-fold ministry, and is the central verb in the passage. The results of the equipping of the saints can be found in Eph. 4:13,14, and this passage stresses the ministry of the parts to the welfare of the whole (Westcott 1950 63; Abbott 1964 119,120).

The "work of service" and "the building up of the Body of Christ" further define the function of the ministry. Again, whether one believes that the ministry is to be accomplished by equipped saints, or by the ministry offices, these phrases describe the function and purpose of the ministry. The word used for "service" is the same used for deacon in other parts of the Scriptures. It links leadership with service, and makes the case for "servant-leadership" in the Body of Christ. The word "building up" literally pictures the raising of a building, and shows what a practical role that the ministry described in Eph. 4:12 is to play.

Jesus Christ is Apostle, Prophet, Evangelist, Pastor, and Teacher. When He ascended, He gave gifts to men, which are the spoils of His victory (Eph. 4:8-10). These gifts are the ministry offices listed in Eph. 4:11, and the men that He appoints to occupy these offices. This dispute, based on the grammar of Eph. 4:12 may not be resolvable with exegesis, but whoever does the work of ministry, the ministry's function should be to "perfect, serve, and build up" the Body of Christ (Eph. 4:12). Enough grammatical evidence does exist to persuade the authors that this text intends that the five-fold ministry to equip the saints for the work of the ministry so that the intended results in Eph 4:12-16 can be realized. Because of this interpretation, theological training with renewal distinctives must be designed to train individuals for full time ministry and lay-leaders in the church. The focus must be to train these emerging leaders, without emphasis on a clergy-laity division, with the skills necessary to, in turn, equip the saints for the work of the ministry.

Implications for Theological Training with Renewal Distinctives

Exegesis of what the Scriptures say concerning the minister and ministry yields some important principles that are vital to delivering theological training. These principles include:

- Ministry is simply service for God and the minister is anyone who renders that service. There is no scriptural division between laity and clergy. Ministry is in essence servant-leadership.

- The establishment of the five-fold ministry including apostle, prophet, evangelist, pastor, and teacher are for the equipping of the saints for the work of the ministry. Together, these five offices represent the fullness of Christ's ministry on the earth toward His Body.

- The equipping of the saints means empowering them to function within their own unique gift-mix and calling to do the work of the ministry. Equipping must therefore be gift-specific and should be directed at the five-fold ministry and people in the church.

- No distinction is made between the laity and the clergy. Both are ministers according to the Bible. They each have different roles in ministry. Both are equally able to offer service to God. Both make up the universal priesthood of the believer.

These interpretations from the Scriptures lead to several practical themes and applications for theological training, which have been designed into the model for theological training outlined in this book. They include:

- Servant Leadership - All theological training must be done in the context of servant-leadership. Ministers are nothing more than those called to serve, and their training must prepare them for this role. The idea of servant-leadership must bring balance to the professional paradigm in place for understanding ministry, which maybe useful, but is not biblical and distorts the perception of ministers as to who they are called to be.

- Equipping the Saints - The main job of theological training is equipping the saints to serve the Body of Christ. The biblical model for equipping yields an understanding that this equipping occur in several ways. The five-fold ministry gifting should be trained to effectively equip the saints for the work of the ministry. Those without a calling to the five-fold ministry should be trained to serve according to their unique gift-mix. This process requires that a student's unique calling and gift-mix be identified and sharpened through the equipping process. This does not bode well for a "cookie-cutter" approach to theological training. It also tears down the distinction of theological training preparing an elite group of ministers for their place in ministry due to the universal priesthood of all believers.

- Spiritual Gifts - Service or ministry is a gift-based (*domata*) function of a believer's life. It occurs as God empowers individuals for service and deploys them according to their gift. Each believer is employed in ministry and therefore should be equipped through theological training either directly by the process or indirectly through ministers who have formal training. This defines the role of theological training and the target it is intended for in the context of the Church. Beyond that, God moves in the life with grace-gifts that function as the Spirit leads (*charismata* – I Cor. 12, 14). Emerging leaders must also be trained to operate in these gifts as well.

From this study of the Scriptures, a definition can be given for the ministry and the minister:

> The ministry is any service rendered on behalf of God, empowered by God and according to one's own unique gift-mix.

> The minister is any believer, whether having the calling

of one of the five-fold ministry or general calling in salvation, who renders service on behalf of God, according to
his or her own unique calling and gift-mix.

These definitions serve to give focus to both the target participants
(the minister) of theological training and their role (the ministry).
Hays asserts that one of the key lenses for interpreting the
Scriptures is the idea of the new creation through which "the church
embodies the power of the resurrection in the midst of a not-yet-
redeemed world" (1996, 198). This rightly describes the role of
New Testament ministers and their ministries as they function in the
world as new creations, imparting that resurrection life to others
whom they serve. It also provides the biblical basis for the training
embodied in renewal-oriented theological training, offered without
emphasis on the traditional clergy-laity paradigm.

CHAPTER EIGHT

Intersections for Change in Theological Training

Bethel Bible School in Topeka, Kansas, was an unlikely site for classes in theology. It was housed in old unfinished mansion in town, which was called by local residents "Stone's Folly," after the gentleman who was unable to complete its construction (Burgess and McGcc 1988, 851). The Stone mansion was rented by Charles F. Parham in 1900, who established Bethel Bible College there in October of that year. He organized the school as a missionary training school and instructed his thirty-four students in Holiness theology (Burgess and McGee 1988, 850).

Parham has been a sickly child. As an infant, he suffered a nearly fatal bout with a virus that weakened him and stunted his growth. At the age of nine, he was stricken with rheumatic fever. A particularly severe bout with a recurrence of rheumatic fever in 1891 left him convinced that he needed to reaffirm a calling he believed he had into ministry. He became a Methodist pastor and was immersed in the Holiness movement of his day, with an acute interest in the supernatural and divine healing (Burgess and McGee 1988, 660).

Parham had been greatly affected by a number of

Holiness evangelists. He was taken by their concept of apostolic power and recent accounts of "xenolalia," or manifestations of the ability to speak in other languages that they had never learned. In 1898, he and his wife founded the "Bethel Healing Home," which offered lodging and training for individuals who were sick and were seeking divine healing, a condition to which Parham was no stranger. At this time, he began to seek God for a greater outpouring of the Holy Spirit. He personally became convinced that the reports of the xenolalia reported among missionaries was a sign of the later day outpouring of the Holy Spirit promised in Joel 2.

In September, 1900, Parham opened up a section of the Bethel Healing Home for intensive Bible study to prepare missionaries for work in the field. He viewed the outpouring of the Holy Spirit as an essential experience for them to have for their upcoming missions work. In late December of that year, he challenged his students to go to Acts 2 where "tongues as an evidence of the baptism in the Holy Spirit was clearly mentioned, and to draw conclusions for themselves as to what this could mean (Burgess and McGee 1988, 850). As a result, one of the students, Agnes Osman, requested at a New Year's Eve gathering, that Parham lay his hands on her and pray that she might receive the baptism in the Holy Spirit as it is recounted in Acts 2. In a service at the school several day later, about half the students at the school were likewise baptized with in the Holy Spirit with the evidence of speaking in other tongues as in Acts 2. News reports soon began to appear about the outbreak of this phenomena in cities as far away as St. Louis. The Bible School in Topeka soon closed after the mansion was sold, but the event that occurred there on New Year,s Eve, 1900 ushered in what can only be described as "The Century of the Holy Spirit" as hundreds of millions of people experienced the baptism in the Holy Spirit. A small gathering at a small Bible school in a small town, studying a simple passage of the Scripture shook the world as we know it today. Topeka lives on in the hearts of hundreds of millions of Spirit-filled Christians who have had the same experience.

The shape of theological training is ultimately determined by the values that inform the training. Much time has been spent reviewing the debate in theological education circles over how to solve the current crisis in theological training. The solutions that have emerged thus far often do not go to the heart of the values that are in operation in the training. It is far easier to try to make surface changes than to reach down to a core values level. In order to accomplish the radical changes necessary to reshape theological training and restore it to the place of relevance in the Body of Christ, changes at a values level are a must.

Likewise, the theological education community has been reluctant to embrace renewal distinctives in its training. This seems to be an instant prescription for irrelevance since most Christians, especially at an international level, are renewal-oriented in their beliefs. What core values must theological education embrace in order to change and become relevant and effective at training emerging leaders once again? What core renewal distinctives and values are essential to theological training? How can renewal-oriented core values be integrated into the process? The answer to these questions determines the shape of the whole enterprise and is of the utmost importance.

Core Shaping Values and Methodologies

Theological training has always been shaped by the shared assumptions of those engaged in the process. At the heart of this shaping process are values. The current crisis that exists in the world of theological training is, in part, a direct result of competing or incongruent values. In order to reshape the enterprise of theological training a new set of guiding values must be established upon which to engineer change. These values should not be established coincidentally by the accidental blending of Christianity with the prevailing cultural assumptions that exist today. They should be deliberately chosen to meet the needs critical in renewal-oriented theological training for the Church as it exists today. They stand in direct contrast with some of the non-biblical values that exist at the heart of theological training today and designed to meet the real and felt needs of the emerging leaders being trained.

The authors assert that a set of five core shaping values are essential to the to design of interdenominational renewal-oriented theological training. These five core shaping values include:

- *Theologia:* This core shaping value represents divine self-disclosure though the authority and inspiration of the Scriptures. In a post-modern culture, it is no longer safe to assume that those desiring theological training share a basic knowledge or consensus on biblical knowledge and values. A new emphasis must be given to a Bible-centered education to facilitate divine self-disclosure through the Scriptures, as Farley has noted, with the basics of the Scriptures and its values accentuated in the curriculum. A new emphasis must also be given to the plenary-verbal inspiration and authority of the Scriptures as a basis for foundational beliefs, assumptions, and Christian values.

- *Paideia*: This core shaping value represents spiritual and moral formation (being formation) that occurs as a result of cognitive knowledge (knowing) and application (doing). A renewed emphasis on spiritual and moral formation issues in theological training is needed. In a post-modern society, it can no longer be assumed that individuals have basic spiritual formation from church, family, or society. Spiritual formation issues must be actively and deliberately addressed in the process of theological training.

- *Ekklesia:* This core shaping value represents a proper biotic-organic and holistic conception of the Church as the living Body of Christ. In a culture that places a high value on self and individualism, the value of the healing community of the Church must once again be emphasized. The present emphasis on church organization must be balanced with the conception of the Church as a living organism. A new organic view of the Church must be adopted and emerging leaders trained to view it as a living web of human relationships. The old clerical paradigms for church ministry must be replaced with a desire to empower and equip the saints for the work of the ministry as active participants. Partnership with the Church in theological training must become an integral part of the process. Service to the Church must become a major goal. Contextualization of the training for the Church's emerging leaders must become a priority.

- *Koinonia:* This core shaping value represents the symbiotic relationship of the believer with other believers and the Church as well as the symbiotic partnership between theological training, the believer, and the Church. The current hunger for meaningful relationships within post-modern culture feeds right into the biblical value of fellowship or *koinonia*. A new emphasis on the Church as a biblical healing community in theological training is needed. Those existing in the context of the current post-modern culture have a hunger for experience and relationship. At its core, theological training is not the transfer of knowledge as much as it is the deepening of a personal relationship with God and with each other in Christian community. A new balance must be established between the Athens way of personal formation and relationship with God and others in the Body of Christ and the Berlin way of reason and knowledge.

- *Pneumatics:* This core shaping value represents the philosophical framework by which the believer relates to God, the Church, life, and ministry through Spirit-filled living. This core shaping value captures the essence of the renewal movement. It seems that God has answered Enlightenment Christianity with an unprecedented outpouring of His Holy Spirit unlike anything that has ever occurred before in the history of mankind. In the past century, over 500 million Christians have been filled with the Holy Spirit around the world, making renewal-oriented Christianity the second largest group in Christianity. A new emphasis on the person, gifts, fruit, nature, and transforming power of the Holy Spirit is called for in theological training. An emphasis on Spirit-filled life and ministry must be integrated into the heart of theological training if it is to remain relevant to the needs of this generation and current with what God is doing in the world today. Theological training must now make room for the Holy Spirit.

These five core shaping values dictate theological training's methodology and form.

Further, the authors also assert that three core-shaping methodologies are indispensable to interdenominational renewal-oriented theological training. Methods are the means for actualizing values. They must not be chosen by chance, but rather embody the best way to express the core shaping values that drive them. They must also be chosen to best suit the object that they express, which in this case is theological training. These three core-shaping methodologies include:

- *Contextualization:* This core shaping methodology expresses the ability of theological training to adapt and design its institutions, curriculum, faculty, student body, and processes for the Church and surrounding culture's unique real and felt needs. This contextualization meets the needs of the Church's specific place in time, space, and cultural context. The process embraces an incarnational theology of culture that seeks to demonstrate Christ to the world in culturally relevant ways by interpreting the culture as well as it interprets the Scriptures.

- *Dynamic Communication:* This core-shaping methodology represents the ability of theological training to adapt its means of communication to be relevant and effective to its mission. All theological training is delivered by means of communication. All emerging leaders trained in the process are, by definition, trained to be communicators. The methods and manners of communication must be culturally relevant and adapted to the target audience if theological training is to succeed in its mission. It can no longer afford to communicate in a set pattern, hoping that the participants will adapt to its culture and methodology. Theological training must adopt learning styles and methodology that are appropriate for this generation and its worldview. The format, delivery, and environment must be negotiable and best suited to facilitate the process, even if institutions and protocol must change to accommodate the process.

- *Praxis:* This core shaping methodology represents a process where cognitive knowledge is deliberately applied to real-life in the context of ministry resulting in the spiritual and moral formation of an individual's being. Post-modern culture values transparency and honesty. It seeks to develop practical knowledge and skills that answer life's questions and meet real life needs. Theological training must seek to balance the need to transmit knowledge with the need to allow the participant to understand how to apply that knowledge. Theological training must become more skill-based and practical in its application in order to meet the needs of emerging leaders. Knowledge must be linked more intimately to practical application and skills. Theological training begins to assume the role of facilitating dynamic reflection that links cognitive knowledge and application for the participants. This seems to be an ideal route to an individual's spiritual and moral formation. In short, it must take on a more andragogical mindset appropriate for adult learning, rather than a pedagogical mindset appropriate for children.

A further exposition of the nuances of the five core values and three core methodologies is necessary to understand the intricacies of the framework used to design interdenominational renewal-oriented theological training.

An Exposition on the Five Core Shaping Values for Theological Training

Values are the core philosophical framework that shapes any enterprise. Theological training is no different. The authors have developed a matrix of five core shaping values with eight associated characteristics for each value that were used in the process of developing the framework for interdenominational renewal-oriented theological training. The following is a more detailed description of each of these core shaping values and the eight characteristics of each.

Theologia

This current generation faces the challenge of a worldview that is in the process of change. A massive shift in values is occurring in Western culture. The culture is in transition from a materialist worldview that largely rejects God and the supernatural to an integral worldview that once again embraces the supernatural. As Sweet notes, there is an intense soul hunger with the current generation, where "God is hot" due to the failure of rationalism (1999b, 411). The problem is that this new acceptance of the supernatural has no direction. While this new openness to the supernatural is a step in the right direction, the integral nature of the assumption Western culture is embracing allows for a dangerous syncretism of Christianity with other competing philosophies. This generation is in desperate need of something solid to stand on once again. The potency of human reason has largely been exhausted, failing to answer some of man's most basic questions about life and nature. The modernist ideals of human progress and the advancement of mankind have failed as man founders in an atmosphere of uncertainty about his environment. Romanticism and its fantasies about the goodness of man as well as liberal theology and its social gospel have ultimately failed to inspire man to higher levels, and instead people have continued to show forth their depravity in countless ways. This generation is looking for answers, and once again must be reoriented toward a faith in the authority of God's written word. Likewise, the authority and the verbal-plenary inspiration of the Scriptures must once again become a core driving value in theological training. This would mark a major step forward for theological training as it abandons Enlightenment assumptions that diminished the Bible's centrality in the Church and her institutions of theological training.

Theological training has lost its way because it has lost its focus. A disjointed nature in what is taught in theological schools has resulted because there is no one thing that makes theological training "theological" anymore. Edward Farley, in his book *Theologia*, argued that the answer to the problem of fragmentation in theological education was to center it once again on a sapiential and personal knowledge of divine self-disclosure (1983, ix). The authors would take that assertion one step further to include the foundation of that disclosure - the authority and inspiration of the Scriptures. All sapiential and personal knowledge of God must ultimately be based on a foundation that is considered to be inspired revelation.

While a personal sapiential knowledge of God is a necessary

focus for theological training and a good starting place for reorienting the enterprise of theological education, the more basic need is to
first reorient theological training's focus on the verbal-plenary inspiration and authority of the Scriptures. This allows for a solid foundation upon which a personal and sapiential experience with God can
be based. The authors will expand Farley's term, *theologia*, to define
a basic value of divine self-disclosure through the Scriptures in their
verbal-plenary inspired form. The Scriptures, by definition, act as
the basis for divine self-disclosure. Grounding theological training
once again in a foundation of inspired absolute truth will fulfill one
of the most pressing needs exhibited by a generation that is desperately seeking answers through syncretism. *Theologia* is therefore a
core value of renewal-oriented theological training.

Emerging leaders must embrace this value in order to effect the
basic changes necessary in the Church. George Barna, in his book
The Second Coming of the Church, states that only 50% of the
people who consider themselves Christians listen to preaching or
teaching from the Bible once per week. Only 33% read their Bible
and 10% study it in any given week. Less that 4% are given to any
kind of Scripture memorization. Less than 2% percent of the people
who call themselves Christians practice all four of these disciplines
(Barna 1998, 135). This type of neglect is a symptom of compla-
cency in the Church, which is typical of Western culture at this
time. People do not value the Scriptures anymore as is demonstrated by their actions. More deeply, it is a symptom of the disregard for the focus and authority of the Scriptures. Only when
theological training facilitates the actualization of *theologia* for its
participants will the leaders themselves have a proper respect and
focus on the Scriptures. Their reorientation toward the value of
theologia in theological training is essential to cause this type of
reorientation to happen in the Body of Christ as well.

In his book, *Aqua Church,* Leonard Sweet calls for a reorientation of the Church through the use of the Bible as a compass
(1999a, 55). He makes the point that the Bible is not anti-cultural,
counter-cultural, nor a cultural extension. When it is used to
promote these agendas, it becomes distorted. When the Church has
a proper respect for the authority of the Scriptures, it seeks to live
out their content to illustrate truth to the world. This type of incarnational theology that results from living the Scriptures because

they are the focus of one's life is one of the best witnesses that this generation could have. This new generation is visually-oriented. They value experience over reason (Sweet 1999b, 197). They do not want pretense or complicated explanations - they want to see for themselves the truth in action before they will accept what is said (Sweet 1999b, 202-205). The type of witness necessary to win this generation's heart will only come to pass if the Scriptures and their authority are restored to their proper place as the focus of theological training, so emerging leaders can model the truth.

In order to actualize *theologia,* the whole process of theological training must once again produce a competent knowledge of the Scriptures. As was noted earlier, it is a faulty assumption to think that most people entering the theological education process have a basic grasp of the content of the Scriptures as was common in earlier times. The culture as it exists today is a post-Christian culture that has no basic Christian consensus of truth or how to perceive reality. Theological training must once again redouble its efforts to highlight the instruction of the Word of God. With the proliferation of specialty courses highlighting a wide assortment of cultural and political agendas, the Scriptures have not been given their proper place of focus as one of the central values that make theological training unique. There must be a special emphasis on the stories, metaphors, and allegories contained in the Scriptures if theological education desires to reach this generation. Sweet notes that this generation revels in stories and word-pictures (1999b, 425). It desperately needs tangible evidence of the love of God and a reason to continue to hope. Many of the stories in the Scriptures are written as narratives that are there to illustrate God's love and faithfulness. A return to a focus on the Scriptures will provide a basis for reaching this generation in a manner relevant to its cultural world.

A fresh focus in theological training on God's self-disclosure in the Scriptures will return the proper sense of mystery that should be inherent in the Church. Enlightenment Christianity sought to explain God with human reason. Where that reason conflicted with the Scriptures, reason prevailed and the Scriptures were discarded. The proper dialectic tensions that exist in the Scriptures that make them too wonderful to be "figured out" were dismissed in Christianity's enlightenment phase as well. A return to the mystery of the faith is necessary in theological training in order for a sense of mystery to be properly restored to the Body of Christ. The Berlin model for education has caused a grave incongruence within theological education between reason and mystery and must be brought back into balance.

The authors propose a set of eight characteristics that express the value of *theologia:*

- The priority of a living, vital, and dynamic relationship with God.

- A priority on divine self-disclosure through the Scriptures.

- A high view of the authority of the Scriptures in the life of the individual as demonstrated by their actions.

- A high priority of the inspiration of the Scriptures in the formation of an individual's values system.

- A holistic understanding of the Old and New Testament's content, values, and principles.

- The use of the Scriptures as a standard for living and the means of interpreting life.

- The formation of a biblical worldview that is solidly anchored in the Scriptures.

- The fostering of a sense of mystery and awe for God from relationship with Him and through the Scriptures.

Together, these characteristics provide a meaningful expression of the value embodied by *theologia*. When reason is once again put back in its place as "a" means of uncovering the truth, and the authority and the supremacy of the Scriptures are once again restored, a healthy balance will be restored. Revelation will once again rule as a means of understanding and knowing God, as it did for many years before reason became king. Enlightenment Christianity's infatuation with reason and human self-sufficiency must be dealt a death-blow by restoring the Scriptures to their rightful place in theological training. The result will be a new love of the mystery of the faith that will trickle down through the pulpits of the Church into the pews once again.

Paideia

Every means of theological training has a primary focus. The primary focus of interdenominational renewal-oriented theological training is the core value of *paideia*. *Paideia*, as stated earlier in this book, is actually an old Greek term that meant the cultivation of culture and character. The authors will borrow the word and its original meaning to express the value of spiritual and moral formation. Richard John Neuhaus did much to bring the issue of personal formation to the forefront of the debate over how to reengineer theological education. In his book, *Theological Education and Moral Formation* (1992), he emphasized the importance of spiritual and moral formation in the process of theological training. This process has been largely neglected when compared to education in the past (Neuhaus 1992, 57). Theological training has been chasing Scheiermacher's Ghost since the time that the Berlin model for theological training came to prominence in Western education (Neuhaus 1992, 114-118). Since that time, there has been a noticeable emphasis on reason and academic pursuits in theological training rather than a pursuit of spiritual and moral formation of the Church's emerging leaders. This emphasis has proved to be devastating for the Church in that many of its leaders — though they have strong knowledge of subjects like systematic theology, Hebrew, and Greek — many times they do not have the depth of character or spiritual formation necessary to successfully lead a church. If theological training does not emphasize the value of spiritual and moral formation for its participants, then what does make it theological and separate it from other disciplines in its education? The Convergence Model outlined in this book is designed to place the value of *paideia* at the center of the process of theological training once again.

Theological training must emphasize *paideia* in its value system. Many of the basic functions of *paideia* were once transmitted in the home and reinforced by Western society, which shared a basic consensus on Christian character and moral principles. In a post-Christian culture with an intensely integral worldview, it is a mistake to continue to assume that basic spiritual formation will have already taken place by the time an individual begins the process of theological training. Basic disciplines that facilitate *paideia* may be totally absent in such candidates for theological training. The ability to discern the direction of God by "hearing Him" with His "still small voice" may be absent (1 Kgs 19:12). The ability to read God's word devotionally and conduct the personal disciplines necessary to build character and moral stamina such as personal study, Scripture memorization and meditation, as well as prayer and fasting may be foreign to new students. Unless theological training changes to prioritize these pursuits in its curriculum and extracurricular activities, who will model these basic spiritual and moral disciplines for the Church? If emerging pastors and leaders in the Church do not have these disciplines mastered and in operation as a part of their daily life, where will they get the moral character and strength to endure the strains and stresses of the ministry?

One of the other aspects of *paideia* is discovering one's gifting and place in service within the Body of Christ. As one comes to know God through a personal relationship with Him, this sapiential experience causes one to understand oneself more fully. The awareness of calling and gifting flows from spiritual and moral character preparation. The problem to this point, however, is that a lack of *paideia* and an unbalanced emphasis on academic pursuits has led to a lack of awareness of the participant's calling and gift-mix. Students are conversant in church history but cannot validate their own calling into ministry or the gifting that God has placed within them. This is evident in a study conducted by George Barna, which surveyed pastors about their calling into ministry and in particular, into leadership (1998, 35-37). He found that less than 10% of the pastors can articulate God's vision for the church they are leading (1998, 36). This has much to do with the process of personal development that should have taken place in seminary. Only 5% believe they have the gift of leadership (Barna 1998, 36). How can the Church's leaders be so unclear as to whether they have the gift of leadership? The answer is a lack of spiritual formation in their training experience and the inability to discern these things for themselves. Theological training must rise to the calling of spiritual and moral preparation if this generation's leaders are to be properly prepared to lead the Church. It must deliberately plan to help its participants identify their gift-mix and grow in personal awareness of their calling. It must then develop the spiritual and moral character necessary for its leaders to lead from a base of inner character and strength. Clinton points out that there are six essential characteristics of spiritual formation that the author has adapted to form eight essential characteristics that express the value of *paideia* (1984, 42):

- Increasing ability to experience more of God.

- Reflecting an increasing God-like character.

- Reflecting an increasing God-like personality.

- Increasing growth in spiritual disciplines (prayer, devotions, fasting).

- Increasing spiritual health (holistic being).

- Increasing experience of the power of God in daily life and ministry.

- Deepening discipleship (surrender to God).

- Increasing maturity (Col 1:28, 29 - *telos*).

These essential characteristics represent the essence of spiritual and moral formation in an individual's life and are the target of *paideia*. These processes lead to a deepening surrender to God (discipleship) and increasing maturity (Greek word *telos* - Col 1:28, 29) (Gangel and Wilhoit 1994, 15, 16). These processes are at the heart of the theological training.

Enlightenment paradigms with their assumptions of self-reliance and self-sufficiency have ravaged the Church and its leaders. The romanticist view that human progress and reason can solve any problem seems to be dying in Western culture as a basic assumption as this idealism gives way to hopelessness. These assumptions are not dead in the Church, however, and many ministry leaders still rely heavily on their own strength, will, and reason to endure ministry rather than entering into the Sabbath rest prescribed by the Scriptures (Heb 4:8,9). This is because theological formation has failed to provide the proper *paideia* for its participants to encourage a proper balance of spiritual and mental health in the discharge of ministry. Emerging leaders are not trained to understand their basic needs, as human beings, for seasons of daily devotion, weekly Sabbath, and periodic retreat. These normal rhythms in the life of a Christian are not reinforced or taught in the course of theological training to the point where ministers suffer with the same stress and burnout that is common to most professions in Western culture. Unless theological training begins to facilitate this type of spiritual formation in the lives of those graduating from its schools, the trend toward ministerial burnout and dropout will continue unabated in the Church. The Church will also continue to act just like the world because its leaders fail to offer them an alternative model. As Bill Hybels notes, ministers must learn to read their own "gauges," knowing their own spiritual, mental, and physical levels of strength and become acquainted with how to "fill their tanks" in the process of ministry (1991, 32-38). This type of training must become part of the *paideia* that emerging leaders experience in the process of theological training. It is the type of training that defines renewal-oriented training.

Ekklesia

Theological training is designed to function in a dynamic partnership with the local church. New values and assumptions related to the Church and how it functions must be added to the process of theological training if it is to succeed in its mission to this generation. The authors will define these new values and assumptions under the heading of *ekklesia*. Theological training has taken on a life of its own since the advent of the Berlin model in 1810. When Schleirmacher made the concessions necessary for theological education to remain a part of the curriculum at the University of Berlin, it separated the enterprise of theological training from the Church and joined it to the university as another department of professional education. While his intentions were noble, the results of removing theological training from the authority and covering of the Church have been devastating. The university and its reason-based higher criticism rejected the authority of the Scriptures. The university's rigid system of granting degrees, which has become standard in Western culture for access to education at higher levels, has kept many in the church from accessing theological training. Enlightenment thinking and academic-based instruction have supplanted the spiritual formation once prominent in theological training. In many cases, the Church has become divorced from the process of educating its leaders. That brings one back to the whole basic question of what theological training is for and from where does it gain its authority to exist as a separate enterprise?

Theological training must once again form an intimate partnership with the Church if it is to remain relevant and positively affect the very people it is training. The Church has an authentic right to exist since it was founded by God and Jesus Christ Himself (Mt 16:18). This is the same right for existence that is shared by human government as well (Rom 13:1-7). Theological training, as an enterprise separate from the Church, has no right to exist. Its authority to exist, if separated from the Church, is human in origin. In order to respect divine authority, the institutions that deliver theological training must come back into divine order and partnership with the Body of Christ. Theological education must form a partnership and act as an extension arm of the Body of Christ to train and equip its leaders. If business schools were to separate themselves from the business world and conduct their education in a manner that seemed best to them, with no input or relationship with the business world, these schools would soon be irrelevant and out of business. The same is true for the Church and theological training. A proper value of *ekklesia* must be restored to theological training and be expressed through its relationship with the Church.

The process of theological training actually forms the concept of what church means in the hearts of its emerging leaders. The whole concept of *ekklesia* hinges on the paradigms and models conveyed to these leaders, which will later be conveyed to the Church itself through them. The Body of Christ has been hindered for years by an unbalanced emphasis of the perception of the Church as an organization. This is not surprising, considering that the university context in which much theological education occurs would naturally see the Church as another sociological organization subject to the same laws of sociology and administration as any other human group in a society.

The problem with that paradigm is that the Church is not just another sociological organization, it is the living Body of Christ (Eph. 5:22-32). The concept that the Church is an organization has been taken too far. The recognition that the Church is actually a living organism is long overdue in theological training. Theological education cannot afford to abandon the proper training of its participants with business and administrative skills, although it is arguable as to whether it did a good job of this or not anyway. It must balance this organizational model with an organic model for understanding the Church as well.

Such a view is embraced by Christian A. Schwarz, and made popular in his book *Natural Church Development*. Schwarz has conducted an empirical study of growing and non-growing churches around the world in multiple countries, cultures, denominations, and sizes (1999, 13). The result has been the development of an organic paradigm for understanding what facilitates church growth and health and what hinders them. He has produced a list of eight quality characteristics that must be present in any given church in order for it to have a high degree of probability for growth and health which include (1999, 16-48):

- Empowering leadership.

- Gift-oriented ministry.

- Passionate spirituality.

- Functional structures.

- Inspiring worship service.

- Holistic small groups.

- Need-oriented evangelism.

- Loving relationships.

Schwarz makes the point that the factor that is at its lowest level, or the "minimum factor," must be addressed to facilitate growth and vitality once again (1999, 49-60). The author would categorize holistic small groups and loving relationships as an expression of the value of *koinoia*, although they overlap with the essential nature of *ekklesia*. All eight of these factors function in line with biotic or organic, living paradigms rather than organizational paradigms that include (Schwarz 1999, 61-82):

- Interdependence.

- Multiplication.

- Energy transformation.

- Multiple usage.

- Symbiosis.

- Functionality.

They result in a revival of an organic living paradigm for the Church that is much closer to the concept of Church as it is portrayed in the Scriptures (Schwarz 1999, 83-102). Theological training must balance its paradigms for understanding the Church between organization and organism. It must cast off some of the Enlightenment thinking that has dominated the organizational methodology employed to attempt to grow the Church. An organic view of the Church, which is also advocated by Sweet in his book *Soul Tsunami,* is essential for balanced ministry and proper perception of reality (1999b, 253). Sweet also notes that the whole value of health and prevention in Western culture has been elevated as wellness come into vogue rather than curing sickness (1999a, 133). The Church would do well to adopt this paradigm as a part of its methodology as well.

As a part of the values and assumptions associated with *ekklesia,* a new view of the pastor's role in the Church must be adopted. With Schleiermacher's professional paradigm came a sharper division of clergy and laity in the Body of Christ. This division is a cultural construct and not biblical since the Scriptures make it clear that it is the saints who are to do the work of the ministry (Eph 4:12) and those who hold ministry office who should equip them to do so (Eph 4:11). With the burden of the professional paradigm for ministry came an inevitable workload and responsibility for ministry leaders, which has proved impossible for them to bear. As Barna notes, pastors work an average of sixty-five hours per week and juggle sixteen dimensions of ministry each day, most of which they lack the skills and training to handle by themselves (1998, 5). As a result, the average tenure of pastors in their church is less than four years, which is tragic considering that the most productive years of a pastor's life in a church are between years five and fourteen (Barna 1998, 5).

Sweet notes that the present generation is a generation that is "dying to serve" (1999a, 342). They are actively seeking something of meaning to die for as they give themselves away in service (Sweet 1999a, 342). They have realized that the self-centeredness of their parents has not produced happiness, but rather broken relationships, families, and heartache. A proper view of *ekklesia* in theological training must convey that ministry is not doing the work, but equipping others to do the work. Emerging leaders must have the proper *paideia* themselves to recognize their gifts and calling, but must also be trained to help others under their leadership discover their gifts and calling in the Body of Christ for service. This generation is looking for purpose and meaningful opportunities to serve and make a difference. It thinks in a collaborative manner and values teamwork (Sweet 1999a, 187). It seems that in regards to worship that this generation does not want to "sit and listen" but "sing and dance." This is also true metaphorically for service in the church. The concept of team ministry and collaboration between its ministry leaders and church members is an essential component of *ekklesia* and must be transmitted through the process of theological training.

The subject matter that makes up the curriculum of theological training must also change to reflect the values and assumptions just outlined under the heading of *ekklesia*. Barna outlines six pillars of the Church that need to be emphasized for church health and growth (1998, 89). They include:

- Worship (Mt 4:8-10; Jn 4:20-24).

- Evangelism (Mt 28:19).

- Service (Acts 2:44-45; 4:32-34).

- Equipping (Eph 4:11-15).

- Community (Mt 16:18).

- Stewardship (Mt 25:1-29).

It is striking how these recommendations made by Barna overlap with the eight quality characteristics necessary for church health and growth suggested by Schwarz. From the suggestions of Schwarz and Barna, the authors have synthesized a set of eight essential characteristics that express the value of *ekklesia*. These include:

- The essential organic-biotic nature of the Church.

- Functional servant-leadership in the Church.

- Expression of the gift-mix of each believer in the Church.

- Expression of the destiny mix of each individual person in the Church with the accompanying vision and discernment necessary.

- Increasing passion for relationship with, nurture of, and equipping of God's people that make up the Church.

- Functional form, leadership, administration, and management of the Church.

- Heart-felt and inspirational worship of God by the Church.

- Passionate need-oriented evangelism and missions by the Church.

Together, these characteristics provide a meaningful definition for the value of *ekklesia* and a prescription for what to emphasize in order to have a relevant curriculum in theological training. This value is essential to the design of the model for theological training presented in this book.

Koinonia

Enlightenment thinking had as its emphasis the autonomous self. By definition, theological training is preparation for a life of serving others. Enlightenment thought and preparation for ministry are at odds from the very start.

Enlightenment thought conceives of people as islands unto themselves, embracing a self-sufficiency and rugged individualism as the cornerstones of their personal philosophy. Theological training must be designed to counter this secular mindset with teaching and through modeling biblical community or *koinonia*. This value is at the heart of The Convergence Model and its theological training.

This materialistic worldview and its set of assumptions have produced chaos in the personal relationships that exist within Western society. America in particular has the highest divorce rate in the Western world (Long 1997, 43). This generation has been the hardest hit by divorce of any since the founding of America and those with intact family units usually suffer with both parents away at work, leaving little time for meaningful relationship (Zoba 1999, 30, 49-55). The high instance of divorce and separation in Western culture has left this generation longing for meaningful relationships and as sense of connectedness. Long notes that this yearning has turned into a tribalistic mindset within society that has redefined what family means (1997, 70-71). The search for others who can be trusted and the formation of "families" with this common link of trust, is now commonplace. Friends who can be trusted now form the basis of family for this generation (Long 1997, 50). Within this tribal group, healing, comfort, direction, meaning, and assumptions of truth are formed. Only those who are members of the family have a right to comment on the truth (Long 1997, 70,71). This sense of community provides the sense of protection, acceptance, and direction that is lacking in today's broken nuclear families.

Theological training has been lacking in its emphasis on community and fellowship since the advent of the professional model for education at the University of Berlin in 1810. The Berlin professional model, while it emphasizes excellent academics, has diminished the human and relational components of pastoral ministry. The Church holds the answer to this generation's longings in the form of the biblical value of *koinonia*. This Greek word is translated fellowship many times in the Scriptures but represents much more. It represents the relationship between Christian believers in the Church, resulting in Christian community and family relationship. It is the life that flows when believers gather together in biblical community with Jesus Christ and His Spirit in their midst, that forms the essence of the Church (Mt 18:18-20). Enlightenment Christianity has emphasized intellectual pursuits and Bible studies. This was fine for a generation of individualists. This generation hungers for community and relationship. The Church has the answer to this generation's longings in the form of biblical community, but is not equipped to give this gift to those who so badly need it. The answer is a fundamental reorientation of the Church and its priorities to meet the needs of this generation. The solution lies in the process of theological training to adequately prepare emerging leaders to facilitate biblical community in the Church.

Koinonia at its heart reflects the nature and being of God. God exists in community with Himself from all eternity (Gen. 1:1-3). He created man in His image and decided that it was not good for man to be alone (Gen. 1:27; 2:18). He created other human beings for fellowship and longed for fellowship with them as well (Gen. 2:23-25; 3:1-8). It was sin that broke community in the first place, and sin that perpetuates the idea that people can make it on their own as autonomous individuals. As Long notes, one of Jesus' prime missions was to create a new community called the Church. Salvation transforms an individual to become a part of a living community of believers (Long 1997, 91-93). Pentecost was the gathering of people who were scattered by sin and rebellion back into one family again

(Acts 2:5-8). The heart of this generation cries out for such meaningful relationships again. Theological training must be reshaped by the value of *koinonia* in order to accomplish this goal.

The small group paradigm that has emerged in some corners of the Church over the last several decades is, in part, a response to this generation's cry for meaningful relationships. As Long asserts, the Body of Christ must rise up in this generation to meet its longing for belonging with a healing community that ministers comfort and purpose (1997, 87, 137, 138). While Enlightenment Christianity has focused on its Bible studies and discussions about doctrines, the Church must seek to shift its emphasis to meaningful personal and dependable relationships that feed into this culture's tribal mentality and provide a meaningful alternative. The collapse of the nuclear family unit and the chaos and pain that it has created provide a wonderful opportunity for small groups to model *koinonia* for the world to see and experience. The problem is that churches are not equipped to offer such community because its leaders have not been trained in the essential skills to facilitate such community. This must change if the Church is to provide a form of meaningful community that meets or exceeds Western society's current tribal community construct.

The authors propose a set of eight key characteristics that express the core shaping value of *koinonia*. These include:

- Personal community in relationship with God the Father, Son, and Spirit.

- Corporate community and fellowship with God and other believers.

- Healing and nurturing community and fellowship.

- Nurture of loving personal and corporate relationships.

- Holistic small group ministry.

- Emphasis on people and relationships over buildings and programs.

- Healthy multidimensional mentoring relationships (upward, downward, peer).

- Network and dynamic partnership between the Church and theological training.

These characteristics express the core shaping value of *koinonia* in a theological training setting. A new emphasis and training in the values and assumptions associated with *koinonia* are necessary. People and connectedness must be emphasized over organizations and administration. The idea of team ministry in an organic environment is necessary to form this connectedness. Small group skills must be taught. The rapid growth of cell-based churches around the world is also a reflection in the change in the way church is conducted and organized. Small group instruction and cell-church methodology are essential components for theological training if the Church is to be relevant in its outreach to this generation. These characteristics have been at the heart of the design of renewal-oriented theological training.

Pneumatics

Vinson Synan, a noted Pentecostal and Charismatic scholar, has noted that the twentieth century has been the "Century of the Holy Spirit" (2001, ix). The set of values and assumptions associated with this remarkable move of the Holy Spirit will be referred to collectively by the authors as *pneumatics*. Renewal-oriented Christianity has literally changed the face of worldwide Christianity through the introduction of a new set of core values and assumptions to the faith. What is remarkable is that no one denomination or group of people has control over the distinctives that mark the movement. Yet, there are several distinctives that emerge from the renewal movement that have left their collective mark on the global and Western church. These distinctives must be recognized in the Church if it is to be understood as it currently exists in the world of the twenty-first century. Further, theological training ignores these distinctives at its own risk if it does not foster an understanding and at the least an openness to them. Theological training should be specifically designed to embody renewal characteristics and targeted to the interdenominational renewal community.

The *pneumatic* distinctive that is most apparent in renewal-oriented Christianity is a personal and sapiential relationship with God at the new birth and through the Baptism in the Holy Spirit. Whereas Enlightenment Christianity embraces a faith that is largely based on reason, renewal-oriented Christianity incorporates a highly experiential view of Christianity and the believer's personal relationship with Christ. The belief in the born again experience of salvation in which the human spirit literally is recreated has now become mainstream in its acceptance (Jn 3:3-8; 2 Cor 5:17-21). The belief in an experience after the new birth called the baptism in the Holy Spirit with the accompanying sign of speaking with other tongues (*glossilalia*) has also gained wide acceptance as well. These experiences represent a very personal form of Christianity. They also suit this new generation that highly values personal experience as opposed to reason. This aspect of the renewal movements of the twentieth century seems to be God's answer to prepare the Church for the needs of this generation.

The new openness to the supernatural that the renewal movements have fostered over the last century has stood in direct opposition to the materialist worldview that has permeated much of Western culture and the Church, which was blatantly anti-supernatural. The distinctive of the baptism in the Holy Spirit has fostered a new openness to the miraculous, also in direct opposition to a materialist worldview held by society and much of the Christian church. The restoration of the nine-fold manifestation of the gifts of the Holy Spirit, a new openness to the fruit, power, and authority of the Holy Spirit, as well as the five-fold functioning of the ministry offices of the church are also remarkable distinctives associated with the renewal movements over the last one hundred years. These distinctives in particular have broken down the barrier that has traditionally existed in the church between clergy and laity. This construct, reinforced by the professional paradigm for ministry popularized by the University of Berlin in the nineteenth century stands in direct opposition to renewal distinctives. These distinctives hold that the believer is the minister who is to be equipped for ministry by those holding one of the five-fold ministry offices of the church (Eph 4:11-13). The tearing down of this wall has profound implications for ministry in the church of the twenty-first century. It is ideal for a culture that would rather serve than sit in the pews. It also is ideal for this generation that is looking for meaning and purpose in life. The changes necessary to accommodate these distinctives in theological training are profound.

The problem to date is that theological training has been either hostile or closed-minded to renewal distinctives. When the renewal movements were limited in influence and relatively new, this was understandable. Now that renewal-oriented Christianity is the largest group of people that make up the Christian faith (besides the Roman Catholic faith), it needs to be taken seriously by theological education. Many of the established seminaries and universities delivering theological training are denominationally based and still struggling with renewal distinctive and the emphasis on personal and sapiential experience. Some keep the door open to renewal Christianity, while others reject it outright. Though many renewal-oriented seminaries and schools are being established to meet the needs of this vast population of renewal-oriented Christians, many are not yet accredited or offering degreed education which seems to be a must in today's culture. While some in the renewal-oriented circles reject the need for formal theological training, many are suffering because they cannot access it due to personal logistics, finances, or educational barriers. Changes must be made in theological training as it exists today to make it both relevant and accessible to renewal-oriented Christians so that the Body of Christ will have leadership that can function effectively in the church.

One of the most important changes that needs to be made in embracing *pneumatics* is a structure curriculum that includes proper training in the operation of the nine-fold gifts of the Holy Spirit and the five-fold ministry offices in the church. It is not surprising that this has been lacking to date because of a lack of consensus on renewal theology. This is changing due to the work of men such as J. Rodman Williams, author of *Renewal Theology* (1996) which is one of the first attempts at a systematic theology based on renewal distinctives. Christian leaders must be trained in the operation of the gifts of the Holy Spirit and in the specifics of the operation of the five-fold ministry offices. They must also receive focused training on how to help believers identify their individual gifts and on how to equip them and deploy them in service within the Body of Christ. These types of training are largely absent from theological education as it exists today but are essential parts of training emerging leaders that will minister in the twenty-first century church. They also feed right into this generation's hunger for a personal experience with God and their desire to find meaning through active service in the context of community.

The authors propose a set of eight characteristics that express the value of *pneumatics*. These include:

- Emphasis on a personal sapiential relationship with God.

- Understanding and embracing renewal-oriented theology.

- Experience and ongoing baptism in the Holy Spirit.

- Increasing ability to function in the gifts and fruit of the Holy Spirit.

- Increasing ability to function in the power and authority of the Holy Spirit.

- Mobilization, equipping, and releasing of the five-fold ministry along with decreasing of the division between clergy and laity.

- Emphasis on the priesthood of the believer and equipping the saints for the work of the ministry.

- Passion for evangelism and missions as a means to fulfill the great commission through the conversion of unbelievers.

These distinctives characterize the historical Holiness-Pentecostal, Charismatic, and neo-Pentecostal movement of God in the twentieth century and capture the spirit of God's work in the revivals in America and globally over the last three centuries. They are at the heart of renewal-oriented theological training.

When the values of *theologia, paideia, ekklesia, koinonia, and pneumatics* are well defined and then integrated into philosophical framework to reshape theological training, profound changes will occur. These values define some very basic ways to view theological reality. They restore the focus of theological training on divine self-disclosure through the authority and inspiration of the Scriptures (*theologia*). They also define the mission and purpose of theological training — coming to know and understand God more truly, resulting in spiritual and moral formation (*paideia*). These values restore the concept of the Church as an organic, biotic entity (*ekklesia*) and the resulting healing community as the essence of Christian experience (*koinonia*). Finally, these values also prescribe one of the most important ingredients that must be woven into church life (*pneumatics*).

It is said that things rise and fall on leadership. This will be true for the Church of the twenty-first century. For the most part, the Church entrusts the training of its leadership to the realm of theological education. The shape that theological training takes, based on the conscious or unconscious values and assumptions that it embraces, will determine that course of the Church by training its leadership. It is vital that theological training embraces the core values necessary to prepare its leadership to succeed in the future.

An Exposition on the Three Core Shaping Methodologies for Designing or Reshaping Theological Training

Methodology is at the heart of actualizing values. They are the means by which values take shape in the physical world. Values can be actualized by varied methodology, but there are appropriate methodologies that can be chosen for a given set of values that best implement them in a manner consistent with the context and with the desired results. There are several core methodologies outlined earlier that the author considers to be vital for designing or reshaping theological training according to the values just presented. These core methodologies include contextualization, dynamic communication, and *praxis*. Each of these core methodologies must be adequately defined and understood in order to facilitate implementation of the five core values outlined previously. Each of these three core shaping methodologies has eight essential characteristics associated with them that are critical to their actualization in the process of theological training. When added to the five core shaping values, they form an eight by eight matrix of core shaping factors used to design interdenominational renewal-oriented theological training.

Contextualization

As noted earlier, John Cobbs, Jr. and Joseph Hough, Jr. took theological education to task in the early 1980s for its failure to contextualize its content for the participants (Banks 1999, 34-39). Their book, *Christian Identity and Theological Education* (1985), urged the theological education community to take into account the various sociopolitical realities represented in the twentieth century culture. Max Stackhouse followed in the late 1980s with his book *Apologia: Contextualization, Globalization, and Mission in Theological Education* (1988). His was a call to cultural contextualization in theological training. Both books have inspired debate in the theological education community as to how to contextualize theological training to insure that it remains relevant for the job for which it exists.

Contextualization as a methodology is critical to the whole process of theological training. While the authors would not agree with Cobbs and Hough that it should be the focus of theological training, it should be one of the primary focuses in methodology for delivery. Sweet speaks of the new personal and cultural coordinates for understanding reality that this generation embraces (1999a, 81). Many of these coordinates center on the changes that have occurred within the participants that are entering into theological training at this present time. Understanding these new personal and cultural coordinates is vital to the whole way theological training is delivered.

One of the profound cultural and personal shifts in this generation is the multicultural and ethnic nature of those entering into the theological training process. Sweet notes that in 1960, 30% of the evangelicals were non-Western. In 1997, 70% of the world's evangelical population are non-Western (Sweet 1999b, 390). The ethnic composition of society is also rapidly changing. As noted earlier, the Caucasian population of America is about 75% with a zero growth rate, while other ethnic populations such as the African-American, Hispanic, and Asian components of the population have a double-digit growth rate (Barna 1998, 52,53). Barna predicts that with that trend, Caucasians will make up less than half of the population of America by 2050 (1998, 52,53). If the Church is to prosper in a world that is becoming increasingly less Anglo-European in culture and composition, it must learn to function in an ethnically and culturally diverse environment. This will only happen as theological training models are contextualized for increasingly diverse Church. Many emerging leaders will be from non-Western cultures, so theological training must become increasingly less Western in its philosophical mindset and make room for the vast expressions of learning style, cultural expression, and needs of a multicultural setting. Many of the things that are associated with theological training are actually cultural constructs that are not necessarily biblical, but preferential in nature. The ideas of degrees, institutions of education apart from the church, buildings and universities, content of curriculum (Schleiermacher's four divisions of seminary education) and many other trappings that make up the process, are all ultimately negotiable. They are one way of doing theological education, and some of these ideas have caught on in other non-Western cultures. Some of these ideas will have to be modified or discarded in a non-Western setting that does not have access to the wealth to build huge facilities separate from the church for the express purpose of theological education. Other ways of doing theological training will have to yield to manpower limitations as well as limited access to high school level education, let alone masters level degreed seminary training.

Perhaps most important to the methodology employed in contextualizing theological training is the creation of a culture that values other cultures. As Sweet notes, opportunities for local cultural expression must be given place in the process of training the Church's leaders (1999a, 239). This would include diverse styles of worship, church government structures, and liturgy. It would also mean seeing to it that theological training included appropriate instruction that would facilitate a proper understanding of a theology of culture and an understanding of the culture of the current generation in whatever cultural context that may be. In years gone by, contextualization was a buzz-word for those taking the gospel to the nations. In this day, the nations are coming to Western society. Contextualization is no longer just necessary in missions work. It is just as vital to Western society as it experiences a huge shift toward a diverse environment with its strongly integral worldview.

Another profound need for contextualization in theological training is the need to adjust to the educational level of the average candidate entering the learning process. It is also vital that the graduates of the theological training process understand the nature of the audience to which they will be ministering, so that they too can contextualize their message. Barna cites the fact that 50% of the adults in this country are functionally illiterate and cannot read or write beyond an eighth grade level. One million of the current graduates from high school each year have the same difficulties (Barna

1998, 3,4). He also notes that 75% of the adults cannot understand the King James Version of the Scriptures, but that it still by far remains the most popular version of the Bible used in Churches today (Barna 1998, 4).

Because of the congregation's lack of training in basic reading and writing skills, as well as a lack of comprehension for the flow of linear arguments, most sermons are incomprehensible to many of the church population today (Barna 1998, 4). Once again, one must ask who the ministry coming from the pulpits in today's church is for? If it is for the people, then the people must understand what is being preached. Emerging leaders must learn to speak their language — contextualize their message for the less educated. This is difficult for academicians who have been removed from their normal surroundings, have been trained in a largely academic environment, and have been given highly academic skills with which to function. Theological education must train emerging leaders to effectively contextualize their message for their audience. As Long notes, preaching styles must change from linear rational argument and apologetics to a narrative and story focused methodology if they are to be understood by today's church goers (1997, 192). Neither style is wrong. Jesus embraced the character of the Hebrew culture of His time and engaged them with many stories to deliver truth. Paul often chose the Greek route of rational linear argument. Both contextualized their message for their time (Long 1997, 192). So it should be with the leaders of the Church today as they are trained to contextualize their message for a post-modern generation, which in this case is more Hebrew than Greek in its mindset (Long 1997, 192).

Contextualization for the current generation demands a new way of thinking that Sweet calls "chaordics" (1999b, 72-103). A chaordic mentality is one that is flexible and adaptable as the current context dictates. Methodology, teaching techniques and even curriculum and course content are designed to meet the specific needs of the target audience.

The authors propose that contextualization can be best applied to theological training by considering eight factors in order to adapt it to the target context:

- What is God's unique mission in establishing a new or revised process of theological training in a specific area?

- What training does the target city, church, region, and individuals need?

- What are the religious traditions of the targeted participants?

- What point on the continuum of educational philosophy is the right mix of Athens and Berlin?

- What blends the means of knowing God best and complements the strengths, weaknesses, and traditions of the target participants?

- What concept of community best complements the mission of the school, its unique cultural context?

- What are the cultural, educational, and socio-economic orientations of the potential participants?

- What multicultural factors are at work in the city/community?

The answers to these questions should provide a guide for the contextualization of the theological training delivered in any given situation based on key factors. As described earlier, the author sees an application of four of Kelsey's considerations as a key to contextualizing four of the above outline factors. The factors of tradition, educational philosophy, means of knowing God, and concept of community can be determined within the following matrix:

1. **Tradition -** This coordinate represents the socio-religious and cultural orientation of the target group that has been shaped by a particular move of God at a certain context of time, history, and culture. None of the various loci of tradition are inherently better or worse and each has their own specific strong and weak points. Each represents a specific move of God at a specific juncture of history and each has its own distinctives. Deliberate planning for a theological educational institution's tradition is vital to the distinctives

of the school. The tradition coordinate has seven particular loci:

- Nicean - the Catholic and Orthodox traditions.

- Trent - the Catholic Counter-Reformation tradition.

- Augsburg - the Lutheran Reformed tradition.

- Geneva - the Calvinist Reformed tradition.

- Canterbury - the Anglican or Episcopal tradition.

- Northampton - the revivalist, Methodist, and Holiness traditions.

- Topeka - the Holiness-Pentecostal, Charismatic, and Neo-Pentecostal renewal-oriented traditions.

2. **Educational philosophy -** This coordinate represents where the educational philosophy of the theological training being delivered will fall on a continuum between spiritual formation and intellectual formation. Extremes of one or the other causes an unbalanced training and warps the student's perspective. The two extremes that make up two loci on the continuum include:

- Athens - an emphasis on *paideia* or spiritual and moral formation in a manner typical of Greek education.

- Berlin - an emphasis on rational thought, cognitive knowledge, and intellectual formation typical of the professional education offered at the University of Berlin in the nineteenth century.

3. **Knowing God Coordinate -** This coordinate represents the predominate means used to come to know and understand God. One of these means is either deliberately or unconsciously used because of tradition, educational philosophy,

or cultural conditioning. One should be deliberately accentuated to contextualize theological training in the context of culture, tradition, or educational philosophy. The other means of knowing God should be deliberately employed as a means to balance the theological training being delivered. The loci for this coordinate include:

- Contemplative - oriented toward knowing God through sapiential means.

- Discursive Reason - oriented toward knowing God through rational means.

- Affective - oriented toward knowing God through experiential means.

- Praxis - oriented toward knowing God through means of correct action.

4. **Community -** This coordinate represents the way an institution delivering theological training sees itself. This self-conceptualization may be explicit or implicit. The institution may not even realize that it sees itself in a particular manner. The loci that constitute this coordinate tend to be associated with a particular tradition and educational philosophy. The four loci that make up this coordinate include:

- Congregation - sees itself as church-like.

- Apprenticeship - sees itself as a community of experienced mentors.

- Extension - sees itself as a service organization of the Church.

- Partnership - sees itself as in cooperative venture with the Church.

These four factors help to further define the answer to how to contextualize theological training for tradition, educational philosophy, means of knowing God, and concept of community, all of which are vital to shaping theological training. They have been used in the design and structure of interdenominational renewal-oriented theological training.

Dynamic Communication

Though the volume, pitch, speed, and content of the message may vary from place to place, what matters is if the hearer can hear, decode, process, understand, and ultimately apply the message to his or her life. Communication does not occur unless the hearer understands the speaker. Much of whether or not this occurs is based on communication styles. Theological training itself depends on communication. The job of most of those being trained for the process will center on communication. Theological training must be vitally concerned with the way it communicates its education to the participants in its process as well as how those participants are trained to communicate. In a rapidly changing cultural environment in which the change is largely driven by communication issues, it becomes even more important.

As mentioned earlier, technology has vastly changed the way Western society communicates and digests information. Barna points out that because of the rapid increase in communication speed and variety, Western culture has become a society used to intense stimulation, valuing information from a variety of sources in rapid succession (1998, 3,4). One must only think of music videos or advertisements to validate this observation. Barna also notes that the average attention span, due to all of the rapid stimulation and input, has decreased to between six and eight minutes while the average sermon is about thirty minutes in length (1998, 4).

In addition to the low attention spans and thirst for rapid stimulation, communication has also become non-linear in a changing Western culture. Sweet notes that communication within Western society has evolved into a more fluid or mosaic form with a fluid, non-rigid format that rapidly changes direction and contains multiple inputs in one package (1999a, 130). The Internet is a prime example of this type of communication with its advertising communications interspersed with information and personal communications mediums that saturate the user with rapid bundles of varied kind and format. This generation expects this form of communication and has rapidly adapted to coping with this volume and style. It is little wonder that the average Sunday morning service has little to do with their world.

Theological education must train its emerging leaders to be skilled in contextualizing its communication to the form of the culture in which it ministers. It must adapt to what the culture pays attention to, understand what it absorbs, and learn to communicate in clear and meaningful ways (Barna 1998, 57,58). It must also adapt to the need for faster input and word choice in order to speak the language of Western culture (Barna 1998, 58). In a world where technology lends credence to the message, theological education must train emerging leaders to understand and make use of the communications technology that is currently available if it is to remain credible and relevant. This is especially true when it comes to the format of delivering theological training. The author proposes a set of eight characteristics that are essential to dynamic communication. They include:

- Communication through culturally contextualized and relevant means.

- Linear and non-linear or mosaic formats for communication.

- Flexible curriculum that can be adapted within certain limits to the need of the individual.

- Fluid and adaptable means of communication that best suit the target audience.

- Adaptation of communication and training to varied learning styles and culturally conditioned patterns.

- The use of multiple mediums of communication that best fit the subject matter and intent of training.

- The use of varied settings as contexts for communication and training.

• The use of technology to deliver theological training.

These eight essential characteristics capture the essence of the core shaping methodology of dynamic communication. The changes in communication technology have made it possible to deliver theological training in ways not possible only thirty years ago. Sweet points out that today's learner is much more self-directed than ever before (1999a, 235). He advocates a dynamic learning environment where students are able to access their own learning needs, direct their own access to sources of training to meet those needs, and have critical access to evaluate their own progress (1999a, 235).

Beyond these considerations, a variety in dynamic communication adapted for each learning situation is vital. The days of the classroom lecture are gone. While lecture has its place in education, varied learning styles must be considered. Openness to online and distance training formats are vital and even preferred for some classes and subjects. Personal formation in the life of a student requires one-on-one contact. Access to online learning and distance education at remote sites would save valuable time and resources otherwise spend in travel. It would also allow students to remain in their home environment, where what is learned can be immediately applied in their own ministry contexts. These forms of dynamic communications methodology not only increase the effectiveness of theological training, but could also potentially increase access to training by diminishing costs. At the same time, this form of dynamic communication increases the relevance of the training to the society it is charged with reaching and prepares emerging leaders to function in the cultural context represented by this postmodern generation. Dynamic communication methodology is at the core of renewal-oriented theological training.

Praxis

Another vital methodology that must be integrated into the process of theological training is the actual application of what is learned to a real-life environment. The authors will refer to this core shaping methodology as *praxis*. When a *praxis* methodology is built into the theological training process it allows the participants to learn and apply what they have learned in the context of ministry. With the advent of the professional model for theological education, academic pursuits have been emphasized, often to the neglect of practical skills and their application. As noted earlier, theological training was first conducted in this country in the context of Log College, in which the student was in intimate contact with the instructor, who was also often engaged in active ministry work (Fraser 1988, xi, 6-9). This style of instruction was often more of an apprenticeship reading during one part of the day and actual practice in ministry during the other part (Fraser 1988, xi). The evolution of the university model in Western education changes this format. Instead of a connection with their ministry contexts, students were now removed from their real-life contexts of ministry and placed in a classroom. Rather than immediate application of what was learned, students were isolated in an academic environment having little in common with everyday life, and taught large volumes of academic knowledge that they were expected to retain and apply years later after leaving school. This model for theological training has produced a large disconnection between the student and the Church, as well as the theological school and the Church. Both the school and the student have often also become disconnected from culture and the Church in this process as well. This has set up well meaning students for failure in ministry when they return to their ministry context and theological schools for potential irrelevance as more and more people question the need for a formal theological training (Barna 1998, 27).

Sound theological training is vital to emerging leaders, especially if it engages real-life issues and skills that they will encounter in serving the Church and if what is learned can be immediately applied. The authors propose a set of eight essential characteristics that express the core shaping methodology of *praxis*. These include:

- The contextualization of all cognitive knowledge presented for the needs of the target participants, the Church, and its cultural context.

- Application of cognitive knowledge to practical real and felt needs appropriate to the target context.

- Skill-based instruction that is appropriate for the participants, their gift-mix, and destiny-mix.

- Training of the participants while they remain vitally connected with their context of ministry.

- Use of dynamic upward and peer mentoring structures to facilitate the learning process.

- A cohort-based system of delivery that encourages peer relationships with those active in ministry in the community context.

- Facilitation of dynamic reflection for the participants that helps to link cognitive and applied knowledge.

- An andragogical approach to training and communication.

Sweet makes the case that Western culture has made the transition into a learning culture over the past several decades (1999a, 228). With the rate of change in society, culture, and the Church, relevant theological training today is essential for the Church to succeed tomorrow.

Learning paradigms must emphasize a practical application of knowledge if they are to remain vital and relevant. The process must organize the vast array of facts into organized information that can be digested by the participants. From there, the goal must always be to integrate information into reality and then into practical application (Sweet 1999a, 228). This is best accomplished in a learning environment that is hot with practical opportunities to apply what is learned (Sweet 1999a, 21). Current seminary models that remove students from a real environment, isolate them from the real world, lead them through a series of academic exercises, and declare them fit for ministry are not adequate for ministry preparation (Barna 1998, 27). New ways to deliver theological training and encourage *praxis* must be implemented. Methods of delivery that involve remote clusters in which the teacher travels to students for most of the instruction in a cohort setting seem more ideal for theological training than removing students completely from their environment. This would also provide an ideal opportunity to establish partnerships between schools and churches to partner in the training process. The cost of theological training could be cut by conducting remote classes in existing church facilities and using qualified adjunct professors from local churches. In the process, the whole enterprise of theological training could be transformed to provide a more meaningful experience and product. *Praxis* is at the core of the design of The Convergence Model. Its partnership with the local church facilitates *praxis*. The courses are designed to be practical and application oriented.

Core Shaping Dimensions of Theological Training

Every model for theological training operates along the line of several defined dimensions. This is also true for theological training. The authors have adopted Dearborne's five-fold model for the specific dimensions involved in theological training and modified them for the purposes of this dissertation and the development of its model with input from Clinton's *Leadership Training Models* (1995a, 4-15; Clinton 1984, 80-98). These five dimensions include:

- Institution - The physical and philosophical aspects of the community delivering theological training.

- Process - The total means used to deliver the theological training.

- Faculty - The people responsible for facilitating the learning.

- Student - The participants in the learning process.

- Curriculum - Every item of the training program which contributes either explicitly or implicitly to the input, experimental, dynamic reflection, or spiritual and moral formation aspects of theological training.

Each of these dimensions has certain characteristics, which must be considered in the process of designing theological training. It would be a faulty assumption that merely changing one of these dimensions and their characteristics, such as curriculum, would solve a problem or set of problems. Each dimension exists in dynamic relation to the others. All must be addressed if meaningful change is to occur.

CHAPTER NINE

The Convergence Model and Its Core Shaping Factors

What minister would pay $750 and fly across the country to far away California to spend a week in someone else's church? The answer – dozens of them each year! The Church on the Way in Van Nuys, California sees this happen several times each year. The church is a thriving ministry several miles north of Los Angeles that has given birth, among other ministries, to its own Bible College and Seminary called "The Kings College." In addition to several more traditional graduate and doctoral level programs for minister, the college offers a unique program called "The School of Pastoral Nurture'" a favorite of the school's founder, Chancellor and Pastor, Jack Hayford.

For what many would consider a modest cost, several dozen ministers at one time are given the opportunity to attend sessions of the School of Pastoral Nurture and have direct contact with Pastor Hayford and several ministry specialists in what resembles more of a personal mentoring model for learning than a "school." These ministers come in to the church and meet for hours each day with Pastor Hayford for personalized teaching, reflection, question and answer times, as well as personal problem solving and prayer. Individuals that have been involved in the School of Nurture do not receive a diploma, certificate, or grade, but claim they receive something far more valuable – answers to nagging questions and the support and encouragement they need to carry on the difficult and demanding work of the ministry.

Pastor Hayford considers this School of Nurture an expression of his love for the local church and its pastors, much the same way that he views the national conferences that the church has held for pastors in years gone by. The emphasis on personal ministry to individual pastors in an intimate setting expresses his value for the local church and compassion for the pastors of local congregations who often face seemingly impossible circumstances in their ministry. The make up of the groups attending cross many ethnic, denominational, and traditional lines. The teaching, personal mentoring, and environment are renewal oriented in their distinctives. The response has been overwhelming and the results equally gratifying.

The School of Nurture represents a trend in theological training that emphasizes renewal distinctives. It also represents a trend toward a more personal mentoring model for delivering that training in partnership with the local church. It illustrates practical, application oriented training that strikes at the heart of what theological training should be – a means of forming and shaping leaders for work in the local church for the work of practical ministry. It is representative of many such movements that are popping up nationally and internationally. It is unlikely that these models will render traditional theological education irrelevant, but those in traditional circles would do well to examine this type of model for training, learn from its benefits, and integrate them into the theological training they deliver.

Millions of emerging leaders in the renewal movements sweeping through the world at this moment are looking for new direction as to how to prepare to fulfill their ministry in the Church. History makes it clear that times of renewal have always led to radical change in the way theological training is done. The current crisis of effectiveness in theological education makes it all the more clear that a new way of training individuals for ministry must emerge. This new way of training individuals for ministry must be interdenominational in nature and emphasize renewal distinctives and values if it is to be relevant to the very people it seeks to train. It must also seek to balance excellent academics with an emphasis on formation of the heart, balancing Athens and Berlin in the pursuit of theological training.

In order to make these changes, theological education must be reconstructed from the ground up. Changes to existing structures and paradigms will not do – the changes needed are radical and do not involve merely adjusting existing ways of doing things. A new set of core values must exist at the core of the endeavor. A new framework and shape must be built. Each dimension of the training must be considered deliberately and then reengineered to fit the needs of today's emerging leaders. The proposal for change required to reengineer theological education to produce the kind of training needed can leave no component of the endeavor untouched. The convergence of God's renewal on a global basis, the interdenominational and renewal distinctives of the movement, and the current crisis that exists in theological training have produced a God-given opportunity for change. For the purposes of this book, the model that has been developed for interdenominational renewal-oriented theological training will be referred to as "The Convergence Model."

Building a Framework for Renewal-oriented Interdenominational Theological Training

In light of the shifts outlined in Western culture and the tremendous renewal occurring in the Church on a global basis, it is imperative that the Church and its theological training be reworked to become relevant. Theological training must begin to address the interdenominational renewal-oriented emphasis in the Church. This means that the basic way that theological training is delivered, its contents and curriculum, its students and faculty, its basic core philosophies and focus, and the institution itself must be open to review, critique, and revision. In this section the authors propose a framework for The Convergence Model for theological training, which encompasses the types of paradigm shifting consistent with the current needs of the interdenominational renewal-oriented churches. The framework is based on a matrix of eight core shaping factors, each of which have eight characteristics associated with them for shaping the framework. This eight by eight matrix for shaping the framework of theological training consists of five core shaping values and three core shaping methodologies.

This section also summarizes the theory-based process developed by the authors to design a means of theological training. This process is developed along five core shaping dimensions associated with theological training, each of which has eight characteristics associated with it. This five by eight matrix was used to shape The Convergence Model for theological training that the authors have developed for the interdenominational renewal-oriented community.

The Mission

The authors have reported the results of their research into the theological education debate over the last two decades. The debate over how to fix what is broken seems to have one central point of agreement — that theological training has become fragmented and that something must be done to fix the fragmentation. Evidence of the fragmentation of theological training can be seen in the research results from the study of the American church and its theological education and the Church in Western nations as well as its theological training. The authors agree with David H. Kelsey (1992) that theological training should be focused knowing and understanding God in a progressively fuller way, or as he would say, "To Understand God Truly." The authors propose that the mission of theological training should be reduced to one clear mission - to know and understand God more truly. Based on this statement, the mission and mission statement for this model of theological training has become:

- **Mission:** To facilitate the understanding and knowing of God more truly.

- **Mission Statement:** The mission of The Convergence Model is to facilitate the understanding and knowing of God more truly.

This mission and mission statement were adopted as the centering purpose for the Convergence Model. The mission is grounded in the biblical foundation of eternal life (Jn 17:3 - knowing God) and coming to know and reverence God, which is the basis for true knowledge and wisdom (Prv 1:7). The authors believe that centering this model for theological training will avoid the fragmentation of the education that occurs when other centering themes are used as the mission of theological training. This mission and mission statement defines the distinctive character and nature of The Convergence Model and guides the purpose and goals of the institution. It also serves as a frame of reference for decision-making and policies developed for The Convergence Model and the center for all educational programs at the institution. The mission will also be used as a standard for assessment of outcomes in the participants who are educated by this model for theological training.

The Purpose

Each institution has a central means to accomplish its mission. That central means exists as the institution's purpose. The debate over how to reshape theological education over the last twenty years has accentuated the division over the purpose of theological training. As was documented through the research in this book, the theological education community is sharply divided along the lines of educational philosophy. One side represents the "Athens" model that places an emphasis on *paideia* or spiritual and moral formation that is typical of Greek education. The other side favors the "Berlin" model with its emphasis on rational thought, cognitive knowledge, and intellectual formation. While both are important to theological training, the author believes that an Athens-like model is more typical of historical theological education over the age of the Church and is most likely to best facilitate the mission of The Convergence Model. The authors have adopted *paideia* - the spiritual and moral formation of the participants - as the centering focus of the institution. As such, the purpose statement for The Convergence Model has become:

- **Purpose Statement:** The purpose of The Convergence Model is *paideia* which is the spiritual and moral formation of its participants.

The purpose statement evolves directly from the mission distinctive of the model. It is the authors' conviction that *paideia* - the spiritual and moral formation of a person - is the biblical means to coming to understand and know God more truly. *Paideia* is a direct result of instruction (1 Tm. 3:16), causing one to grow in the knowledge and wisdom of the Lord (Prv. 1:7). It takes place in the context of community or *koinonia* (Acts 2:42-48).). *Paideia* is something that occurs as a result of the process of proper theological training - it cannot be self-induced or forced, only facilitated. It is the holistic transformation of a human being that occurs as a result of the work of the Holy Spirit in their life in response to processing various experiences (Rom. 12:1,2;

2 Cor. 3:16). This spiritual and moral formation results in deepening devotion to God (discipleship) and maturity of a person toward what God has created them to be

(Col. 1:28, 29 - *telos*). In theological training, *paideia* occurs holistically as knowledge and other inputs are integrated into the participant's lives and they begin to prize and act on that knowledge. Behavior changes as they begin to act on the new knowledge (knowing linked with doing). The individual begins to reorder their system of what is valued (affective or values-based knowledge). As a result of this process, a spiritual and moral formation takes place that transforms the participant (*paideia*).

The Goals

The goals of an institution represent the desired outcomes in the lives of the participants in the process of theological training. They are an expression of the institution's purpose and mission, being tied directly into these two dimensions. The mission of The Convergence Model is to "facilitate the understanding and knowing of God more truly." The purpose of The Convergence Model is *paidiea* or the spiritual and moral formation of the participants, which leads to understanding and knowing God more truly. The goals of The Convergence Model must therefore be tied to the purpose in order to accomplish the model's mission.

When the authors discussed *paideia* as a core shaping factor for theological training, they set forth a set of eight characteristics that give evidence of spiritual and moral formation. The authors have adopted these eight characteristics of *paideia* as a framework to center the goals of The Convergence Model, and as such, center the goals of the model in its purpose and mission. The eight goals of The Convergence Model, designed to facilitate *paideia* are:

- Increasing ability to experience more of God and His presence in the lives of the participants.

- Increasing God-like character in the lives of the participants.

- Increasing God-like personality in the lives of the participants.

- Increasing growth of the spiritual disciplines in the lives of the participants.

- Increasing holistic spiritual health in the lives of the participants.

- Increasing experience of the power and authority of God in the daily life and ministry of the participants.

- Increasing discipleship as represented by deepening surrender to God in the lives of the participants.

- Increasing maturity as evidenced growth in personal witness, understanding of gift-mix, and progression toward God-given destiny in the lives of the participants.

These goals serve as guidelines for the measurable objectives and student profiles for desired outcomes that have been developed for the school. The goals and resulting objective and profiles have been used to shape the process, faculty, students, and curriculum of the institution. They address the centrality of knowing and understanding God through the process of spiritual and moral formation by expressing their end-result.

The Core Values and Methodologies

Any model for theological training begins at the level of thoughts and ideas. Each institution or system is a complex blending of these thoughts and ideas that mix together to give the institution a distinctive life or essence. The authors agree with Malphurs that values are the end that an institution is striving for. They are also the basic reasons, sometimes written and many times assumed, for what an institution does (1996, 31-41). Through the process of research for this dissertation, the authors have distilled a set of five core values, outlined in the last chapter, that were used in shaping this model for theological training. These core values for The Convergence Model are:

- *Theologia* - divine self-disclosure through the authority and inspiration of the Scriptures.

- *Paideia* - spiritual and moral formation (being formation) that occurs as a result of cognitive knowledge (knowing) and application (doing).

- *Ekklesia* - a proper biotic-organic and holistic conception of the Church as the living Body of Christ.

- *Koinonia* - the symbiotic relationship of the believer with other believers and the Church as well as between theological education, the believer, and the Church.

- *Pneumatics* - the philosophical framework by which the believer relates to God, the Church, life, and ministry through Spirit-filled living.

These core values define a distinct way of viewing theological reality. They all relate back to the mission, purpose, and goals of The Convergence Model. The core value of *paideia* is at the center of realizing the mission of the school, serving as the means for coming to understand and know God more truly. The core value of *theologia* represents the foundation of truth in the Scriptures that is the basis for spiritual and moral formation when applied. *Koinonia* is the proper biblical context of community in which theological training should take place. The Church as the living biotic Body of Christ is the context for ministry as the institution delivering theological training partners with the Church to train its emerging leaders. *Pneumatics* is the value that describes the renewal distinctive of Spirit-filled life, ministry, and walk with God that must be woven into the very fabric of theological training. These core values have been woven into the author's model for theological training. Actualization of *theologia, ekklesia, koinonia, and pneumatics* in the fabric of the school will produce the *paideia* that is the purpose of the educational process, thereby fulfilling the school's mission. These core values represent the division of subject matter in the curriculum as well, so that the curriculum focuses on the institution's core values.

In addition, the author's research has distilled three core methodologies that represent applied values for shaping the institution, as outlined in the last chapter. Methods are a means for actualizing values. They were chosen as the best means for fulfilling the mission, purpose and goals of The Convergence Model. They also take into account the need to adapt the model for the geographic and cultural coordinates that are unique to this model. The core methodologies distilled by the authors for application in this model of theological training are:

- **Contextualization** - the ability of theological training to adapt and design its institution, curriculum, faculty, student body, and processes for the Church and surrounding culture's real and felt needs.

- **Dynamic Communication** - the ability of theological training to adapt its means of theological education to be relevant and effective to its mission.

- *Praxis* - a process where cognitive knowledge is deliberately applied to real-life in the context of ministry, resulting in the spiritual and moral formation of an individual's being.

These core methodologies were woven into the design of The Convergence Model in each of the institution's dimensions. They assist in the implementation of the five core values in line with the goals, purpose, and mission of the school. The core values and methodologies are of prime consideration in any decision made concerning the institution, process, faculty, student body, or curriculum of The Convergence Model.

Each of the eight core values and methodologies were assigned eight characteristics for actualizing them in the author's model of theological training. This eight by eight matrix of core shaping factors was applied to each of the five core dimensions of the model, resulting in eight questions for each dimension that were used to actually form the model for theological training.

The Core Philosophy

Every institution operates on philosophical assumptions that are either implicit or explicit. The practices and the methods that are employed in theological training emanate from these underlying philosophies. These philosophies relate to assumptions about God, truth, reality, values, and the educational process. The result is a framework for delivering the education offered by the institution in a manner that actualizes these assumptions so as to fulfill its goals, purpose, and mission.

The assumptions about God and truth relate strongly to the institution's theological and religious statement of faith. The Statement of Faith for The Convergence Model, reflecting the resulting institution's core values are:

- **God** - God is a triune Being, existing as One God, who is eternal, transcendent, omnipotent, personal, and revealed in the form of the Father, the Son, and the Holy Spirit.

- **The Father** - God the Father is the first person of the Trinity who is infinite, sovereign, eternal, and unchangeable, and who is to be worshipped, honored, and obeyed.

- **Jesus Christ** - is the second person of the Trinity, who was made man and was without sin, fully God and fully man, united in one person. He was born of a virgin, lived and died in the flesh on earth for mankind's sin, and rose again for the believer's justification.

- **The Holy Spirit** - is the third person of the Trinity who convicts, teaches, and indwells believers as they submit to Him. His baptism and infilling invite the gifts, fruit, and power of the Holy Spirit into the life of a believer.

- **Baptism in the Holy Spirit** – A belief in an experience subsequent to salvation, called the baptism in the Holy Spirit, in which the believer is filled with God's power to be His witness and work God's works in the discharge and service of ministry.

- **The Bible -** The Bible to be God's inspired Word in a plenary-verbal sense, given as a means for divine self disclosure to man. It is inerrant in the original writing, complete in its revelation, and authoritative for life, faith and conduct.

- **The Church -** is the visible expression of the Body of Christ in its universal and local expression. It is organic in nature, being a living body of believers that exist in community with each other and God.

- **Salvation -** All people are born in sin and need the redemptive gift of Christ's sacrifice on the cross to free them from an eternity apart from God and grant eternal life. This redemption is only through the substitutionary sacrifice of Jesus Christ on the Cross and His death, burial, and resurrection which conquer sin and death. It is provided by grace alone to all who believe, through personal faith in His work and atonement.

- **Last Things -** The future, personal, literal return of Jesus Christ to earth to establish His Kingdom, conquer and subdue a personal being who is the source of all evil named Satan and the devil, and to fulfill the purposes of the Father - that Jesus Christ might become all in all, Lord over creation.

This Statement of Faith represents the standard biblical and philosophical assumptions that are woven into the educational process for The Convergence Model. They are also the standard philosophical assumptions that will be used to shape the institution's faculty, student body, and curriculum. They represent renewal-oriented distinctives that add to the institutions interdenominational and renewal-oriented ethos.

Core Shaping Educational Philosophy

In addition to the assumptions concerning the faith, there are also basic philosophical assumptions concerning the educational process that were woven into the model, representing the core shaping delivery model for presenting the training offered through The Convergence Model. The authors have integrated a core delivery model for delivering theological training based on the developmental model of education.

All institutions delivering theological training have a primary delivery model for delivering their theological training. This is also true for this model. Two primary delivery models for theological training and education in general are the traditional model and the developmental model. The core shaping methodologies of contextualization, dynamic communication, and *praxis* of The Convergence Model are more amenable to a developmental model for delivering theological education than traditional model for education, called the "banking model" by Clinton (1984, 12).

The traditional model for education is based on a Greek concept of knowledge. This paradigm values the acquisition of knowledge as the goal of education in a formal setting such as a classroom. The transfer of knowledge is mainly on a cognitive level, "depositing" knowledge from the teacher's "knowledge account" to the student's "knowledge account," hence the metaphor of the banking model set forward by Clinton. The structure for the traditional model for education is very organized and formal, emphasizing degrees symbolic of acquired knowledge and accreditation as a means of building credibility and prestige. Learning is most often passive and transmitted through lecture, book, and essay. The active presuppositions at work in the traditional model include (Clinton 1984, 12):

- Education is going to a school building to gain knowledge.

- The primary purpose of education is to impart cognitive knowledge.

- Knowing is more important than doing.

- Ideas are more important than people.

- Information should be organized and delivered in cognitive categories.

- The teacher has the right to determine what is learned.

- Open competition to see who can learn the best is valuable.

- Degrees should represent a symbol of acquired cognitive knowledge.

Most universities, colleges, and many Bible colleges and institutes operate consciously or subconsciously based on the traditional model. Most accrediting agencies indirectly reinforce this model as well.

A developmental model for theological training is much more able to provide an environment that can actualize the core shaping methodology of *praxis*. Bodies of knowledge in theological training and in general are expanding so rapidly that it is now practically impossible to master a discrete area of cognitive knowledge. The developmental model is a holistic approach to training that approaches the acquisition of knowledge in three different realms (Clinton 1984, 14). These realms include the cognitive (factual knowledge), experiential (skills-based), and affective (reflective intuitive-based knowledge or values).

A dynamic tension between these three realms in the process of theological education results in the spiritual and moral formation of the participants. The goal of the developmental approach to training is the growth of the individual rather than merely the acquisition of knowledge. The setting for training using the developmental model can and should be varied since it presupposes practical application. A blend of formal educational structures and non-formal structures are ideal for training, especially along the affective and experimental lines of knowledge. The teachers in this process are seen more as facilitators that encourage the links for the participants between cognitive, experiential, and affective knowledge. Students are active in this sort of learning process and often negotiate what is to be learned and the manner in which it is to be learned.

Degrees and accreditation may still be present, but instead of representing accumulated knowledge, they show the student's attainment attaining to certain prescribed competencies that represent the desired outcome of the educational process. Active student participation in the training process includes skilled-based experience designed to apply the cognitive input from a class. It also involves dynamic reflection by the student on the linkage between cognitive and practical application of the knowledge based on their personal experience. The advocates of a more traditional model of training acknowledge the value of this type of dynamic reflection (Rouch 1974, 27).

The developmental model is ideally suited for actualizing the core shaping methodology of *praxis* in theological training and will be adopted for the purposes of the model for theological training expressed in The Convergence Model. It also allows for the core shaping value of dynamic communication to be actualized as well due to the need for varied methodology to address the different categories of knowledge. To summarize, the main points of the developmental model of theological training include (Clinton 1984, 14):

- A holistic approach to training including cognitive, experimental, and affective knowledge.

- Seeing education as personal growth through spiritual and moral formation as opposed to the accumulation of knowledge.

- Consisting of formal and non-formal structures to facilitate the acquisition of the three types of knowledge.

- Possible use of degrees and accreditation in the model, but as a symbol of obtaining desired competencies rather than accumulated knowledge.

- Students as active participants in the process of training who negotiate some of the learning goals based on their needs and who engage in dynamic reflection and discussion to tie together cognitive, experimental and affective knowledge based on experience.

- Teachers who act more as facilitators who specialize in tying together cognitive, experimental, and affective knowledge rather than prescribing a body of knowledge that is to be learned through lecture.

- Methods that are varied in order to impart the three different kinds of knowledge, utilizing dynamic communication strategies.

As with the traditional model of education, there are active presuppositions made with the developmental model of education. These include: (Clinton 1984, 14):

- It is profitable for people to *do* and *be* as well as to *know*.

- Experimental and affective knowledge must be acquired in addition to cognitive knowledge.

- People are unique individuals who all have different paths to their optimum growth potential.

- Education is growth rather than just the accumulation of knowledge.

- Education can take place anywhere and is best done in varied settings to facilitate the acquisition of all three types of knowledge (experimental, affective, and cognitive).

- Students must be taught with a variety of learning styles and formats in mind since they all learn differently.

- Teachers should act in the role of facilitators that seek to help link cognitive, experimental, and affective knowledge together.

The developmental model for theological training encourages the actualization of the core shaping methodologies for contextualization, dynamic communication, and *praxis*. It also leads to a philosophical basis for the development of curriculum a triad of knowing (cognitive), doing (experimental), and being (spiritual and moral formation). As Gangel and Wilhoit observe, the process of increasing knowledge (cognitive input) and integration of that knowledge into one's life (experimental and dynamic reflective components — doing) lead to a prizing of the knowledge and experience in one's own value's system (affective knowledge) (1994, 15, 16). Behavior begins to change based on cognitive input and a new willingness to value the truth that has been learned. This is the essence of spiritual and moral formation, leading to deepening discipleship and increasing maturity. It follows from this model that the curriculum of the school should all have knowing, doing, and being competencies and goals attached to each class or activity. This process of knowing, doing, and being become dynamically linked in the training process, resulting in spiritual and moral formation and the fulfillment of the mission of The Convergence Model - to know and understand God truly.

The curriculum will have some spectrum of knowing, doing, and being competencies associated with each class providing for (Clinton 1984, 41-48):

- Input - (knowing) cognitive knowledge:

  - Cognitive - information centered (acquire knowledge).

  - Experimental - task centered (function in ministry).

  - Affective - values centered (develop values).

- Experience - (doing) ministry application of cognitive input:

  - Activities - stimulate learning.

  - Application - apply inputs.

- Dynamic Reflection - (processing) correlation of cognitive and experiential knowledge and experience:

  - Discover relationship between input and experience.

  - Teach how to evaluate life and ideas.

- Learn the ability to relate ideas in the cognitive, experimental, and affective realms.

- Forces accountability for learning transfer.

- Forces accountability for spiritual and moral formation.

- Forces the application of learning in all realms to real life.

- Promotes the idea that learning occurs in the midst of life and is a life-long task.

- Spiritual and Moral Formation - (being) coming to know and understand God more truly because of the educational experience:

  - The person begins to experience more of God.

  - The person begins to reflect a more God-like character.

  - The person's personality becomes more God-like.

  - The person's everyday relationships become more God-like.

  - The person increasingly knows the power of God in everyday life.

  - The person increasingly knows the power of God in their ministry.

The developmental model actively focuses on the core shaping value of *paideia* as defined by the author. It also helps to actualize the three core shaping methodologies adopted by the author. As such it is an ideal method for the model of delivering theological training that the author proposes. For these reasons, the authors have adopted this model for delivering theological training through The Convergence Model. As such, the educational philosophy active in The Convergence Model has the following core assumption at work:

- **Holistic Approach** - A holistic approach to training which includes cognitive (factual), experimental (practical), and affective (value-based) components at each point in the educational process.

- **Formation** - An emphasis on personal spiritual and moral formation (*paideia*) for the participants as opposed to the accumulation of knowledge as the purpose of education. The basic assumption is that education is growth and transformation rather than merely the accumulation of knowledge.

- **Fluid Structure** - The use of formal and non-formal structures to facilitate the acquisition of cognitive, experimental, and affective forms of knowledge, both at central and decentralized locations. The basic assumption is that learning can take place anywhere, and is best facilitated in a variety of settings.

- **Active Participation** - The active participation of the students in the process of training through the use of dynamic reflection, communication, and adapted to meet their real and felt needs. The basic assumption is that all students are adult learners with unique gift and destiny-mixes, as well as a unique learning styles, that requires them to be an active part of the learning process.

- **Facilitators** - Faculty who act to facilitate the learning process, who specialize in tying together cognitive, experimental, and affective knowledge, rather than merely prescribing a body of knowledge through lecture.

- **Contextualization** - Contextualization of the training to meet the unique needs of culture, tradition, gift-mix, and destiny-mix of the participants.

- **Dynamic Communication** - The use of dynamic communication methods appropriate for the culture of the participants and varied in medium, setting, and delivery to best communicate what is being taught.

- *Praxis* - Structured and deliberate *praxis* in each learning experience, geared toward applying the cognitive knowledge that is taught in the context of the participant's ministry and aimed at a process of dynamic reflection that links knowing and doing, leading to spiritual and moral formation. The assumption is that it is profitable to do and be in addition to know, and that experimental and affective knowledge are required in addition to cognitive knowledge.

This core delivery philosophy is consistent with The Convergence Model's desire to facilitate spiritual and moral formation in the lives of the participants in the institution's theological training. It was woven into all dimensions of The Convergence Model as the institution, process, faculty, student body, and curriculum was designed, which are the subject of the next chapter.

Dimensions of the Model

The authors have adopted Dearborne's five dimensions of theological education as core shaping dimensions for the model (1995a, 4-15). These dimensions represent dimensions that are common to all means of theological education, all of which must be addressed in order for an effective design or reshaping of a means of theological education to take place. The dimensions of theological education include:

- **Institution** - The physical and philosophical aspects of the community delivering theological training.

- **Process** - The total means used to deliver the theological training.

- **Faculty** - The people responsible for facilitating the learning.

- **Student** - The participants in the learning process.

- **Curriculum** - Every item of the training program which contributes either explicitly or implicitly to the input, experimental, dynamic reflection, or spiritual and moral formation aspects of theological training.

The authors applied each of the core values and methodologies and their associated characteristics to each of these five dimensions to produce the model for theological training. The mission, purpose, goals, and educational philosophy were used to guide the process. All of these factors were used to formulate eight questions for each of the dimensions, the answers to which produce the model. The result is a proposal for change in theological education that takes into account all five dimensions of the endeavor. It is called The Convergence Model for theological training.

CHAPTER TEN

The Convergence Model and Its Dimensions

W hen one talks of change, it is important to define not only the nature of the change but also exactly what is to be changed. As outlined in the prior chapters, theological education is in the midst of a time of deep soul-searching to determine how to bring it back toward a greater effectiveness. Many changes are being suggested and implemented, but most seem to fall short of their mark. The authors believe that this is because most of these attempts at change are flawed because they do not address all the necessary dimensions of change. Since they only address a part of the change necessary, they deal primarily with paradigm refinements and adjustments rather than paradigm shifting.

Only paradigm shifting will provide the necessary change to make theological education relevant once again. Only a deep shift in the core values and shaping factors of the enterprise will solve many of the significant problems that exist as barriers to effective theological education today. These significant paradigm shifts will take place as the all dimensions of theological education are defined and systematically addressed with appropriate solutions. Changes in classes will not produce the change necessary since they are only one-fortieth of the dimensional aspects of theological education. Changes in curriculum alone will no longer do, since they represent only one-fifth of the picture. All dimensions must be defined and readdressed.

Dimensions of the Model

The authors have adopted Dearborne's five dimensions of theological education as core shaping dimensions for the model (1995a, 4-15). These dimensions represent dimensions that are common to all means of theological education, all of which must be addressed in order for an effective design or reshaping of a means of theological education to take place. The dimensions of theological education include:

- Institution - The physical and philosophical aspects of the community delivering theological training.

- Process - The total means used to deliver the theological training.

- Faculty - The people responsible for facilitating the learning.

- Student - The participants in the learning process.

- Curriculum - Every item of the training program which contributes either explicitly or implicitly to the input, experimental, dynamic reflection, or spiritual and moral formation aspects of theological training.

The authors applied each of the core values and methodologies and their associated characteristics to each of these five dimensions to produce the model for theological training in this dissertation. The mission, purpose, goals, and educational philosophy were used to guide the process. All of these factors were used to formulate eight questions for each of the dimensions, the answers to which produce the model. For convenience, the model will be described by category of core shaping dimension.

The Dimension of Institution

The dimension of institution represents the physical and philosophical aspects of the community delivering theological training. There are several key characteristics that influence the core shaping dimension of institution, some of which were adapted from a discussion on theological education by Clinton (1984, 81). The eight characteristics that the author has distilled for the core shaping dimension of institution include:

- Tradition - The coordinate representing the socio-religious and cultural orientation of the institution.

- Community - The coordinate representing how an institution sees itself in terms of a congregation, apprenticeship, extension, or partnership.

- Incorporation - The legal status of the corporate institution, either a tax-exempt Internal Revenue Service code 501(c)3 organization or a for-profit corporation.

- Financial Base - The source of money, materials, or their equivalent for funding the institution.

- Research Base - Access to systematically organized data, biographical, and research material that is useful to the institution.

- Facilities - The physical location(s) that the training is delivered.

- Administrative Base - Staff and equipment available to facilitate the operation of the institution.

- Ethos - The perceived qualities of the training context such as enthusiasm, relevance, competence, adequacy, community, growth, and expectations.

These characteristics of the institution must be addressed when defining or reshaping a means of theological training. They cannot be left to chance or ignored because each has consequences in shaping the institution. The tradition and community are all expressions of the core shaping methodology of contextualization. The corporate status is a legal decision made by the governing board as to how the corporation relates legally to the government and has far reaching consequences in the design of the institution. Examples include tax and accounting implications for the institution as well as implications for government control and oversight. Many of the characteristics of the institution's ethos are a result of the synergy of these characteristics and the reaction of the people and organizations involved with the institution.

These eight shaping characteristics can be reduced to eight questions that when answered, form the basis for shaping the dimension of institution:

1. Which of the coordinates of tradition (Nicean, Trent, Augsburg, Geneva, Canterbury, Northampton, or Topeka) most closely represents the socio-religious and cultural orientation desired for the institution?

2. Does the institution see itself as a community most like a congregation, apprenticeship, extension, or partnership?

3. Does the institution desire to incorporate as a non-profit IRC 501(c)3 corporation or a for-profit corporation if in the United States or similar corporate structures if incorporated elsewhere?

4. What is the financial base consisting of money, materials, or their equivalent that will be used to fund the model for theological training?

5. What kind of research base consisting of systematically organized data, biographical, and research materials will be available for the institution to use?

6. Where will the physical location(s) for delivering the theological training be?

7. What administrative support base of volunteer and paid staff will be available to facilitate the operation of the institution?

8. What perceived qualities of ethos - including enthusiasm,

relevance, competence, adequacy, community, growth, and expectations - can be controlled, improved, and monitored?

All of these questions must be answered in accordance with the mission, purpose, goals, core values and methodologies, as well as the educational philosophy of the institution in order to shape the means of theological training accordingly.

Tradition

The characteristic of tradition is important in orienting the institution to its proper socio-religious and cultural coordinates. The authors drew heavily on the work of David H. Kelsey to understand the way that the characteristic of tradition affects the institution (1992, 30-59). Kelsey's concept of tradition is framed in the metaphor of a hamlet community that exists by the side of two crossroads. Often, hamlets and cities form where two roads intersect because of access and commerce. Kelsey pictures the seven major Christian traditions as hamlets that have formed at the intersection of Christian history and a move of God:

- Nicean: the Catholic and Orthodox tradition.

- Trent: the Catholic Counter-Reformation tradition.

- Augsburg: the Lutheran Reformed tradition.

- Geneva: the Calvinist Reformed tradition.

- Canterbury: the Anglican or Episcopal tradition.

- Northampton: the Revivalist, Methodist, and Holiness traditions.

- Topeka: The Holiness-Pentecostal, Charismatic, and neo-Pentecostal or renewal-oriented traditions.

These traditions exist as "hamlets" that have formed at the intersection of the road of Christian history and the road of a distinct move of God. Each tradition represents a valuable move of God at a particular time and place. Each tradition contains something unique that expresses the move of God despite its weaknesses. This paradigm for viewing the traditions represented in the Church and in individual expressions of theological training is a valuable way to frame an understanding of the importance of being interdenominational. Each has strong and weak points. Each tradition has value and is welcome by God, though stained with man's imperfections.

The model that the authors have developed for theological training is decidedly renewal-oriented in nature. It therefore carries the distinctives that follow the Topeka tradition. Its training is contextualized for renewal-oriented Christians in that renewal distinctives are expressed in The Convergence Model's process, faculty, student, and curriculum dimensions. This is an expression of the core value of *pneumatics,* which carries the following characteristics:

- Emphasis on a personal, sapiential relationship with God.

- Understanding and embracing renewal-oriented theology.

- Experience an ongoing baptism in the Holy Spirit.

- Increasing ability to function in the gifts and fruit of the Holy Spirit.

- Increasing ability to function in the power and authority of the Holy Spirit.

- Mobilization, equipping, and releasing of the five-fold ministry.

- Decreasing of the division between clergy and laity.

- Emphasis on the priesthood of the believer and equipping the saints for the work of the ministry.

- Passion for evangelism and missions as a means to fulfill the Great Commission through the conversion of unbelievers.

With the worldwide increase in the renewal-oriented Christian population, a Topeka-based tradition for The Convergence Model is in line with a great need for this type of distinctive in theological education. The Topeka tradition and its distinctives were applied to the model for the interdenominational renewal-oriented community, which is severely lacking in options for renewal-oriented theological training. The personal and sapiential emphasis of the Topeka tradition also seems to best contextualize the education being offered to the post-modern culture in Western society since it is highly relational and experience-oriented in nature.

Community and Ethos

The coordinate of community represents how a means of education sees itself. Many times the way that an institution conceives of itself is implicit rather than explicit. The perception that the faculty, students, and outside world have of the institution often vary greatly as well. It is important that the institution understand the way it pictures itself so that decisions about process, faculty, students, and curriculum can be made with this picture in mind. Again, David H. Kelsey was responsible for shaping the author's conception of this characteristic, and suggested three different ways that an institution can perceive itself (1992, 50-57). The authors add the fourth way, which better describes the way he sees the model designed in this book:

- Congregation: sees itself as church-like.

- Apprenticeship: sees itself as a community of experienced mentors.

- Extension: sees itself as a service organization of the Church.

- Partnership: sees itself as in cooperative venture with the Church.

The way an institution sees itself works its way out into the processes, the faculty and students it attracts, and the curriculum that it offers. The authors conceive of this model of theological training as a dynamic partnership between the institution and the Church. It is the author's conviction that there is no biblical authority for a means of theological training to exist apart from the Church. The Church was given God's authority to exist (Mt. 16:18) and carry out His purposes on the earth

(Mt. 28:18-20). Other institutions were called into being by God's authority as well (Rom. 13:1-8). These institutions have the authority to empower other institutions to carry out God's purposes, such as those delivering theological training. Institutions delivering theological training do not have biblical authority to exist as stand-alone institutions away from the Church, but should exist in symbiotic relationship with the Church to accomplish Christ's purposes with the Church and by the Church's authority. When the Church is divorced from the process of theological training, both suffer. When both are joined in God's purpose, both gain.

The coordinate of community that best describes the relationship that The Convergence Model has with the Church is that of partnership. The model exists in symbiotic relationship with the Church. That partnership will express itself in several ways:

- As the model is presented to an informal group of ministry peers in the city where it is implemented for review and blessing.

- As key pastors of the city's renewal community are added to the governing board of the resulting institution.

- As key renewal-oriented churches in the target city are invited to join a formal partnership with the institution in theological training, encouraging their members to obtain training and contribution on a regular basis to the institution.

- As adjunct professors from the local church are added to the faculty of institution to teach courses in their area of academic or practical expertise.

- As key renewal-oriented churches in the city enter mentoring agreements for the *praxis*-oriented part of the courses that require a field mentor.

- As individual church sites in the city offer the use of their facility to conduct some of the classes taught through the institution.

As can be seen, the characteristic of community affects each dimension of the institution. The concept of community and partnership with the local church in is also an expression of the values of *ekklesia* and *koinonia*. The partnership with the local church is an expression of the symbiotic relationship that should exist between theological training, the believer, and the Church. The partnership also values the proper biotic-organic and holistic picture of the living Body of Christ and its authority on the earth to conduct Christ's mission (*ekklesia*). The dynamic partnership between the local church and institution will also help to contextualize the theological training being delivered for the unique real and felt needs of the city, since the pastors of the city in their experience are all too familiar with them.

The ethos of the school should be in many ways the outcome of other factors in the institution. It consists of the perceived qualities of the training context such as the enthusiasm, relevance, competence, adequacy, level and quality of community, status of growth, and expectations and their fulfillment. Many times these qualities are subjective and hard to measure, existing as a "sense" that students and faculty have about the school. These qualities exist on the level of assumptions and perceptions and vary appreciably from person to person. These qualities are as hard to measure as they are to control, but play a very important part on the overall education of the students.

The ethos of the institution will reflect the school's distinctives of interdenominational and renewal-oriented Christianity. No one denomination, group, or church will exert major control over the ethos so that it can continue to have an interdenominational feel that respects the many traditions within Christianity and their strengths and contribution to the Church. The selection of administration and faculty for the school will indirectly impact the ethos of the institution, so it is important that each member have a living vital relationship with God and that they have a renewal distinctive in operation in their lives. The student body and their selection also play an important part in the ethos, and the selection of committed

Christians who are grounded in a church body and in active service there is important. The ability of the faculty to contextualize its learning experiences and the content and shape of the curriculum will be used to influence the perception of the school's adequacy and relevance. Close contact and knowledge of the student body will help to fulfill expectations and communication of the institution's mission, purpose, goals, values, and educational philosophy will all help to instill realistic expectations in the faculty and students.

Incorporation, Facilities, Financial, Administrative and Resource Bases

The characteristic of incorporation is a vital factor for the dimension of institution, especially if the school is to function in a Western setting. The decisions made about incorporation have far reaching effects on the means of theological training across each dimension. In the United States, the choice comes down to either operating as a corporation or as an unincorporated entity, possibly in association with another entity. There are advantages and disadvantages to either way of organizing this dimension of the institution. The authors propose that the model adopted minimize the costs associated with the institution so that the theological education delivered is as accessible as possible to the target group being trained. Much of the solution lies in the realm of partnership with the local church which provides potential for meaningful contextualization of the training, existing facilities for the education to be located in, and possible qualified adjunct professors to deliver the education.

Much of the cost of theological training is tied up in the physical plant where theological education is delivered. The traditional model for education has several presuppositions that make the physical location of the institution central in concern. Some of the assumptions at work in the traditional model, either implicitly or explicitly include:

- Education is going to a school building to gain knowledge.

- The facility is an expression of academic credibility and excellence.

- The student should come to the school for his or her education.

- The students should leave their environment, if necessary, for education.

As a result of these assumptions, theological training has been traditionally centered in specific locations and centers on the building in which the education occurs. Large and elaborate physical plants have been established to support the education and require a significant investment of capital to operate and maintain. This has also facilitated the extraction of individuals from their context of ministry in order to obtain their education. It has also restricted access to theological training for individuals who cannot relocate for logistical reasons or cannot afford the expense of education and relocation. This type of model may not work well in developing countries, in which capital is scarce and ministers must often work full time while in active ministry.

American church history and the history of its theological training demonstrate that many effective models of theological training are not facility-centered. All of these models are associated with the revivals that have taken place over the last three hundred years. The Log Cabin College movement occurred after the First Great Awakening to take theological training to the frontier of the Colonies since access to theological training at established schools and universities was often impossible for the frontier pastors. This is how theological training started in frontier cities, such as Pittsburgh, in their log cabin colleges in the late 1700s. The Second Great Awakening saw the establishment of Methodist circuit riders and apprenticeship in churches on the frontier that paired established pastors and with those entering the ministry. The Holiness-Pentecostal revivals saw the establishment of Bible schools and institutes that often met in churches and other central buildings to deliver theological education. Finally, the theological education by extension movement (TEE) is associated with the latest Charismatic and neo-Pentecostal movements that are sweeping the globe. In the TEE model, the education is offered at remote sites away from the central institution and at a greatly reduced cost.

The authors propose a decentralized model for theological

training through partnership with local churches. The facilities for conducting theological training would consist of a selected cluster of location in local church buildings throughout the target city. One of those local church sites will be used as the central office for the school, and be the location where school records, administration, and the library are located. A formal partnership for the theological training process should be established between the school and several selected local churches. This partnership should exist as an agreement for the institution to provide the program, instructors, and degree or certification for the training. The local church partner would provide a space for the institution to conduct its classes, adjunct teachers who are qualified to teach, mentoring opportunities for the students to apply what they are learning, and monthly monetary support for the theological school. The training becomes easily accessible to those in the community since it would be resident in the community at an easily identifiable spot. It would have a much lower cost associated with it for the student because the cost of purchase, debt service, maintenance, and utilities normally associated with a building would be absent. It would also provide greater access to application of the knowledge gained in the training process since it would allow students to stay in their ministry context, church, and city while they are being educated.

A decentralized cluster of sites in target cities is in line with the mission, purpose, goals, core values and methodologies of The Convergence Model, as well as its core philosophy. The core philosophy for education is a developmental model rather than a traditional model. One of the active assumptions of this model is that training can take place anywhere and is best done in varied settings to facilitate the acquisition of cognitive, experimental, and affective knowledge. By locating the training in local churches, the education will be closest to ministry where "the walls talk" rather than in a more remote facility that is disconnected from a ministry environment. This will facilitate the core shaping methodologies of contextualization and *praxis* in the educational process. Location of the training in a church setting will also demonstrate the values of *ekklesia* and *koinonia*. The training will be associated with the local church in the target city, demonstrating relation and high regard for it. The training will also be done through a partnership relationship that provides a context of living community to facilitate the training process.

It is essential that students and faculty have access to adequate research materials and services so that they can facilitate and supplement their learning experiences. Traditionally, this exists as a discrete library that is housed in a central location where all of the classes are held. Some forms of accreditation require that this library consist of a certain number of volumes. Often, this results in a large investment of capital for the purchase of materials that may already exist in other institutions in the city. When combined, their libraries represent hundreds of thousands of books and other research materials.

The institution should concentrate on forming access alliances with existing libraries in the target city's seminaries rather than concentrate capital on duplicating existing libraries. This would also express the core value of *koinonia* as agreements are formed with the city's existing seminaries.

The administrative base is critical to the operation of the institution. The institution should have several key administrative positions, all of which report directly to the school's Board of Directors. These positions include:

- Chief Executive Officer (CEO) of the school who functions as the president and is represented on the schools Board of Directors as a non-voting member and directs the school's operation, CFO, and CAO.

- Chief Financial Officer (CFO) of the school who functions as the treasurer on Board of Directors and directs the school's financial operations and personnel.

- Chief Academic Officer (CAO) of the school who is responsible for the academic operations and to pursue the school's prescribed academic outcomes.

All of the people holding these positions should have the credentials, experience, and demonstrated competence necessary for their areas of responsibility. Both the CFO and the CAO will report to the CEO and all will be in submission to the Board of Directors. As partnership develops in the target community between the school and the existing churches, these roles should be filled in part with key qualified clergy from the community to further cement the church and school partnership dynamics.

The Dimension of Process

Another core shaping dimension in theological training is process. Process includes the total means used to deliver theological training. Most institutions are aware of some of the characteristics of process that shape the institution. Many institutions do not understand their own defining characteristics of process, and are therefore powerless to understand how to change them to effect different results. Process is also highly interrelated with all of the other dimensions. A change in any of the other characteristics of the various dimensions can render a process characteristic ineffective or completely useless in furthering the mission, purpose, and goals of the institution. The process has several characteristics, many of which exist on a continuum rather than as discrete points. It is important to address all of these characteristics of process when designing a means of theological education. The eight characteristics of the core dimension of process include:

- Knowing God Orientation - The coordinate expressing the main way the institution uses to facilitate the understanding and knowing of God, emphasizing contemplative, discursive reason, affective, or *praxis* orientation.

- Degree Orientation - The organization of the training process around the attaining of certificates, diplomas, degree, or a combination thereof.

- Accreditation Orientation - Conformance of the institution to standards of accreditation in all of its dimensions.

- Structured Time Orientation - The nature of quantification of non-formal and formal learning processes.

- Outcome Continuum - Tendency to base the results of the training on a continuum between cognitive goals and practical competencies.

- Educational Philosophy Continuum - The location on the continuum between an Athens (spiritual and moral formation) and Berlin (cognitive and rational thought-based) philosophical modes of training.

- Delivery Model Continuum - The location on the continuum between the traditional and developmental models of theological training that the educational process is centered on.

- Extraction Continuum - The location on the continuum between the participant's complete extraction from their context of ministry and complete residence in it during the training experience that the process of theological training is centered on.

The Knowing God Orientation of an institution that delivers theological training greatly shapes its ethos and curriculum. Many times this orientation is implicit rather than explicit based on the institution's distinctives, traditions, faculty, history, or student body. The institution's orientation toward degree and accreditation greatly shapes the curriculum and structured time characteristics of the process dimension as well. In addition to these orientations, and institution delivering theological training must locate itself on several different continuums. The balance of Athens (spiritual and moral development) with Berlin (cognitive and rational-based thought) in the institution determines where it falls on the educational philosophy continuum. The institution must decide where it is appropriate to fall on the continuum between a traditional delivery model and a developmental model for delivering theological training because the decision greatly effects the type of curriculum and faculty needed. Core values influence where on the continuum of extraction (removal of the individual from their context of ministry) and extension (bringing the training to the individual to allow them to stay in their context of ministry).

The dimension of process and the eight characteristics associated with it can be reduced to a series of eight questions that can be used to shape it:

1. Will the process for knowing and understanding God be

oriented more toward contemplation, discursive reason, affective experience, or *praxis* or a balanced combination thereof?

2. Will the training process be organized around the attaining of certificates, diplomas, degrees, or a combination thereof, or will another means of certifying that the participants have fulfilled the mission, purpose, and goals of the process be used?

3. Will the training process conform to a standard form of accreditation or not be accredited?

4. How will the process of theological training be quantified for time of instruction?

5. Will the outcome of the process be centered on cognitive or competency goals or a combination thereof?

6. Where on the continuum of educational philosophy between Athens and Berlin will the process be located?

7. Where on the continuum of delivery will the training be located between traditional and developmental models?

8. Where on the continuum of extraction from the participant's context of ministry will the training be delivered between complete extraction from the context to complete residency in the context?

Once again, all of these questions must be answered in accordance with the mission, purpose, goals, core values and methodologies, as well as the educational philosophy of the institution in order to shape the means of theological training accordingly. As noted, many of them exist on a continuum rather than as discrete points in the structure of the institution, so that they must be located on that continuum as they are actualized.

Knowing God, Degree, Accreditation and
Structured Time Orientations

The mission stated for The Convergence Model is to facilitate the understanding and knowing of God more truly. This mission is accomplished by the purpose of the school, which is the spiritual and moral formation of its participants. Every school has a predominate means of coming to know God. This dominant means of coming to know God is shaped either consciously or unconsciously by the traditions, educational philosophies, cultural conditioning, faculty, and student body as they are mixed in the process of training. An understanding the different means of coming to know God and their strengths and weaknesses is valuable in planning to facilitate this characteristic of process.

David H. Kelsey distills four predominant means of knowing God that are associated with the theological training process (1992, 72). They include:

- Contemplative - Orientated toward knowing God through sapiental means.

- Discursive Reason - Oriented toward knowing God through rational means.

- Affective - Oriented toward knowing God through experimental means.

- *Praxis* - Oriented toword knowing God through means of correct action.

Different traditions have embraced one of these means of knowing God as their predominate way to know and understand God. For instance, the Nicean, Trent, and Canterbury traditions tend to gravitate toward the contemplative means of knowing God. The Augsburg and Geneva traditions tend to emphasize discursive reason. The Northampton tradition tends to emphasize *praxis* and the Topeka tradition emphasizes affective means as a dominant means of knowing God.

Since the model is targeted toward the renewal community, it can be expected that most students will come to the school with a bias toward knowing God through affective means. The typical student can be expected to have a strong desire to experience God in their daily life. This experiential expectation in coming to know God can be considered a strong point, especially since *paideia* is directly related to spiritual and moral formation through personal experience. An orientation toward affective means is also a weakness, in that it often looks down upon discursive reason and intellectual pursuits, a common attitude found in renewal circles.

The authors have deliberately designed The Convergence Model to encourage an affective orientation toward knowing and understanding God by stipulating its mission and purpose around an experiential pursuit (*paideia*) that is transformative in nature and only possible through a living relationship with the Holy Spirit. The authors also have designed the curriculum of the school to balance out the most prominent weakness of this knowing God orientation, by compensating with excellence in academics that involve discursive reason. These nuances work themselves out in the curriculum of the school by balancing affective and discursive reason.

The model for professional education that originated at the University of Berlin in the early nineteenth century has left its mark on Western education in a powerful way. When theological education was included in the university's curriculum in 1810, it became associated with professional education, and the degree system caught on as well in seminaries. As education increased through the twentieth century, the degree system has become the standard paradigm for summing up a person's educational achievements in both secular and theological pursuits. This is true for the Western world as well as increasingly true internationally. The degree system has also become strongly entrenched in the reputable forms of accreditation that are available for schools as well.

The authors have concluded through their research on theological education's history as well as a study on Western culture that the degree and accreditation paradigms are here to stay for the foreseeable future. They are often the primary measures of credibility that individuals use to sum up the competence of an individual and an institution. The authors have concluded that they are essential parts of a model for theological training if it is to be contextualized for the needs and culture as they exist at the beginning of the twenty-first century.

Both the degree and accreditation paradigms have significant problems associated with them. Degrees represent a level of achievement that is often based on attaining a certain number of hours of instruction and passing certain cognitive milestones in attaining knowledge. The problem is that the individual with the degree may have no idea how to apply what they have learned, and simply be good at academics or taking tests. Accreditation likewise has problems associated with it. The standards for accreditation are carefully chosen to provide quality standards for training, which represent certain minimums for an institution. The problem is that no set of standards can apply to every school efficiently due to its unique characteristics, resulting a "box" that the school must fit into that sometimes affects its ability to carry out its mission, purpose, and goals. While there is some flexibility offered in choosing an appropriate accrediting agency, there still are a large number of areas that are nonnegotiable that can shape the institution in ways that are inconsistent with the mission of the school, thus turning it into something that God never intended it to be. Despite these weaknesses, the paradigm of degreed and accredited education has so permeated Western and international cultures, the authors feel it is best to use them in this model, in order to properly contextualize the theological training being offered.

The authors have designed The Convergence Model to begin its operation as an undergraduate college based on a seamless education concept that leads to graduate and post-graduate degrees. The model is not designed to train only those in ministry, but to grant access to training at an undergraduate level to any who desire to prepare for service in the Body of Christ consistent with their gift and destiny-mix. Graduate and post-graduate education through the Convergence Model is reserved for those who are active in an area of ministry and who can demonstrate a calling to ministry through active service to the Body of Christ.

The certificate and degree system developed for the school is based on a semester hour system in which each semester hour is equivalent to fifteen hours of class time. The certificate and degrees that will be offered through within The Convergence Model include:

- Certificate in Ministry (C.Min.) - A one-year undergraduate course of study that emphasizes cognitive knowledge of the Scriptures and their application to ministry as well as resulting in spiritual and moral formation. (30 semester hours)

- Associates Degree in Ministry (A.Min.) - Equivalent to a two-year undergraduate degree that emphasizes a series of general studies courses focused on contextualization, cognitive knowledge of the Scriptures, with distinctive emphasis on formation for ministry, and spiritual and moral formation. (63 semester hours)

- Bachelors Degree in Ministry (B.Min.) - Equivalent to a four-year undergraduate degree providing a broad general studies offering to facilitate contextualization, cognitive knowledge of the Scriptures, detail in application to ministry, as well as broad offering for spiritual, moral, and ministry formation. (126 semester hours)

- Masters Degree in Ministry (M.Min.) - Equivalent to a two-year masters degree providing the practical knowledge, skills, experience, and spiritual and moral formation necessary for pastoral ministry. (72 semester hours)

- Masters Degree in Urban Ministry (M.Urb.) - Equivalent to a one-year masters degree that specializes in providing the practical knowledge, skills, experience, and spiritual and moral formation necessary to function in an urban ministry context. (36 semester hours)

- Masters Degree in Missiology (M.Miss) - Equivalent to a one-year masters degree that specializes in providing the practical knowledge, skills, experience, and spiritual and moral formation necessary to function in cross-cultural missions. (36 semester hours)

- Doctor of Ministry (D.Min.) - Equivalent to a three-year doctoral degree for ministry composed of two-years equivalent of study and one year equivalent dissertation work in practical leadership and ministry (36 or 60 semester hours)

The curriculum itself should be designed around a semester hour orientation that equates each semester hour of credit with fifteen hours of instruction. This means that a three semester hour class is equivalent to forty-five hours of class time or instruction. All of the certificates and degrees consist of three semester hour courses that will be offered over a ten-week period for four and one-half hours per week. There will be three semesters scheduled per year to allow for time between semesters for personal and logistical concerns. This also satisfies most standard accreditation systems, holding to a high standard for training delivery.

The authors propose a varied format of delivery including formal and non-formal delivery methods that will require adaptation for the structured time for classes. Modular classes that are offered will meet the forty-five hours required for a three-semester hour course by a combination of class time and independent study time, with at least twenty hours of structured onsite class time. Independent study classes offered by video, audio, or Internet for some of the more cognitive subjects will meet a required forty-five hours for three semester hours through the demonstrated time in input, reflection, reading, and session writing. The variety of methods by which the classes will be delivered is in line with the school's core methodologies of dynamic communication and contextualization to meet the needs, logistical concerns, and varied learning styles of the participants.

Outcome and Educational Philosophy Continuums

The education philosophy of the school is highly influenced by the tradition, knowing God orientation, the degree and accreditation orientation, as well as the delivery model, faculty, and student population. David H. Kelsey describes the two educational philosophies as Athens and Berlin (1992, 33, 34). Kelsey describes the Athens educational philosophy as a more Greek-oriented model that has an emphasis on *paideia*, which centers on formational issues. He describes the Berlin model as training that centers on rational and intellectual means to formation. The two possible extremes on an educational philosophical continuum as defined by the authors would be:

- Athens - an emphasis on *paideia* or spiritual and moral formation in a manner typical of Greek education.

- Berlin - an emphasis on rational thought, cognitive knowledge, and intellectual formation typical of the professional education offered at the University of Berlin in the nineteenth century.

These two extremes exist on a continuum and an institution's educational philosophy is located somewhere between the two extremes. The Convergence Model falls to the far left of the continuum, emphasizing the Athens-like educational philosophy that focuses strongly on *paideia*:

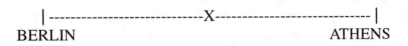

| --------------------------X---------------------------- |
BERLIN   ATHENS

Tradition is a major influence in deciding where the school falls on the continuum between these two points. The Nicean, Trent, and Canterbury traditions tend to be more contemplative in their preferred means of knowing God and gravitate more toward a contemplative means to know God and an Athens-like spiritual and moral formation preference. The Augsburg and Geneva traditions gravitate toward the rational and intellectual means of knowing God through discursive reason, and are more on the Berlin end of the continuum. Northamption and Topeka fall somewhere between the two, but more toward an Athens-like expression of philosophy in training, showing a preference for affective and experimental means of knowing God and a more formation-oriented route.

The Convergence Model is decidedly Topeka in tradition and centered very heavily on an Athens-like model of training. The authors believe that spiritual and moral formation are at the center of theological training, as is expressed in the purpose of the model, which is the facilitation of the spiritual and moral formation of the participants in the educational process. The process of this formation, or *paideia*, occurs in partnership with the Holy Spirit, who actually causes and directs the formation process. The training itself cannot produce the *paideia* - it can only facilitate the process of *paideia* occurring. In a more Berlin-oriented model of training, the assumption is that the training itself produces the change in the individual as they engage in discursive reason. The active assumption of the Athens model is that the change takes place as cognitive input is received, the individual reflects on the input and applies it to life, and the Holy Spirit in partnership with the individual and the training process changes the person's heart and transforms their being.

The Athens orientation of the model is in line with the purpose of the school, which is the spiritual and moral formation of the participants. It matches the goals of the model as well, which all center on *paideia*. The developmental philosophy of training best facilitates an Athens-like orientation as well. The tradition orientation of Topeka also best disposed to a more affective sapiential training experience. Authorss have formed this model based on an Athens orientation, believing that as spiritual and moral formation take place, a person is prepared for ministry. The skills and information taught cannot be the center of a means of theological training or the means begins to fragment. With the mission of facilitating the understanding of God more truly and the purpose of spiritual and moral formation, the institution must reflect these qualities at each level. The curriculum is therefore saturated with courses that all have knowing, doing, and being outcomes that are specified along the mission, purpose, and goals, that are facilitated with an Athens philosophy of training.

The outcome orientation of The Convergence Model is decidedly toward competency goals that express the desired results of the educational process. There are two poles on this continuum that express the way institutions seek to express and evaluate the desired results of its training These poles include:

- Cognitive-based - The outcomes are viewed and evaluated more in terms of degrees, grades, semester hours, accumulated knowledge and professional accomplishment rather than the results in the adequacy, competency, and degree of transformation and formation that have taken place.

- Competency-based - The outcomes of the institution are viewed and evaluated more in terms of the ability for the participant to perform a skill competently and in terms to the increase in discipleship and maturity due to spiritual and moral formation in the participant's life.

The model falls on this continuum much further toward the competency-based outcome orientation:

COGNITIVE   COMPETENCY

As a result of this deliberate orientation toward a competency basis of evaluation and desired result, the curriculum and each of the courses have knowing, doing, and being competencies and outcomes attached to them. This triad ties each course back to the mission, purpose, goals, values, methodologies, and educational philosophy. The model strives for cognitive and experimental competencies with each course as well as affective or being based outcomes. The competency orientation of the school is much more in line with the Athens and developmental educational philosophies as well as the affective and experiential knowing God orientation of the school.

Delivery Model and Extraction Continuums

Two other important characteristics of process include the delivery model and the extraction continuums associated with the educational model. The delivery model is a core shaping philosophy of the institution and ranges from a traditional delivery philosophy to a developmental philosophy on the other extreme. The assumptions and mechanics of the traditional and developmental models were reviewed in this chapter under the core philosophy section of this model. The authors stated a decision to form The Convergence Model around a developmental philosophy of training and therefore the school exists far toward the right of the continuum:

TRADITIONAL   DEVELOPMENTAL

As such, the model will actualize its training according to a developmental philosophy of education. There will be an emphasis on a holistic approach to the training rather than just cognitive knowledge. Formation will be emphasized and structures will be fluid to facilitate this end. Students will be active participants in the process and the teachers will act as facilitators. A high value will be placed on contextualization and *praxis* orientation, as well as varied and dynamic means of communication in the educational process.

The desire to express the model's core shaping methodologies dictates its place on the extraction continuum. Training can be offered by having the participants relocate or travel to a central location to receive their training and live in at the new central site. In this case they are completely extracted from their community, church, work, social, and many times relational networks. Training can also be brought to the individuals so that they do not have to leave their networks of context. In this case the training allows for almost all of their residence work to be done in their home context. This characteristic of process falls somewhere in between complete extraction and complete residency.

The authors have developed The Convergence Model to function as a near complete residence model for the process dimension. It is the authors' conviction that substantially removing a student from their church, community, family, and friendships damages the theological training. The student is not able to apply the cognitive knowledge that he or she learning immediately and must defer this important aspect of learning for months or years until they return to their context of ministry or establish a new one. Extraction also removes students from their support and sponsoring networks, such as church, family, friendship, and place of employment, leaving the student with artificial church, mentoring, and friendship networks in the extraction environment. These disconnects do not facilitate the type of spiritual and moral formation that The Convergence Model strives for. As such, it has adopted the cluster concept of training that is centered at various sites around the city in various partner churches to minimize extraction as much as possible. The model falls far toward the residence poll of the continuum:

| ---X----------- |

EXTRACTION   RESIDENCY

This allows for the participants to remain in vital mentoring and authority relationships with their pastor and church, actualizing the values of *ekklesia* and *koinonia*. It allows students to apply the cognitive knowledge that they gain as soon as possible in their own context of ministry, actualizing the value and methodologies of *paideia*, contextualization, and *praxis*.

The Dimension of the Faculty

One of the most critical core dimensions to consider in designing or shaping a means of theological training is that of the faculty chosen to facilitate the learning process. Faculty includes all the people directly responsible for facilitating the learning experiences that contribute to theological training. The faculty who actually facilitate the process of theological training for an institution contribute greatly to the *ethos* of the institution in either a positive or negative manner. Their academic specialty is important, but depending on the nature of the mission, purpose, goals, and philosophies of the institution, the experience that the faculty has could be just as important or even more important. The authors have distilled eight critical factors that should be considered when shaping the dimension of faculty for a means of theological training:

- Gift-mix - The individual gift-mix of the faculty members dictate which area of specialty they can best facilitate in the educational curriculum.

- Education - The education background, experience, and area of concentration of the faculty members determine where they best fit in the educational process and are essential to the accreditation process.

- Experience - The faculty member's actual ministry experience is essential to the educational process to assure a dynamic link between cognitive and experimental knowledge.

- Relationship - The relationship of the faculty to the school is important to the process, whether the relationship is formal, informal, adjunct, or tenured.

- Orientation - The personal orientation of the faculty member's philosophies, assumptions, and values in relationship to academic and practical skills determines their placement in the institution and process.

- Fluidity - The faculty member's ability to adapt and contextualize for the any given set of factors that influence the institution and process.

- Compensation - The pay, benefits, and non-tangible compensation afforded a faculty member for his or her work.

- Communication - The ability of the faculty members to apply dynamic means of communication to the delivery of theological training as it best fits the context and requirements of the process and institution.

A calling to and experience in ministry may be of critical importance to many of the learning experiences that would be used to shape theological training. Experience in ministry is critical because much of what is learned is "caught" rather than taught, necessitating a model for the participants to imitate. The relationship of the faculty facilitating the theological training to the institution has many financial and practical implications that must be contextualized for the mission, purpose, and goals of the individual institution. The orientation of faculty to academic or practical skills is a critical determining factor along with gift-mix in determining what area of curriculum the faculty member can best facilitate.

When the eight factors that influence faculty are considered, they can be reduced to a series of eight questions that shape the dimension of faculty:

1. What is the individual gift-mix of the faculty members that can be used to place them in a position to best facilitate theological training in the institution, process, and curriculum?

2. What educational background and experiences have shaped the faculty member's concepts and philosophies of theological training, and where would they best fit in the institution,

process, and curriculum?

3. What actual ministry experience does the faculty member bring to the institution that would assure a dynamic link between cognitive and experimental knowledge in the institution, process, and curriculum?

4. Will the relationship of the faculty member to the institution be formal, informal, temporary, permanent, adjunct, or tenured in nature?

5. Is the faculty member most oriented to academic or practical training or skills?

6. Does the faculty member display a fluidity as expressed in the ability to adapt to changing curriculum, process, and contextualization needs?

7. What will be the nature of the pay, benefits, or non-tangible compensation for the work done by faculty?

8. Does the faculty member have the ability use varied styles of communication in delivery and the ability to contextualize the training being delivered for the target individuals?

Gift-mix, Education, and Experience

The proper choice of faculty represents one of the most important aspects of an institution delivering theological training. As with any business or church setting, it is the people who make the business, not the business that makes the people. This is especially true in a church or training setting where ministry and training are concerned, since so much of what is learned is "caught" rather than taught though the faculty's actions, attitudes, and character rather than just their words.

The Convergence Model's mission does not include the preparation of academicians for teaching in more Berlin-oriented schools. Many schools already do a more than adequate job of this by employing faculty that have little or no real-life experience in ministry and therefore are qualified to teach and reproduce academicians. The mission, purpose, goals, values, and methodologies of The Convergence Model dictate that the faculty have a high degree of experience in ministry and ideally still function in active ministry during their time as a teacher at the school. The authors have personally experienced the disconnection that occurs in theological training when an instructor with little or no experience attempts to teach a highly skilled and experienced-based curriculum such as pastoral ministry. Based on the definition of training and *paideia* offered in this book, individuals who have had enough cognitive knowledge given to them to attain a degree, but have had little or no experience in applying that knowledge, would not be qualified to teach that subject. This individual may have earned good grades (traditional model of education), and may have demonstrated the ability to reason (Berlin model), but has not had the chance to apply the cognitive knowledge to life and connect with the reflection and *praxis* necessary to produce adequate spiritual and moral formation. Experience is therefore of high importance to a model such as the author's which has an Athens orientation and a *praxis* methodology. The faculty member's training experience is usually decided by standards of accreditation. Their gift-mix must line up with the area that they are teaching as well according to the accreditation standards, and as demonstrated by experience. The trait of an experienced practitioner in faculty members is not as obvious in the accreditation material, though it is mentioned, but of high importance to The Convergence Model.

Relationship and Compensation

The relationship characteristic of faculty is just as important to the institution as it is to the faculty member. The mission, purpose, and goals of the school have much to do with determining the relationship of the faculty to the school. Traditional forms of theological training have produced central facilities that facilitate extraction, expecting the students to come to them for their training. This training is costly because of the buildings, programs, and faculty that must be in place to support the large budgets that result. In a traditional setting, faculty is, in most cases, tenured and have expensive benefits attached to their salaries as well.

The Convergence Model is designed to minimize extraction and to minimize the cost of the training for the students. In order to do this, a non-traditional delivery format has been developed that has already been partially described herein. In addition to locating the training in the community within local church facilities to maximize church partnership, student access, and minimize costs, the relationship of the teaching faculty to the institution was also adjusted to address these same factors.

Orientation, Fluidity, and Communication

The tradition, core values and methodologies, as well as nature of a school dictate the orientation, fluidity, and communication characteristics necessary for the faculty of the school. The orientation of the faculty includes their personal philosophies, assumptions, and values. These must substantially agree with the school's mission, purpose, core values and methodologies, and philosophies so that the faculty member can embody them for the student body. While the academic requirements to teach at the school are clear, the importance of the faculty's orientation, fluidity, and communication skills are of equal importance.

The faculty member must have a renewal orientation to fit with the school's tradition, knowing God orientation, and value for *pneumatics.* This renewal orientation of the faculty members also helps to ensure the same values for *theologia, ekklesia,* and *koinonia* so that they are conveyed to the student body. Many traditional schools have a denominational litmus test for faculty so that they must subscribe substantially to a certain confession. The interdenominational nature of The Convergence Model would encourage the make up of the faculty to be from a variety of denominational backgrounds but with a renewal distinctive.

In addition to the renewal distinctive, the faculty would also need to have a high degree of experience functioning in the body of knowledge they are teaching so as to be able to link cognitive and practical knowledge by facilitating dynamic reflection in the participants. This dictates that the orientation of the faculty will have to be practical rather than purely academic. It also dictates the necessity of having practitioners teaching rather than faculty who are only academically oriented to the body of knowledge being taught, allowing them to actualize the core methodology of *praxis* in a classroom setting.

Given the core methodologies of contextualization and dynamic communication, the faculty members will have to display a highly fluid nature in their ability to adapt to the institution's processes, students, and curriculum. One of the goals of The Convergence Model is to contextualize the theological training being delivered for the individual students so that a variety of learning styles, cultures, and ministry contexts can be addressed through the training. This will be done in a non-traditional setting in partnership with the local church in the target city, and in varied locations throughout the city. Given these parameters, the faculty of the school will have to be fluid in their thinking and teaching to cope with the environment in which the training takes place. They will not be going to a central location to engage in set curriculum and classes in a classroom full of young and inexperienced people contemplating ministry. They will be going to a variety of locations, teaching a fluid curriculum adapted for the student's needs, and teaching people engaged in ministry within the church who are adult learners.

The context just described will require the application of dynamic communication to be successful. The nature of dynamic communication includes:

- Communication through culturally contextualized and relevant means.

- Linear and non-linear or mosaic formats for communication.

- Flexible curriculum that can be adapted within certain limits to the need of the individual.

- Fluid and adaptable means of communication that best suit the target audience.

- Adaptation of communication and training to varied learning styles and culturally conditioned patterns.

- The use of multiple mediums of communication that best fit the subject matter and intent of training.

- The use of varied settings as contexts for communication and training.

- The use of technology to deliver theological training.

The nature of the contextualization process could involve coordinates for culture, previous experience and training of the participants, as well as adjustments for their mixture of learning styles, as well as gift and destiny-mixes. It will also involve the use of a variety of formats besides lecture, so that a variety of learning formats can be accommodated in the training process. The nature of dynamic communication also implies that the training may take place outside the classroom in a place that is most adapted to facilitate the application of what is being taught.

The Dimension of the Student

The students who participate in the process of theological training are a core dimension as well. Many times this dimension is overlooked as a factor that shapes the institution and process of a means of theological training. Random acceptance of students for economic or logistical reasons can greatly affect a school. In addition, the quality and character of the students that result from theological training speak louder than advertisements or catalogues. Admission policies and guidelines for the institution are sometimes lax or not followed, affecting the composition of the participants and the other dimensions of theological training as well. This can be due to financial constraints that dictate a liberal entrance policy for students. It can also be due to denominational or institutional requirements that stipulate liberal entrance policies. The shaping effect of the composition of the student body has a great impact on the *ethos* of the institution and should not be left to chance. The authors have distilled eight critical characteristics that influence the shaping dimension of the student:

- Gift-mix - The individual gift make up of the participants involved in the process of theological training.

- Destiny-mix - The God-designed destiny for the participants in the process of theological training.

- Education - Prior learning experiences and preparation that the participants have had both formal and informal.

- Experience - The ministry experience that the participants bring with them to the training process.

- Qualifications - The minimum spiritual and moral requirements that the participants possess upon entering its training process.

- Context of ministry - The context and the nature of the participant's ministry as they enter the process of theological training.

- Church context - The degree to which the participant is grounded in, recommended by, and sponsored by a local church body.

- Learning style - The preferential learning style-mix of the participant in the process of theological training.

The entrance qualifications for theological training need to be based on accountability with a local church. A vital relationship with Jesus Christ and evidence of a probable calling to service in a particular area of ministry are other factors to be considered. The participant's dynamic link to a church is vital as well to the whole process since this most often serves as their context of ministry, accountability, and support. The more a participant and the institution delivering theological training understand about the participant's gift-mix and destiny-mix orientation, the more effectively the curriculum can be individualized and targeted for personal growth and adapted to personal learning style preference.

A series of eight questions have been distilled to shape the dimension of the student in theological training:

1. What is the individual gift-mix of the participant?

2. What is the destiny-mix of the participant?

3. What prior training experiences have shaped the participant?

4. What level and kind of experience does the participant bring with them to the training process?

5. Does the participant meet the minimum moral and spiritual requirements for participation in the training process?

6. What is the participant's context of ministry as they enter the process?

7. To what degree is the participant grounded in, recommended by, and sponsored by a local church?

8. What is the preferential learning style-mix of the participant?

Gift-mix, Destiny-mix, Learning Style, Education, Qualifications, and Orientation

In a more traditional setting for theological training, the institution, process, faculty, and curriculum are designed to educate the students in a group paradigm with little ability to address individual characteristics. To address the students as individuals is time consuming and not cost effective. This often leaves the students lost in the maze of the training process and sometimes results in an end product that does not understand their relationship to what they have learned. The Convergence Model is designed to work in dynamic partnership with the local church and to form its emerging leaders to be vital parts of that church community. As such, the nature of the model's mission and design will dictate that there be a much more individualized attitude toward the student body than is normally found in traditional theological training.

God has designed each individual with unique gifts and purpose (Ps 139:13-18). This means that each individual who comes to the school has already been endowed with a unique profile of gifts and destiny, which God is working out in their lives. A foundational part of the educational process is to know as much about the student's individual gift-mix and destiny-mix before the training begins so a course can be prescribed for them to sharpen these gifts and mature them toward their individual destiny. Added to these factors is the unique learning style and personality of the individuals as they enter the learning process. Both of these factors should be formally assessed as well, in order to contextualize the training as specifically as possible for the incoming student.

The Convergence Model requires the participation of anyone entering the school in some form of ministry in a local church. Because of the nature of the school, no person will be admitted for theological training who is not firmly planted in a local church body and who is not functioning is some form of service to that local church. Partnership with the local church in theological training dictates that the school is educating the local church's members for ministry. The proper actualization of *ekklesia* through this partnership demands that it educate individuals who are a part of the church community. This also respects the value of *koinonia*, since the school will only educate those who are in fellowship and community with the local church. In addition, the nature of theological training at the school is not only cognitive, but also highly *praxis*-oriented. It is based on the immediate application of cognitive knowledge in a real-life ministry context so that through dynamic reflection, this cognitive and experimental knowledge can be linked to produce the desired affective, spiritual, and moral formation in the student. Without a working context of ministry in the local church, this would be impossible.

Church Context and Context of Ministry

As was just stated, the church context for the student is vital to the overall training within The Convergence Model. No students will be admitted without a local church that sponsors them in the process. The nature of the local church partnership that the model's process is built on demands a high degree of involvement with the local church in the educational process. Each incoming student will need to be certified as a vital part of the local church in the target city. He or she will have to be recommended by a local church pastor who will also have to give evidence that the student is vitally involved in some area of service to their church. In addition, a meeting and interview with potential students will include the pastor who is sponsoring them to verify their part in the church and to verbally access the student's gift and destiny-mix as well as to begin to set goals for their training. The sponsoring church will also be given opportunity to sponsor all, or part of the student's training expenses with matching funds from the school as they are available.

Summary

When all of the dimensions of theological education are defined and properly addressed, the kinds of change necessary to make the enterprise more effective once again will be restored. This chapter has addressed the first four dimensions of theological education and how they must be changed to make theological education more relevant once again as is represented in The Convergence Model. The next chapter will address the dimension of curriculum and the portion of that dimension that deals with the actual class offerings.

CHAPTER ELEVEN

The Convergence Model and the Dimension of Curriculum

M ost efforts to revitalize theological education begin, and often end, with the curriculum. The Convergence Model of theological training will end with the dimension of curriculum and the various course offerings common to theological education. The order is deliberate. For years, it was assumed that true change could occur if one dimension (curriculum) or a fraction of that curriculum (classes) were modified in some way. This type of change often ignored the other four dimensions of theological education (Institution, Process, Faculty, and Student) in part or completely. The result was different classes with the same results – irrelevance.

The curriculum and classes prescribed in this chapter must be understood in light of the other four dimensions described earlier. If change is made only in the classes offered or in the curriculum from which they flow, the nature of the change will be one of paradigm adjustment rather than paradigm shifting. The core values and shaping factors that truly determine the effectiveness of theological training will lie dormant. The result will be more of the same thing – in the classroom and in the results it produces. When the dimension of curriculum is changed along with the other four dimensions of theological education, a true platform for change and new relevance emerges.

The Dimension of Curriculum

The most commonly emphasized core dimension in theological training is curriculum. The word curriculum is a Latin word that means "a race course or prescribed path" (Gangel and Hendricks 1988, 51). Curriculum refers to every item of a training program which either explicitly or implicitly contributes to the input, experimental, dynamic reflection, or spiritual and moral formation aspects of theological education (Clinton 1984, 81). Beyond the materials and courses offered, it refers to the formal and non-formal learning experiences structured to deliver the theological training. Curriculum is usually organized along one or more of several dimensions (Gangel and Hendricks 1988, 52-54):

- Chronology: historical order of the content.

- Complexity: simple to more complex content.

- Thematic: organized by theme of literature or content.

- Pedagogical: personally experienced events to more remote events.

The content of the curriculum should actualize the mission, purpose, goals and values of the institution delivering theological training. The institution's core shaping values, methodologies, and delivery model should be used to shape the institution along each dimension, including theological training. There are eight critical characteristics involved with the core shaping dimension of curriculum. Some of these characteristics were described by Clinton and adapted (1984, 81). Some of them exist on a continuum upon which the individual institution must locate itself. They include:

- **Formal Functions** - The main learning experiences consisting of scheduled courses, lectures, activities, learning experiences, and their requirements associated with theological training.

- **Non-formal Functions -** The peripheral learning experiences consisting of seminars, workshops, lectures, small group experiences, and other input activities that exist on the periphery of the theological training but contribute to the training.

- **Materials** - The written input for theological training such as texts, workbooks, and manuals.

- **Outcomes** - The cognitive, experimental, and affective results centered knowing, doing, and being that represent the desired results of the theological training process.

- **Curriculum continuum** - The location on the continuum between completely open and completely closed that the curriculum content of the theological training is located.

- **Pedagogical continuum** - The location on the continuum between pedagogical and andragogical teaching philosophies and methods that the process of theological training is located.

- **Individualization continuum** - The location on the continuum between completely individualized training and total group-oriented training that the process of theological training is located.

- **Spatial continuum** - The place on the continuum between linear (one input/subject at a time) and spiral (multiple mosaic-like inputs) that the curriculum content of the theological training is located.

Learning experiences must contain a proper balance of formal and non-formal functions so that different learning styles can be addressed. The outcome competencies are designed around a triad of knowing (cognitive) doing (experimental), and being (affective and formation issues) that represent what the ideal outcome of the theological educational process should be. A continuum of curriculum design exists that ranges from open (highly adaptable to change based on the needs of the participants) and closed (prescribed and unbending). A balance between pedagogy (child-based learning) and andragogy (adult-based learning) are important for contextualization of the theological training for the target participants. Ideally, the curriculum should be individualized for each participant, but time, resources, and efficiency dictate that this would most often be impossible. A continuum between individualization and group-targeted curriculum exists that is important to address explicitly in order to contextualize the curriculum for the institution's mission, purpose, and goals. The spatial continuum addresses how the curriculum will be delivered. Most traditional schools offer theological training in a highly linear subject by subject manner. Another approach dictates that these subjects or competencies be interwoven throughout the curriculum and progress in a spiraling rather than linear manner.

The eight characteristics associated with this dimension can be reduced to eight questions for shaping the dimension of curriculum:

1. What is the nature and mix of formal functions that will be offered in the process of the theological training?

2. What is the nature and mix of the non-formal functions that will be offered in the process of theological training?

3. What material will be used to facilitate the process of theological training?

4. What outcomes will be prescribed for the process of theological training that can be designed into the curriculum?

5. Where on the continuum between totally open and totally closed will the curriculum fall?

6. Where on the continuum between pedagogical and andragogical instruction will the curriculum fall?

7. Where on the continuum between totally individualized and totally group-based will the curriculum fall?

8. Where on the continuum between linear and spiral competencies will the curriculum fall.

Curriculum, Pedagogical, Individualization, and Spatial Continuums and Outcomes

The curriculum of every school exists on several continuums that radically shape a school's course offerings and structure. The curriculum continuum represents the location on the continuum between completely open and completely closed on which the school's curriculum is located. In an ideal world, the curriculum would be completely open and be tailored, designed, and expressed for each individual student and their gift and destiny-mix, learning style, needs, and preference. This is not possible in the real world due to constraints on time, financial limitations, and the nature of educating a group of students at the same time. In addition, many times accreditation prescribes that the curriculum be similar to course offerings in nature with other similar institutions and that the curriculum be set in some sort of formal format (i.e., TRACS 2000, 33). The Convergence Model maintains the standards for accreditation by operating with a relatively closed curriculum that is formally prescribed in writing and substantially formed:

OPEN   CLOSED

The curriculum course structure and content are relatively closed and designed to prevent the proliferation of class offerings that can dilute the effectiveness of instruction. Too many times there is a multitude of offerings in an attempt to educate individuals for a variety of ministry specialties. This requires many ministry and academic specialists and increases the overall cost of the training. The model offers one undergraduate track in Christian Ministry for the certificate, associates, and bachelors degree programs to avoid this type of proliferation. It will offer three distinct specialties at the masters level programs in Ministry, Urban Ministry, and Missiology. The courses prescribed will be relatively inflexible for each track. The flexibility to contextualize the training will exist within the classes themselves, where the individual instructors will be expected to adapt the learning experience as much as possible for the individuals involved.

Education pedagogy is of primary concern in curriculum. There is a continuum that exists between pedagogical (child-oriented) and andragogical (adult-oriented) education in every curriculum. The target of The Convergence Model is the adult population in the interdenominational renewal-oriented community. As such, the training should have a substantial andragogical orientation to it if it is to be properly contextualized:

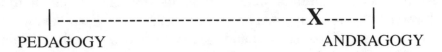

| ----------------------------------**X**------ |
PEDAGOGY   ANDRAGOGY

Proper andragogical instruction assumes that the instruction is being directed primarily at a self-directed adult learner. Andragogy assumes that the individuals being taught rely heavily on their own initiative in the learning process. This affirms the necessity of cognitive input through the learning process that the learner must then apply to real-life learning situations and experiences through dynamic reflection. The andragogical process has four distinct phases as the author has adapted from information from J. Robert Clinton (1984, 41-48):

Input - (knowing) cognitive knowledge:

- Cognitive - information centered (acquire knowledge).

- Experimental - task centered (function in ministry).

- Affective - values centered (develop values).

Experience - (doing) ministry application of cognitive input:

- Activities - stimulate learning.

- Application - apply inputs.

Dynamic Reflection - (processing) correlation of cognitive and experimental knowledge and experience:

- Discover relationship between input and experience.

- Teach how to evaluate life and ideas.

- Learn the ability to relate ideas in the cognitive, experimental, and affective realms.

- Forces accountability for learning transfer.

- Forces accountability for spiritual and moral formation.

- Forces the application of learning in all realms to real life.

- Promotes the idea that learning occurs in the midst of life and is a life-long task.

Spiritual and Moral Formation - (being) coming to know and understand God more truly because of the educational experience:

- The person begins to experience more of God.

- The person begins to reflect a more God-like character.

- The person's personality becomes more God-like.

- The person's everyday relationships become more God-like.

- The person increasingly knows the power of God in everyday life.

- The person increasingly knows the power of God in ministry.

There are also some basic assumptions that are in effect in andragogical learning environments that the author has adapted from some of Clinton's writings (1984, 86):

- The learner has a drive to learn certain input segments and will take the initiative to do so.

- The learner has a reservoir of experience that can be used to facilitate the learning experience as they relate the cognitive input to life and experience within their context of ministry.

- The learner is motivated by the drive to enhance their present circumstances and those of others.

- The learner has a need and desire to immediately apply what is being learned to life and ministry, being more performance that subject-oriented.

Pedagogical instruction is more lecture-oriented due to the insufficient knowledge and experience of the students. It also assumes that the student has less self-motivation for learning and best learns by subject rather than by performance. It is also much more future-oriented than oriented toward immediate application. Andragogical instruction best contextualizes the training for the model's adult targets for theological training. It best meets their needs and learning styles. It also facilitates the core value and methodology of *paideia* and *praxis*.

As was stated, it is impractical to expect the curriculum The Convergence Model to be completely individualized for the students. The instruction will take place in a group and cohort format for the most part because it is the author's conviction that these atmospheres best facilitate *koinonia* for the students involved. This will give the students the ability to interact with peers in ministry and the local church. The benefit gained from such a group experience will help to reduce any liability in the school's inability to completely individualize the curriculum for each student. The Convergence Model therefore falls more toward the group-orientation on the individualization continuum due to its cohort structure:

INDIVIDUALIZATION   GROUP-ORIENTATION

As proper contextualization occurs, a balance between complete individualization and complete group-orientation in the curriculum will result.

The spatial orientation of the curriculum is another characteristic that must be defined in order for the curriculum to have the desired impact and for it to meet the mission, purpose, goals, values, methodologies, and philosophies of the school. The point on the curriculum's spatial continuum describes the place between linear (one-subject and input at a time) and spiral (multiple mosaic-like inputs) that the curriculum content takes. Traditional theological education, especially when influenced by the Berlin educational philosophy, takes a highly linear form that often expresses itself in one subject having one major theme, objective, or competency associated with it. The Convergence Model has adopted a non-traditional approach that introduces a spiraling mosaic-like set of competencies and outcomes that are associated with the curriculum. As such, it would be toward the spiral side of the spatial continuum:

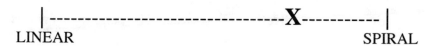

|------------------------------------**X**----------|
LINEAR   SPIRAL

There are several programs of study offered at the school, grouped by degree:

- Certificate in Ministry (C.Min.)
- Associates Degree in Ministry (A.Min.)
- Bachelors Degree in Ministry (B.Min.)
- Masters Degree in Ministry (M.Min.)
- Masters Degree in Urban Ministries (M.Urb.)
- Masters Degree in Missiology (M.Miss.)
- Doctor of Ministry Degree (D.Min.)

The undergraduate programs are seamless in regards to their design, leading to a masters degree in one of three specialized areas. The Masters Degree in Ministry is seamless in design, leading to a Doctor of Ministry Degree. There are prescribed courses associated with each degree.

Each of the programs described above and all of the courses that are offered have spiraling competencies and outcomes that are associated with them. The progression of the courses and the seamless degrees are linear in nature, as with traditional training. This is necessary to conform to accreditation standards and to contextualize the delivery of the training in a format that would be expected by most individuals as they have been conditioned by Western models of education. The spiral nature to the curriculum exists at the level of each program and course's outcomes and competencies.

Each course must have a formal design that prescribes outcomes for the triad of knowing, doing, and being. Appropriate taxonomy will be used to describe the knowing, doing, and being objectives for each course:

- Knowing (Cognitive) Objectives - The participants will know....

- Doing (Experimental) Objectives - The participants will know how to...

- Being Goals (Affective) Objectives - The participants will be...

A list of suggested wording for taxonomies for each of these areas, as adapted from Clinton's writings, are:

COGNITIVE DOMAIN - (Knowing)

1.0   Knowledge

    1.10   Knowledge of specifics
          1.10.1 Knowledge of terminology
          1.10.2 Knowledge of specific facts

    1.20   Knowledge of ways and means of dealing with specifics
          1.20.1 Knowledge of convictions
          1.20.2 Knowledge of trends and sequences
          1.20.3 Knowledge of classifications and categories
          1.20.4 Knowledge of criteria
          1.20.5 Knowledge of methodology

    1.30   Knowledge of universals and abstractions of a field
          1.30.1 Knowledge of principals and generalizations
          1.30.2 Knowledge of theories and structures
          1.30.3 Intellectual Abilities and Skills

2.0   Comprehension
    2.10   Translation
    2.20   Interpretation
    2.30   Extrapolation

3.0   Application

4.0   Analysis
    4.10   Analysis of the elements
    4.20   Analysis of relationships
    4.30   Analysis of organizational principles

5.0   Synthesis
    5.10   Production of a unique communication
    5.20   Production of a plan or proposed set of operations
    5.30   Derivation of a set of abstract relations

6.0   Evaluation
    6.10   Judgement in terms of internal evidence
    6.20   Judgement in terms of external criteria

EXPERIENTIAL DOMAIN - (Doing)

1.0   Exposure - Consciousness of an experience
    1.10   Sensory
    1.20   Response
    1.30   Readiness

2.0   Participation
    2.10   Representation
        2.10.1   Covertly
        2.10.2   Overtly
    2.20   Modification

3.0   Identification
    3.10   Reinforcement
    3.20   Emotional
    3.30   Personal

4.0   Internalization
        4.10   Expansion
        4.20   Intrinsic

5.0   Dissemination
        5.10   Informational
        5.20   Homeletic

AFFECTIVE DOMAIN - (Being)

1.0   Receiving (Attending)
        1.10   Awareness
        1.20   Willingness to receive
        1.30   Controlled or selected attention

2.0   Responding
        2.10   Acquiescence in responding
        2.20   Willingness to respond
        2.30   Satisfaction in response

3.0   Valuing
        3.10   Acceptance of a value
        3.20   Preference of a value

4.0   Organization
        4.10   Conceptualization of a value
        4.20   Organization of a value system

5.0   Characterization by a value or value system
        5.10   Generalized set
        5.20   Characterization

A preliminary set of objectives expressed as a student profile can also be developed based on these standards:

1. **Christian Worldview** - A commitment to a Christian Worldview centered on the inspiration of the Scriptures and God's self-disclosure through them.

2. **God's Presence** - A passion for the knowledge, understanding, and experience of God and His presence.

3. **God-like Character** - A continuous growth in God-like character as expressed in servant leadership and conduct.

4. **God-like Personality** - A continuous growth in God-like personality as expressed in fellowship (*koinonia*) and relationships.

5. **Discipleship** - An increasing discipleship to Christ as expressed by application of the spiritual disciplines to life and ministry.

6. **Holistic Lifestyle** - A commitment to a balanced and healthy holistic spiritual, mental, and physical life and the ability to reckon with one's gift and destiny mixes.

7. **Pneumatic Life** - A commitment to a pneumatic life as evidenced by increasing experience of the power of God in daily life and ministry.

8. **Prophetic Focus** - A commitment to a biblical organic view of the Church as well as local, national, and international witness as evidenced by a lifestyle of evangelism and discipleship.

Each course must also be related back to one or more core values of the school through its objectives.

The spiraling nature associated with the curriculum is introduced based on the emphasis given at each level of degree. While all levels of the curriculum must have knowing, doing, and being objectives that are associated with them, each degree level spirals toward increasing emphasis on the continuum of knowing, doing and being:

DEGREE	EMPHASIS
• Certificate in Ministry	Knowing
• Associates Degree in Ministry	Knowing
• Bachelors Degree in Ministry	Knowing/Doing
• Masters Degree in Ministry	Doing/Being
• Masters Degree in Urban Ministries	Doing/Being
• Masters Degree in Missiology	Doing/Being
• Doctor of Ministry	Being

The overall curriculum spirals toward the "being" emphasis as the student progresses through the seamless degree process, ultimately fulfilling the mission and purpose of the school.

Formal and Non-formal Functions and Materials

A school's formal and non-formal functions, as they relate to course offerings, are normally the central factor considered in a model for theological training. While they are of central concern since they are what the potential student sees as the "school" itself, they are really an expression of the mission, purpose, goals, values, methodologies, and philosophies that the school hold to in either their explicit or implicit form. The following format for the school's class offerings are a direct result of the school's mission, purpose, goals, values, methodologies, and philosophies as they were outlined earlier in this chapter. They represent the actualization of these qualities and the author's consideration of all of these factors. They also represent the author's synthesis of research into American church history, the history of its theological training, as well as the research into contemporary Western culture and the current debate in theological education. They attempt to meet the unique needs of the interdenominational renewal-oriented community in the twenty-first century.

Certificate and Undergraduate Programs

The certificate and undergraduate programs are meant to offer theological training to the interdenominational renewal community. This training is targeted toward individuals who are active participants in these churches, to facilitate their spiritual and moral development, rendering them more fit for service within the Church. The degrees are designed through location, cost, and entrance requirements, as described previously, to grant access to theological training to those who may not be able to access such training because of economic, logistical, or educational barriers that currently exist in the city. The certificate and undergraduate programs offered at the school consist of three distinct programs:

- A Certificate Program (One-year, 30 semester hours).
- An Associates Degree Program (Two-year, 63 semester hours).
- A Bachelors Degree Program (Four-year, 126 semester hours).

As was mentioned, all of the programs are seamless and encourage the participants to continue through masters level studies by allowing each degree to build on each other. All classes offered are three semester hour classes, which account for an equivalent of forty class hours for the three semester hours. Classes are numbered by program:

- 100 Level - Certificate, first year Associates and Bachelors Degrees.
- 200 Level - Second year Associates and Bachelors Degrees.
- 300 Level - Third year Bachelors Degree.
- 400 Level - Fourth year Bachelors Degree.
- 500 Level - Masters Degree level.
- 600 Level - Reserved - Future Masters Level.
- 700 Level - Doctoral Degree Level

The actual courses could vary greatly depending on the needs of the institution, its specific mission and emphasis based on calling, and the faculty and student make up. A potential list of classes offered can be found in Appendix D.

Summary

It is prudent to end this section describing the dimension of curriculum with a caution – the Dimension of Curriculum represents only one of the dimensions that must be considered when designing or renewing theological training. Traditionally, it has received the most attention because it is one of the more visible parts of the process – the product that the "consumer" buys. With this dimension being only one fifth of the picture, changes in curriculum only affect the enterprise of theological training in part. A dynamic equilibrium exists with other dimensions so that changes in one dimension affect other dimensions and these changes can actually be nullified if other critical dimensions of the process are not considered or trained. Consider the fact that the actual classes offered exist as one of eight factors to be considered in the continuum of five dimensions, each with their own eight factors. That means that the classes offered make up one-fortieth of the big picture of what the theological training becomes. The future of theological training does not rise and fall on changing one-fortieth of the picture. It rests on understanding the institution's mission, purpose, core shaping values and methodologies. From there, the proper orientation of the five dimensions can be chosen deliberately and with God's guidance to actualize the shape of the institution. If this is done properly, the question of what classes to offer will nearly take care of itself.

CHAPTER TWELVE

A Well-Furnished Heart – Restoring the Spirit's Place in the Leadership Classroom

W hen God sends renewal, He never does so in a haphazard manner. There is always purpose and substance to what He does, that is often far beyond our ability to comprehend. The renewal that has taken place since 1900 is just now being understood in part from the vantage point of several decades of time that have passed. The renewal that has taken place over the last twenty years, with hundreds of millions of souls born into His kingdom will likely take decades to understand in part as well.

Leadership training and equipping is a task where there is no luxury to wait those decades. The renewal movement in this country is beginning to see fifth and sixth generation leaders that are attempting to steer the church on a true course towards the future. It is the task of this generation to equip these emerging leaders in the most effective ways possible. The task is made even more complicated by the global nature of the need for training, which bridges nearly every culture, language, and ethnic group on the face of the earth. Divine wisdom is needed and the flexibility to rethink even the most basic foundations of theological training in order to contextualize the process for today's emerging leaders wherever they may be. At stake may be the continued progress of this present move of God which now seems to be intensifying, but also showing signs of the need for strong skillful leadership. Will history look back on our time and say that we gave this next generation of leaders the tools they needed to do their job?

Theological training has always changed to meet the challenges brought on by God's renewal. This is illustrated by the Log Cabin College of the Great Awakening on the American frontier, the stand-alone seminary of the 1800s, the Bible college movement of the Pentecostal and Holiness renewals, or the theological education by extension movement in the last several decades. The format of theological training must not be considered sacred, but rather a wineskin made to hold God's "new wine" as He pours it out from heaven. God forbid that we hang onto the old wineskins from the past, no matter how effective they have been, lest they burst and we lose the new wine that He is pouring out on the Church. Those involved in theological education would be foolish to think that things can remain the same in the realm of training for emerging leaders in light of the massive renewal and the evidence of the past.

The current crisis in the classroom is drawing no little attention in the church and in theological education circles. At its core, the crisis is a crisis of values rather than methodologies. Methods flow from values. Values are at the heart of any endeavor and explain why things are done in a particular way. Values that captured the movement of God at one time become worn out and need to be renewed or replaced. Many of the values fueling the current way of doing theological education are simply worn out or are in bad need of balance. The values shift brought on by renewal has accentuated the problems in the classroom. In many places, theological education is struggling to be relevant and in some cases struggling for its very life. The core of the struggle often comes down to a clash between the Berlin philosophy of theological training which emphasizes an academic and knowledge-based approach toward knowing God and a more Athens and Topeka-like approach to knowing God which is more sapiential and experiential in nature. For theological training, it is not a matter of "which" philosophy to choose, since both are vital to the process, but rather how to balance each to produce training that provides training that is rich in cognitive, practical and experiential components.

The core values of renewal gravitate toward spiritual formation as a center for theological training. This formation, or *paideia*, involves not only the formation of the soul through the impartation of knowledge, but the true "culturing" of the soul with applied formation experiences that prepare the student for actual ministry in real-life contexts. Not only does a more *paideia*-laden education make sense in light of renewal distinctives, but this mode of education also seems to make sense in light of current post-modern culture and the unique needs of today's emerging leaders.

Renewal distinctives are no longer the exception to be viewed as some sort of peculiar way of experiencing Christ. They have in fact become the defining factor in Christian experience over the last twenty years. Renewal distinctives have broken down the artificial distinction between clergy and laity necessitating accessible theological training to "equip the saints for the work of the ministry." A renewal emphasis on the role of the five-fold ministry and the gifts of the Holy Spirit in ministry have created a whole new category of training necessary that did not exist several decades ago. The emphasis of justification by faith, personal evangelism, and the conscientization of the renewal movement as it begins to address the social, political, economic, and injustice issues within the cultures it has penetrated will require a whole new way of thinking about how to educate today's emerging leaders. These types of changes will not involve a mere adjustment to existing paradigms for theological training, but will require paradigm shifts in thinking to address needed change. In many cases, these changes fly right in the face of existing structures for education that have deeply entrenched vested interests such as fixed endowments and issues of tenure. It should be interesting to see whether the pressure for more contextualized training that the renewal has brought overwhelm these vested interests, bend them to suit new needs or simply pass them by to establish new means of training.

If theological training is to be relevant for today's emerging leaders, it must address all five dimensions of the endeavor. In the past, change has centered on curriculum and subject matter. These changes have been inadequate because they have not addressed the other dimensions involved in the enterprise. The dimension of institution must be restructured to fit the economic and cultural context of the participants being trained. The faculty and student dimensions themselves must be addressed to be sure that those delivering the training are themselves practitioners that are experienced in what they are teaching. The students must be a vital part of a local assembly so that they can immediately apply what they have learned in the context of ministry and in partnership with the local church. This makes a strong argument for the process dimension of the training to be designed with minimal extraction of the student from their local home and church environment, rather than relocation to a distant place to receive the training. Spiritual and moral formation of the participants must become the centering purpose and a more sapiential experience for the participants that forms their character, gift-mix, and personal relationship with God. The training must never surrender a Berlin excellence at academics, but this must be balanced with an Athens emphasis on formation. Core values that reflect renewal distinctives (*pneumatics)* must be integrated into the training in a meaningful way. In addition to spiritual and moral formation (*paideia)*, and emphasis on the renewal view of the authority and inspiration of the Scriptures (*theologia*) must be central. A proper relationship of theological training to the Church must be established as theological training once again partners with the local church in the effort to train emerging leaders (*ekklesia* and *koinonia*). When these values are at the core of the effort, they not only reflect renewal distinctives but move the effort to train emerging leaders into the realm of relevancy for most of the Christians that are alive today.

The authors have proposed a form of renewal-oriented training called The Convergence Model that brings all of the renewal, contextual, and values-oriented issues to bear on the process of theological training. It is a seamless approach to theological training that we believe has the best chance of training in various cultural and geographic settings. It is contextualized for renewal Christianity and takes into account the need for degreed and accredited education for today's emerging leaders. Various institutions, including those that the authors are involved with personally are struggling to actualize this model for theological training, which if chronicled could be the work of another book on these matters. The desire of the authors of this book are that meaningful dialogue take place on the nuances of renewal in theological training and that we somehow capture the transforming power of the current renewal to pass on to the next generation of emerging leaders that they might lead well. Ultimately, there will be no perfect means that will act as a universal model. May God grant us His wisdom on how to capture this renewal and pass it on to the next generation.

Selected Bibliography

Abott, T. K. *The International Critical Commentary.* ed. by S.R. Driver, A. Plummer, and C.A. Briggs. Edinburgh: T. & T. Clark, 1964.

Aleshire, Daniel, and Jonathan Strom, ed. *Fact Book on Theological Education.* Pittsburgh: The Association of Theological Schools, 1996.

Anderson, Allan H., and Walter J. Hollenweger, eds. *Pentecostals After a Century.* Sheffield: Sheffield Academic Press, 1999.

Banks, Robert. *Going to Church in the First Century.* Beaumont: Christian Books, 1980.

_____. *Paul's Idea of Community.* Peabody: Hendrickson, 1998.

_____. *Reenvisioning Theological Education.* Grand Rapids: Eerdmans, 1999.

_____, and Julia Banks. *The Church Comes Home.* Peabody: Hendrickson, 1998.

Barker, Joel Barker. *Paradigms: The Business of Discovering the Future.* New York: Harper Collins, 1992.

Barrett, David. "The Status of Christianity and Religions in the Modern World". *World Christian Encyclopedia,* Oxford: Oxford Press, 2001.

Barna, George. *The Second Coming of the Church.* Nashville: Word, 1998.

Barnes, Albert. *Notes on the New Testament – Ephesians, Phillipians, and Colosians.* ed. Robert Few. Grand Rapids: Baker, 1965.

Blair, Christine E. "Understanding Adult Learners: Challenges for Theological Education." *Theological Education* 34, no.1 (1997) : 11-24.

Bowers, Paul., ed. *Evangelical Theological Education Today:* Vol. 2, *Agenda for Renewal.* Nairobi: Evangel Publishing, 1982.

Brereton, Virginia Lieson. *Training God's Army: The American Bible, 1880-1940.* Bloomington: Indiana University, 1990.

Brown, Colin, ed. *Dictionary of New Testament Theology.* Vol. 1, by L. Coenen. Grand Rapids: Zondervan, 1975.

Burgess, Stanley M. and Gary B. Mc Gee, eds. *Dictionary of Pentecostal and Charismatic Movements.* Grand Rapids: Regency, 1988.

Caird, G.B. *The Apostolic Age.* England: Booksprint, 1955. Reprint, England: Duckworth, 1993.

Calian, Samuel Carnegie. *Where's the Passion for Excellence in the Church? – Shaping Discipleship Through Ministry and Theological Education.* Wilton: Morehouse, 1989.

Calvin, John. *John Calvin's Sermons on Ephesians.* trans. Arthur Golding, 1577. Original French, 1562. Carlisle: Banner of Truth, 1975.

Cetuk, Virginia Samuel. *What to Expect in a Seminary: Theological Education as Spiritual Formation.* Nashville: Abingdon Press, 1998.

Chopp, Rebecca S. *Saving Work: Feminist Practices of Theological Education.* Louisville: Westminster John Knox, 1995.

Clinton, J. Robert. *Leadership Training Models.* Altadena: Barnabas Resources, 1984.

Conn, Harvie M. and Samuel F. Rowen, ed. *Missions & Theological Education in World Perspective.* Michigan: Associates of Urbanus, 1984.

Copeland, Robert M. *Spare No Exertions: 175 Years of the Reformed Presbyterian Theological Seminary.* Grand Rapids: Eerdmans, 1986.

Davies, Richard E. *Handbook for Doctor of Ministry Projects: An Approach to Structured Observation of Ministry.* Lanham: University Press, 1984.

Day, Heather F. *Protestant Theological Education in America: A Bibliography.* ATLA Bibliography Series, 15. *Metuchen: Scarecrow Press, 1985.*

Dearborn, Tim A. "Editorial: Theology at the Front Line." *Themelieos* Vol.17, no.1 (1990): 3-5.

_____. "Preparing Leaders for the Future Education...Today." Seattle: Seattle Association for Theological Education, 1995a. Photocopied.

_____. "Preparing New Leaders for the Church of the Future." *Transformation* Vol.12, no.4 (1995b): 7-12.

Eadie, John. *The John Eadie Greek Test Commentaries.* Vol. 2. *Ephesians.* ed. W. Young. Grand Rapids: Baker, 1979.

Ferris, Robert W. *Renewal in Theological Education: Strategies for Change.* Wheaton: Wheaton College, 1990.

Farley, Edward. *Theologia: The Fragmentation and Unity of Theological Education.* Philadelphia: Fortress Press, 1983.

_____. "Toward Theological Understanding: An Interview with Edward Farley." *The Christian Century* 115, no.4 (F 4-11 1998): 113-115.

Fletcher, John C. *The Futures of Protestant Seminaries.* Washington, D.C. : Alban Institute, 1983.

Ford, Leroy. *A Curriculum Design Manual for Theological Education.* Nashville: Broadman Press, 1991.

Fraser, James W. *Schooling The Preachers: The Development of Protestant Theological Education in the United States,1740-1875.* Maryland: University Press of America, 1988.

Gambrell, Mary Latimer. *Ministerial Training in Eighteenth - Century New England.* New York: Columbia University, 1967

Gangel, Kenneth O. "Delivering Theological Education That Works." *Theological Education* 34 (Autumn 1997): 1-9

_____. and Howard G. Hendricks. eds. *The Christian Educator's Handbook on Teaching.* Grand Rapids: Baker, 1988.

_____., and James C. Wilhoit, eds. *The Christian Educator's Handbook on Adult Education.* Grand Rapids: Baker, 1993.

_____., and James C. Wilhoit, eds. *The Christian Educator's Handbook on Spiritual Formation.* Grand Rapids: Baker, 1994.

Gingrich, F. Wilbur, and Arnot, William F. *A Greek-English Lexicon of the New Testament.* Chicago: The University of

Chicago Press, 1957.

Goodwin, Thomas. *An Exposition of Ephesians, Chapter 1 to 2:10.* Vol. I. city unknown: Sovereign Grace Book Club, 1958.

Hammer, Richard R. *Pastor, Church, and Law.* Springfield: Gospel Publishing House, 1983.

Harris, R. Laird, Gleason L. Archer, Jr., and Bruce K. Waltke, eds. *Theological Workbook of the Old Testament.* Vol. 1. Chicago: Moody, 1980.

Hart, D.G., and R. Albert Mohler,Jr. *Theological Education in the Evangelical Tradition.* Grand Rapids: Baker Books, 1996

Hastings, D. D., J. *Dictionary of the Apostolic Church.* Vol. 1. New York: Scribner's, 1951.

Hatch, Edwin. *The Influence of Greek Ideas on Christianity.* New York: Harper & Brothers, 1957.

Hayes, Richard B. *The Moral Vision of the New Testament.* San Francisco: Harper San Francisco, 1996.

Hendrikson, William. *New Testament Commentary: Exposition on Ephesians.* Grand Rapids: Baker, 1967.

Hodge, Charles. *Systematic Theology.* Vol. 1. Grand Rapids: Eerdmans, 1952.

Holmes, Arthur F. *The Idea of a Christian College.* Grand Rapids: Eerdmans, 1987.

Hough, Jr. Joseph C., and John B. Cobb, Jr. *Christian Identity and Theological Education.* Chico: Scholars, 1985.

Hybels, Bill. "Reading Your Gauges." *Leadership* (Spring 1991) 32-38.

Jaeger, Werner. *Early Christianity and Greek Paideia.* New York: Oxford University, 1961.

Johns, Cheryl Bridges. *Pentecostal Formation.* Sheffield: Sheffield Academic Press, 1993.

Joy, Charles R. *Harper's Topical Concordance.* New York: Harper and Row, n. d.

Kelsey, David H. *To Understand God Truly: What's Theological About a Theological School.* Louisville: Westminster John Knox Press, 1992.

_____. *Between Athens and Berlin: The Theological Education Debate.* Grand Rapids: Eerdmans, 1993.

_____. and Barbara G. Wheeler. "The ATS Basic Issues Research Project: Thinking about Theological Education." *Theological Education* 30, no. 2 (Spring 1994) 71-80.

_____. "Reflections on a Discussion of Theological Education as Character Formation." *Theological Education* 34, no. 4 (Autumn 1988) 62-75.

Kinsler, F. Ross. *The Extension Movement in Theological Education.* South Pasadena: William Carey Library, n.d.

Kitagawa, Joseph Mitsuo. *Religious Studies, Theological Studies and the University-Divinity School.* Scholar Press, 1992.

Kraft, Charles H. *Christianity with Power.* Ann Arbor: Servant, 1989.

Land, Stephen J. *Pentecostal Spirituality.* Sheffield: Sheffield Academic Press, 2001.

Leith, John H. *Crisis in the Church: The Plight of Theological Education.* Louisville: Westminster John Knox Press, 1997.

Lincoln, Andrew T. *Word Biblical Commentary.* Vol. 42. *Ephesians.* Dallas: Word Books, 1990.

Long, Jimmy. *Generating Hope: A Strategy for Reaching The Post-Modern Generation.* Downers Grove: InterVarsity, 1997.

Lorant, Stefan. *Pittsburgh: The Story of an American City.* Pittsburgh: Esselmont Books, 1999.

Malphurs, Aubrey. *Values Driven Leadership: Discovering and Developing Your Core Values for Ministry.* Grand Rapids: Baker, 1996.

Mancuso, Anthony. *How to Form a Nonprofit Corporation in all 50 States.* Berkley: Nolo Press, 1997.

McKenzie, S. J., John L. *Dictionary of the Bible.* New York: MacMillian, 1965.

Messer, David E. *Calling Church & Seminary into the 21st Century.* Nashville:Abingdon Press, 1995.

Monser, Harold E. *Topical Index and Digest of the Bible.* Grand Rapids: Baker, 1983.

Moore, Allen J., ed. *Religious Education as Social Transformation.* Birmingham: Religious Education Press, 1989.

Neuhaus, Richard John, ed. *Theological Education and Moral Formation.* Grand Rapids. Eerdmans, 1992.

Niebuhr, H. Richard. *Christ and Culture.* New York: Harper & Row, 1956.

Newbegin, Leslie. *Foolishness to the Greeks.* Grand Rapids: Eerdmans, 1986.

Otis, Jr., George. *The Twilight Labyrinth.* Grand Rapids: Chosen, 1997.

_____. *Informed Intercession*. Ventura: Renew, 1999.

Pacala, Leon. *The Role of ATS in Theological Education 1980-1990*. Atlanta: Scholars Press, 1998.

Pratney, Winkie. *Revival*. Springdale: Whitaker House, 1983.

Review of Graduate Theological *Education in the Pacific Northwest: Review, Post-Publication Summaries and Reactions*. Vancouver: The M.J. Murdock Charitable Trust, Sept. 1994. Photocopied.

Robertson, Pat. *The Secret Kingdom*. Nashville: Thomas Nelson, 1982.

Rouch, Mark. *Competent Ministry: A Guide to Effective Continuing Education*. Nashville: Abingdon, 1974.

Ryken, Leyland, James C. Wilhoit, and Tremper Loggman III. *Dictionary of Biblical Imagery*. Downers Grove: InterVarsity, 1998.

Schreiter, Robert J. "The ATS Globalization and Theological Education Project: Contextualization from a World Perspective." *Theological Education* 30, no. 2 (Spring 1994) 81-88.

Schwarz, Christian. *Natural Church Development*. Carol Stream: ChurchSmart, 1996.

Seymour, Jack L., and Donald E. Miller. *Contemporary Approaches to Christian Education*. Nashville: Abingdon Press, 1982.

Solivan, Samuel. *The Spirit, Pathos, and Liberation*. Sheffield: Sheffield Academic Press, 1998.

Stackhouse, Max L. "Contextualization and Theological Education." *Theological Education* 23, no. 1 (1986): 67-84.

_____. *Apologia: Contextualization, Globalization, and*

Mission in Theological Education. Grand Rapids: Eerdmans, 1988.

Strauss, Anselm, and Juliet Corbin. *Basics of Qualitative Research - Techniques and Procedures for Developing Grounded Theory.* Thousand Oaks: Sage, 1998.

Sweet, Leonard. *Aqua Church.* Loveland: Group, 1999a.

_____. *Soul Tsunami.* Grand Rapids: Zondervan, 1999b.

Synan, Vinson, ed. *Aspects of Pentecostal-Charismatic Origins.* Plainfield: Logos International, 1975.

_____. "Century of the Holy Spirit." Virginia Beach: Spirit Link, Regent University, Fall 2000, 1.

_____. *The Century of the Holy Spirit.* Nashville: Thomas Nelson, 2001.

Thayer, Joseph Henry. *A Greek-English Lexicon of the New Testament.* Grand Rapids: Zondervan, 1978.

Trench, Richard C. *Synonyms of the New Testament.* Grand Rapids: Eerdmans, 1980.

Unger, Merrill F. *Unger's Bible Dictionary.* Chicago: Moddy Press, 1966.

Walther, James Arthur, ed. *Ever A Frontier: The Bicentennial History of the Pittsburgh Theological Seminary.* Grand Rapids: Eerdmans, 1994.

Westcott, Brooke Foss. *St. Paul's Epistle to the Ephesians.* Grand Rapids: Eerdmans, 1950.

Whang, Henry Kyuil. "A New Model for Theological Education in Korean Church Context: Centered on the Curriculum for Minor Schools." Ph. D. diss., Regent University, 1999.

Wheeler, Barbara G. "The Faculty Members of the Future: How are They Being Shaped." *The Christian Century* 115, no.4 (F 4-11 1998): 106-109; 111.

_____., and Edward Farley, ed. *Shifting Boundaries: Contextual Approaches to the Structure of Theological Education.* Lousiville: Westminister John Knox, 1991.

Williams, J. Rodman. *Renewal Theology.* Grand Rapids: Zondervan, 1996.

Wink, Walter. *The Powers that Be.* New York: Galilee Doubleday, 1998.

Wiersbe, Warren W. and David W. Wiersbe. *Making Sense of the Ministry.* 2d ed. Grand Rapids: Baker, 1989.

Witmer, S.A. *The Bible College Story: Education with Dimensions.* New York: Channel Press, 1962.

Wood, Charles M. "Theological Inquiry and Theological Education." *Theological Education* XXI, no. 2 (1985): 73-93.

Wuest, Kenneth S. *Wuest's Word Studies From the Greek New Testament.* Vol. 2, First Peter. Grand Rapids: Eerdmans, 1980.

Zoba, Wendy Murray. *Generation 2K: What Parents Need to Know About the Millennials.* Downers Grove: InterVarsity, 1999.

APPENDIX A

An Excursis on Spiritual Formation

The Hebrew and Greek Scriptures are a rich source of information on spiritual formation. They produce a rich understanding of the linkage between knowledge, wisdom, and understanding and the basic element for acquiring them – the fear of the Lord. They are strongly linked to the concept of spiritual formation as well. This linkage lies at the heart of what spiritual formation is – it begins with the fear of the Lord and is imparted by a sapietial knowing of God Himself. This sapiential knowing is at the heart of spiritual formation and should be the goal of theological training if it to be based on a biblical foundation.

The Fear of the Lord

There are several key passages in the Scriptures that address the basis of spiritual and moral formation. The Scriptures, as the plenary-verbal inspired Word of God, are the ultimate source of truth and the standard by which truth is to be judged. (2 Tm. 3:15, 16; 2 Pet. 1:20-21). They must therefore be the source of and basis for understanding spiritual and moral formation as well. There are many verses that address the topic of spiritual and moral formation that can be found in the Book of Proverbs. The first is found in Prv. 1:7 which in the English text states:

> The **fear of the LORD** is the **beginning of knowledge**; Fools despise **wisdom** and **instruction**. (Prv. 1:7, NAS, *emphasis mine*)

The Hebrew text reads:

יְרְאַת יְהֹוָה רֵאשִׁית דָּעַת חָכְמָה וּמוּסָר
אֱוִילִים בָּזוּ׃

This text contains several key phrases that establish some basic principles for spiritual and moral formation. They include:

- The "fear of the Lord" (יְרְאַת יְהֹוָה) - The fear of the Lord is represented here to be a basic requirement to gain knowledge, wisdom, and understanding. It is presented as a prerequisite for acquiring this type of knowledge. The phrase "יְהֹוָה יְרְאַת" implies a reverence or awe for God in the context of relationship with Him, and is therefore impossible to gain outside this context.

- Knowledge, Wisdom, and Instruction *begin* (רֵאשִׁית) with a relationship with God. Outside this relationship with Him, it is therefore impossible to acquire them.

Knowledge and Wisdom

The word for knowledge is דָּעַת which comes from the Hebrew root word "יָדַע" which is translated "knowledge" and "know" in the Scriptures. The root occurs a total of 944 times in the Old Testament, expressing various shades of knowing. Some of its uses are (Harris, Archer, and Waltke 1980, 366):

- God's knowledge of man (Gen. 18:19; Deut. 34:10).
- Man's knowledge (Isa. 1:3).
- Knowing of skills (Gen. 25:27; 2 Chr. 8:18; 1 Sam. 16:16).
- Learning in general (Isa. 29:11).
- To have acquaintance or relationship (Gen. 29:5; Exod. 1:8).
- To have sexual intercourse with (Gen. 4:1; 19:8).
- To know secular matters (Deut. 13:3, 7).

The form used in Prv. 1:7, דַעַת, refers in particular to a personal, experimental kind of the knowledge. The verse reveals that all knowledge begins in the context of the knowledge of God. A true grasp of knowledge in its proper context and meaning is therefore only available to those who know God as their redeemer and creator (Banks 1999, 74).

This is also true for wisdom (חָכְמָה) and understanding (מוּסָר). The word for wisdom in the Hebrew text covers the whole gamut of human experience. It can mean (Harris, Archer, and Waltke 1980, 282):

- Technical skill or craftsmanship (Exod. 28:3; 31:3, 6).
- Execution of strategy or tactics well (Isa. 10:13).
- Administration (Deut. 34:9; 2 Sam. 14:20).
- Leadership (Isa. 11:2).
- The exercise of prudence (Ps. 37:30; Prv. 10:31).

One striking feature of wisdom is that it is personified in the Scriptures in Proverbs 8, strongly connecting it with the nature and character of God. As such, it is no wonder that an understanding of wisdom is only possible in the context of a relationship with God and based on the truth in His inspired Word.

Spiritual Instruction *(paideia)*

In Prv. 1:7, instruction (מוּסָר) is also mentioned. It translates as "instruction" and is from the Hebrew root "יָסַר" which conveys the meanings of discipline, chastening, and instruction. The Septuagint text gives another key to the understanding of this word when it uses the Greek word "παιδείαν" (*paideian*) to translate מוּסָר. The use of παιδείαν in the Septuagint to translate the Hebrew word מוּסָר ties in the concept of *paideia* with the New Testament in 1 Tm. 3:16 where "instruction" (παιδείαν) is also mentioned (Harris, Archer, and Waltke 1980, 386-387).

One of the outcomes of the Scripture's inspiration is its ability to be used to "train" (παιδείαν) people as 2 Tm. 3:16 notes. The word *paideia* denotes instruction that relates to the whole training and education of a child, including the cultivation of the mind, moral life, commands, admonitions, and cultivation of the soul. Linking the Scripture in 2 Tm. 3:16 and Prv. 1:7 together, an intimate and experiential knowledge of God is necessary for instruction, or as it would be called, "training," to take place properly. This training is dynamically linked with knowing and doing. Training in the context of relationship with God produces proper spiritual and moral formation (*paideia*). Training outside this context is either warped or impossible. A sapiential knowledge of God is indispensable for true instruction and formation to take place.

APPENDIX B

An Excursis on the Church

The target of theological training is the Church. Theological training is meant to produce leaders that are properly formed for their ministry in the Church and the end result of this training will determine the course of the Church's future. A biblical understanding of the word "church" as it is found in the Scriptures is vital to the whole process of theological education. The Hebrew and Greek texts are pregnant with clues that help to shed light on what is meant by the word "church" in the Scriptures. This appendix contains a more detailed examination of the word "church" from an exegetical standpoint.

The word church in English is related to the Scotch word *kirk* and the German word *kirche*. Both are related to the Late Greek word *kyriakon*, which is translated "the Lord's house" (McKenzie 1965, 133). The Classical Greek word used in the Scriptures that is translated church is the word *ekklesia* (ἐκκλησία) and means "an assembly of citizens in a city for legislative or deliberative purposes." The word was used to describe a gathering of citizens with full rights in legal assembly to conduct the business of a city or state (McKenzie 1965, 133-134). Trench points out that ἐκκλησία in *Koine* Greek is "a summons or a call" (1980, 2). The construction of the word ἐκκλησία reflects this definition in that the root word is *kaleo* (καλέω) which means "to call." It was used as early as the fifth century B. C. for the "call" (καλέω) sent "out" (ἐκ) for the citizens of a city to assemble. This was the assembly of the *polis* (πολις) that Athens was known to have as many as thirty to forty times per year. In these meetings, the citizens gathered to confer about changes in the law. The assembly conveyed the idea of a special or privileged group with full rights as citizens who gather for this purpose. Later, the root word *ekkaleo* (ἐκκαλέω) was used to mean a summons to an army to assemble. It is no wonder that the writers of the New Testament and the translators of the Septuagint used ἐκκλησία in the majority of the cases for the word church or assembly (Brown 1975, 291-305).

Less frequently than ἐκκλησία, the words *paneguris* (πανήγυρις) and *sunagoge* (συναγωγή) are also used in the New Testament to mean an assembly. The word συναγωγή is used only ten times, such as in Jas. 2:2, and is root word for the English word synagogue used for a Jewish assembly. Most of the occurrences of συναγωγή in the New Testament refer to the Jewish place of assembly for worship. The use of this word in Jas. 2:2 could be a reflection of how ancient this book is, reflecting tha,t at the time of its writing, the Christians may have still meeting mingled with Jews in the synagogue, rather than separately in a church. It refers more to a "collection of things brought together" whether people or objects. It is also used of festive assemblies and for the place of assembly called the synagogue (Brown 1975, 292). The word πανήγυρις has a more distinctly religious feel to it. Whereas ἐκκλησία has the meaning many times of a general assembly, πανήγυρις has the meaning of a solemn assembly for the purposes of festal rejoicing, such as in the Septuagint Greek translation of Ezek. 46:11, Hos. 2:11 and 9:5, Isa. 65:10 and in the New Testament in Heb. 7:23 and Rev. 21:4 - the Marriage Assembly of the Lamb (Trench 1980, 6-7).

In the Old Testament, the Hebrew root *qahal* (קהל) is used exclusively for the word "assembly." In the Septuagint, the word קהל is translated ἐκκλησία more than one-hundred times. The word קהל is used to mean an assembly or the act of assembling (Deut. 9:10; 10:4), often with a religious element to the assembly. It is also used to describe a great multitude (Gen. 28:3; 35:11). Also in the Old Testament is the Hebrew root word *edah* (עדה) which refers to a community as a whole or the assembly of a community. The word עדה is always translated into Greek as συναγωγή, and occurs frequently in the Pentateuch (Brown 1975, 292-294). Hastings makes the following conclusions about the words that occur in the Old and New Testaments that are translated into the English words church or assembly (1951, 204):

- קהל (*qahal*) - is the Hebrew word for "assembly" and is most often translated by the Greek word ἐκκλησία in the Greek Septuagint, inferring meaning on the New Testament usage of the word.

- עדה (*edah*) is the Hebrew word for "congregation" and is always translated by the Greek word συναγωγή in the Greek Septuagint, being consistently used to describe a congregation of believers.

- ἐκκλησία (*ekklesia*) is the Greek word for "church" or "assembly" in the New Testament, sometimes having a secular meaning (Acts 19:32,39,41) but most often a spiritual meaning.

- συναγωγή (*sunagoge*) is the Greek word used in the New Testament, always referring to an assembly of religious believers.

- πανήγυρις (*paneguris*) is the Greek word used in the New Testament to denote a solemn or religious gathering, such as the Marriage Gathering of the Lamb (Heb. 12:23, Rev. 21:4).

The way that these words are used in their context in the Old and New Testaments yields data to accomplish the interpretation of the meaning of church.

The word ἐκκλησία is used two times in the Synoptic Gospels by Jesus in Mt. 16:18 and 18:18. In Mt. 16:18, Jesus refers to the Body of Christ as "My church" which would be built upon the revelation that Jesus is the "Christ, the Son of the Living God" (Mt. 16:16). It is clear in this instance that Jesus Himself formed the group as "My church," and with the reference in Mt. 18:18, commands it to continue and overcome conflict.

Luke does not use the root ἐκκλησία in his Gospel, but uses it twenty-three times in the Book of Acts. He always uses it of the local church assembly, usually the church in Jerusalem, exhibiting it as a prototype church (McKenzie 1965, 134). He uses ἐκκλησία to describe the whole redeemed fellowship of believers (Acts 5:11; 9:31; 12:1) as well as a specific local assembly of believers (Acts 8:1,3). Luke also adopts it in a secular usage to describe assemblies of people (Acts 19:32,39,41) and Israel as an assembly of witnesses (Acts 7:38).

Paul uses ἐκκλησία sixty-five times to describe the local church in a fixed geographical location and also to describe the worldwide church, with the later usage especially occurring in the books of Ephesians and Colossians (McKenzie 1965, 135). Paul's language is especially picturesque when he describes the church as the "Body of Christ," picturing all things to be in subjection to Him (Eph. 1:22,23). He intends to make His manifest wisdom known through the church (Eph. 3:10), through which He will actualize His complete authority over all created things (Col. 1:18). He also poetically compares His relationship to the church as that of a bride and her bridegroom, He being the husband of the church and the church His bride (Eph. 5:22-32). Paul speaks of the church as a group of believers in a certain geographical location (1 Thes. 1:1; 2 Thes. 1:1) as well as an assembly for the purpose of public worship (1 Cor. 11:18; 14:19,35).

The New Testament themes that involve the church are merely carry-overs from Old Testament themes. The root word ἐκκλησία is used in the Septuagint for the root word קָהַל in Deut. 4:10; 23:2;

and 31:30 to denote the assembly of God's people. This language carries over to the references in Acts 7:38 and Heb. 2:12 to the same Old Testament assemblies.

The mention of the church in the Scriptures is not limited to a specific use of the literal Hebrew, Greek, and English words mentioned. Throughout the Scriptures, the vivid imagery used as a metaphor to describe the church is important to understand the meaning of what the church is. Some of the most common metaphors assembled by the author directly from the Scriptures and from other sources include metaphors of a house (1 Tm. 3:15, Mt. 10:35), family (Rom. 8:14, Eph. 3:15), nature (1 Pet. 5:2,3; Jn. 10:16), and body (1 Cor. 6:5; Col. 1:24) (Joy n. d., 139-150; Monser 1983, 105).

The concept of community is also central to understanding what is meant by church. God created man in His image (Gen. 1:26). The very idea of community is embodied in the concept of the Trinity, and finds its expression in the living Body of Christ. God did not make man to be alone, but rather to dwell with others as one (Gen. 2:18; 20-24). The idea of two or more becoming one in fellowship expresses the very nature of the Godhead, and defines the biblical concept of community. This concept lies at the heart of what the church is - a community of believers in fellowship with one another who become one through the sharing of this fellowship.

The idea of community begins with the Trinity, the three persons of the Godhead who have been in community as "One God" from all eternity. This community was expressed in the first man and woman and expanded first to their family, and then to the tribes that made up Israel. Banks points out that the concept of community began with the household (Deut. 8:10 18), centered later around the tabernacle of God (Exod. 26; 36:4) and was celebrated at the various festival gatherings in Israel (Exod. 23:14-19). Jesus deepened this concept by applying it to the family of God (Mk. 3:31-41). It was the Holy Spirit Himself who baptized believers into one community that the New Testament refers to in Acts 2:42-48 (Banks 1998, 24-28).

The original Christian community was home-based, meeting in people's homes rather than a building called the church. The idea of a building being called "the church" is foreign to the Scriptures and confuses the Scriptural identity of the church (Acts 2:43; 16:40;

20:8; Rom. 16:1,5; 1 Cor. 16:19; Col 4:15; Phlm. 2). The bond in these homes was similar to that of a family. The fellowship that knit the community together is described by the Greek word *koinonia* (κοινωνία). It implies an intimacy and bond of unity. This bond of κοινωνία is what fuses a local body of believers together, which is an expression of the non-local Body of Christ that exists as a universal body of believers in various places and at various times (Col. 1:18; 24). This κοινωνία creates unity in the midst of tremendous diversity (Rom. 3:22-23) and is the physical representation of Christ's love (Banks and Banks 1998, 146). In the context of this κοινωνία, the church worshipped, ate meals together, prayed, gave testimony, operated in the gifts of the Spirit, learned the ways of God, and matured in Christ (Banks 1980, 32). All of these things took place in the highly relationship oriented context of community that is a defining mark of the church.

The exegetical consideration just outlined, as well as the metaphors and the church's connection to the concept of community, yield several conclusions important to theological training. These include:

- The Church is a living organism: The Church is clearly a living organism rather than an organization. The metaphors that describe the church are pregnant with life and demand that the church be thought of in this way.

- The Church is universal: The Body of Christ exists in all parts of the world and crosses the ages of time from the Old Testament through the New Testament to the present day. Local assemblies are merely an expression of this universal assembly. The Church is composed of multicultural and multiethnic peoples but it transcends these differences in the unity of fellowship.

- The Church is local: The local gathering of believers is an expression of the universal church of Christ and meets in a certain geographical location, which in the New Testament times was in homes.

- The Church is a community: Fellowship or κοινωνία is the

key glue that holds the church together in unity. This fellowship is an extension of the Old Testament concept of community that existed from the creation of mankind, was developed in the people of Israel, and expanded upon in Jesus Christ and His church. It is this sense of community that was the context for teaching, maturity, and growth in Christ. The bond of community also fused diverse peoples together across racial and cultural divides. As such, community or *koinonia* should be a central value in theological training.

• The Church is one with Christ: The metaphors involving Christ's body, His bride, and His sons show the intimacy that He has with the church. The church is God's family by birth.

• The Church is Precious to God: The metaphors of His beloved and His bride show the precious nature of the church to Her Savior.

All of these principles that are defined by the Scriptures lead to a proper understanding of what the church is. The church is a community of witnesses to the good news of Christ and His resurrection, empowered by the Holy Spirit to share that good news, and to live in obedience to Christ as its Lord and Savior (Hays 1996, 194-196).

APPENDIX C

An Excursis on the Minister and Ministry

If the target of theological training is the minister and his or her function will be ministry, then understanding these two words are central to the whole process. Renewal distinctives dictate a different concept of who the minister is and what ministry is all about. The renewal concept of "minister" and "ministry" are solidly backed up by the exegesis of several key New Testament passages. This appendix contains an excursis that examines these two important words and provides a foundation for their meaning and expression in renewal-oriented theological training.

Exegesis of Ephesians 4:11-16

The text for Eph. 4:11-16 deserves special exegetical attention since it is a pivotal text for defining what the ministry is and who the ministers are. In English (NAS) it reads:

11 And He gave some *as* apostles, and some *as* prophets, and some *as* evangelists, and some *as* pastors and teachers,

12 for the equipping of the saints for the work of service, to the building up of the Body of Christ;

13 until we all attain to the unity of the faith, and of the knowledge of the Son of God, to a mature man, to the measure of the stature which belongs to the fullness of Christ.

14 As a result, we are no longer to be children, tossed here and there by waves and carried about by every wind of doctrine, by the trickery of men, by craftiness in deceitful scheming;

15 but speaking the truth in love, we are to grow up in all *aspects* into Him who is the head, *even* Christ,

16 from whom the whole body, being fitted and held together by what every joint supplies, according to the proper working of each individual part, causes the growth of the body for the building up of itself in love.

In the Greek New Testament, Eph. 4:11-16 reads:

11 καὶ αὐτὸς ἔδωκεν τοὺς μὲν ἀποστόλους, τοὺς δὲ προφήτας, τοὺς δὲ εὐαγγελιστάς, τοὺς δὲ ποιμένας καὶ διδασκάλους,

12 πρὸς τὸν καταρτισμὸν τῶν ἁγίων εἰς ἔργον διακονίας, εἰς οἰκοδομὴν τοῦ σώματος τοῦ Χριστοῦ,

13 μέχρι καταντήσωμεν οἱ πάντες εἰς τὴν ἑνότητα τῆς πίστεως καὶ τῆς ἐπιγνώσεως τοῦ υἱοῦ τοῦ θεοῦ, εἰς ἄνδρα τέλειον, εἰς μέτρον ἡλικίας τοῦ πληρώματος τοῦ Χριστοῦ,

14 ἵνα μηκέτι ὦμεν νήπιοι, κλυδωνιζόμενοι καὶ περιφερόμενοι παντὶ ἀνέμῳ τῆς διδασκαλίας ἐν τῇ κυβείᾳ τῶν ἀνθρώπων, ἐν πανουργίᾳ πρὸς

τὴν μεθοδείαν τῆς πλάνης,
15 ἀληθεύοντες δὲ ἐν ἀγάπῃ αὐξήσωμεν εἰς αὐτὸν
τὰ πάντα, ὅς ἐστιν ἡ κεφαλή, Χριστός,
16 ἐξ οὗ πᾶν τὸ σῶμα συναρμολογούμενον καὶ
συμβιβαζόμενον διὰ πάσης ἀφῆς τῆς ἐπιχορηγίας
κατ᾽ ἐνέργειαν ἐν μέτρῳ ἑνὸς ἑκάστου μέρους
τὴν αὔξησιν τοῦ σώματος ποιεῖται εἰς οἰκοδομὴν
ἑαυτοῦ ἐν ἀγάπῃ.

This passage specifies the role of the ministry offices that are listed in Eph. 4:11. These offices are a fulfillment of Ps. 68:18, quoted by Paul in Eph. 4:8, where it says that Christ gave "gifts to men." These ministry offices are Christ's gifts to men after His ascension. Together they express Christ in His fullness, who was Apostle, Prophet, Evangelist, Pastor, and Teacher. Now these gifts are distributed among men, and together function to minister as He did while on the earth, to His people. There is debate about which of these offices is still in existence today, but no debate that in apostolic times, these ministry offices were Christ's gift to the Church after He ascended.

The precise function of the five-fold ministry, or at least those offices that can be agreed to be still valid for today, such as pastor-teacher, is disputed. This point is the heart of the most significant teaching that Ephesians holds for who the ministers are, and also the heart of the problematic nature of this pericope. The problematic nature of the text can be resolved by use of the Greek text, although fine scholars such as Calvin would have disagreed.

The problem centers upon what is the function of the five-fold ministry. One philosophy of ministry, enforced by the King James Version, asserts that the function of the five-fold ministry is to actually *do* the work of the ministry described in Eph. 4:12 (KJV):

11 And he gave some, apostles; and some, prophets; and some, evangelists; and some, pastors and teachers;
12 For the perfecting of the saints, for the work of the ministry, for the edifying of the Body of Christ:

With the comma inserted after "saints" in verse twelve for the King James Version, the clause seems to indicate that the five-fold ministry is responsible for the perfecting of the saints *and* for the work of the ministry, *and* for the edifying of the Body of Christ. Calvin echoed this in his comments on this passage, with his emphasis on the role of the ministry offices (1975, 373-375). He felt that it was the role of the pastor-teacher to preach the word, and thereby perfect the saints, do the work of the ministry, and edify the body. In his thirteenth sermon on Ephesians 4, he states that the "preaching of the Word brings the body to soundness," thereby assigning the "work of the ministry" to the pastor-teacher. There is no emphasis on "equipping the saints *for* the work of the ministry," and the interpretation of Calvin seems to agree with the translation found later in the King James Version and its insertion of commas to divide the clauses in this passage.

There is also a revival in some Reformed circles today of an emphasis on preaching, and preaching alone to accomplish the work of the ministry, such as evangelism and ministry to the body. This model pictures ordained clergy as the ones appointed by this passage to do all the work of the ministry, because they are called to do so. This paradigm is existent in many church settings today, and limits the potential of the Body of Christ to effectively distribute the work of ministry to those who are not called to one of the five-fold ministry. This paradigm is perpetuated in many realms of theological training as a result of a faulty exegesis of this passage of Scripture.

The problematic nature of this passage, and the above assertions, are adequately resolved by examining the grammar of the passage, specifically as it relates to the prepositions that set off the clauses contained therein. The construction of these clauses in Eph. 4:12 are:

πρὸς τὸν καταρτισμὸν τῶν ἁγίων
εἰς ἔργον διακονίας,
εἰς οἰκοδομὴν τοῦ σώματος τοῦ Χριστοῦ,

The change in prepositions from **πρὸς** to **εἰς** is no accident. While it is proper to translate **πρὸς** τὸν καταρτισμὸν as "for the perfecting of the saints," the proper translation of **εἰς** ἔργον διακονίας should be "into" the work of the ministry and **εἰς** οἰκοδομὴν τοῦ σώματος τοῦ Χριστου "into" the building up of the Body of Christ. Because of the switch to εἰς, the meaning should be understood to direct the responsibility of the καταρ τισμὸν (equipping or perfecting) toward the saints, not the professionals holding ministry office in Eph. 4:11. The meaning of the passage in light of the switch to εἰς, would be that the five-fold ministry offices have the responsibility to equip the saints *for* (into – εἰς) the work of the ministry, and *for* (into – εἰς) the edifying of the Body of Christ. The job of the fivefold ministry becomes one of equipping the saints to serve in ministry, according to their God given gifts, under the authority of the pastor-teacher (Westcott 1950, 62). Thus, every believer is charged with a personal service toward God, rather than just those that fill the five-fold ministry offices. Westcott holds that the change of the prepositions clearly shows that the clauses are not coordinate, and that the purposes described in Eph. 4:12 are the spiritual ministry of all the saints, not just those ordained to ministry (1950, 62,63). As Abbott points out, Chysostom treated the clauses as coordinate (1964, 119), so the idea of a professional clergy doing the "work of the ministry" is not new. The εἰς construction seems to negate this fact, however.

The word καταρτισμὸν, is found nowhere else in the Scriptures. It refers to the perfecting or equipping of the saints, in harmonious power for the work of the ministry to the Body of Christ. Gingrich relates the word to medical literature, where it is used to describe the setting of a bone (1957, 419). It refers to the ultimate purpose of the five-fold ministry, and is the central verb in the passage. The results of the καταρτισμὸν of the saints can be found in Eph. 4:13,14, and because this passage stresses the ministry of the parts to the welfare of the whole (Westcott 1950 63; Abbott 1964 119,120).

The work of service (εἰς ἔργον διακονίας) and the building up of the Body of Christ (εἰς οἰκοδομὴν τοῦ σώματος τοῦ Χριστου), further define the function of the ministry. Again, whether one believes that the ministry is to be accomplished by equipped saints, or by the ministry offices, these phrases describe the function and purpose of the ministry. The word used for service (διακονίας), is the same used for deacon in other parts of the Scriptures. It links leadership with service, and makes the case for "servant-leadership" in the Body of Christ. The word building up (οἰκοδομὴν), literally pictures the raising of a building, and shows what a practical role that the ministry described in Eph. 4:12 is to play.

Jesus Christ is Apostle, Prophet, Evangelist, Pastor, and Teacher. When He ascended, He gave gifts to men, which are the spoils of His victory

(Eph. 4:8-10). These gifts are the ministry offices listed in Eph. 4:11, and the men that He appoints to occupy these offices. This dispute, based on the grammar of Eph.4:12 may not be resolvable with exegesis, but whoever does the work of ministry, the ministry's function should be to "perfect, serve, and build up" the Body of Christ (Eph. 4:12). Enough grammatical evidence does exist to persuade the authors that this text intends that the five-fold ministry to equip the saints for the work of the ministry so that the intended results in Eph. 4:12-16 can be realized. Because of this interpretation, theological training with renewal distinctives must be designed to train individuals for full time ministry and lay-leaders in the church. The focus must be to train these emerging leaders, without emphasis on a clergy-laity division, with the skills necessary to in turn equip the saints for the work of the ministry.

The Minister and Renewal Distincives

The exegesis of Eph. 4:11-13 states that it is job of the five-fold ministry to prepare the saints for the work of the ministry. With this understanding, those in the Body of Christ with one of the five-fold ministry gifts are ministers in the sense that they are called to equip the saints for the work of the ministry. The saints are also ministers in the sense of doing the work of the ministry. With this in mind, what do the Scriptures have to say about the minister?

There are six distinct Greek root words that translate roughly into the English word "minister" (Hastings 1951, 37-39):

- διακον (ος ια είν) - The *diakon* root that is recognizable in the English word deacon translates most often minister such as in the word *diakonos* (διάκονος).

- δουλ (ος εία ευειν) - The *doul* root translates most often slave or bondslave such as in word *doulos* (δοῦλος).

- ὑπηρετ (ης εσια είν) - The *huperet* root translates dignified service.

- λατρ (ις εία ευειν) - The *latr* root translates most often spiritual service.

- λευτουργ (ος ια εῖν) - The *leutourg* root that is recognizable in the English words liturgy is a Classical Greek word that referred public service.

- θεραπ (ουν ευειν εία) The *therap* root is translated serve and often used as the word for servant.

In the Old Testament, the Hebrew root שָׁרֵת (*shareth*) is used extensively to describe service or ministry (Unger 1966, 746,747).

The word διάκονος is used in Matthew, Mark, John, and the Pauline Epistles, but is found nowhere else in the New Testament. It is used in

Mt. 20:25-27 to describe Christ as a servant leader and to set the standard for what leadership is from a Kingdom perspective (NAS - *emphasis mine*):

> 25 But Jesus called them to Himself and said, "You know that the rulers of the Gentiles lord it over them, and *their* great men exercise authority over them.
> 26 "It is not this way among you, but whoever wishes to become great among you shall be your **servant**,
> 27 and whoever wishes to be first among you shall be your **slave**;
> 28 just as the Son of Man did not come to be served, but to **serve**, and to give His life a ransom for many."

Constructions of the word διάκονος are used in this verse for serve and servant. It is also interesting that the word "slave" is the word δοῦλος or bondservant. This Scripture sets the standard for what service is in the Body of Christ and how that service should be administered.

Another key passage in the New Testament that deals with service is the Pauline passage in Phil. 2:5-10 that speaks of the essence of service that was illustrated in the incarnation (NAS -

emphasis mine):

> 5 Have this attitude in yourselves which was also in Christ Jesus,
> 6 who, although He existed in the form of God, did not regard equality with God a thing to be grasped,
> 7 but emptied Himself, taking the form of a **bond-servant**, *and* being made in the likeness of men.
> 8 Being found in appearance as a man, He humbled Himself by becoming obedient to the point of death, even death on a cross.
> 9 For this reason also, God highly exalted Him, and bestowed on Him the name which is above every name,
> 10 so that at the name of Jesus EVERY KNEE WILL BOW, of those who are in heaven and on earth and under the earth,

In this passage, Jesus is portrayed as the Son of God who left the trappings of Heaven behind in order to become the God-man through the incarnation and to die to redeem mankind on the cross. He does so by a selfless act of service, as He takes upon Himself the form of a bond-servant (μορφὴν δούλου - the very essence of what a bondslave is). The passage embodies the essence of what ministry is - the laying aside of what are one's rights in order to serve others. Such imagery is also portrayed at the Last Supper in John 13, when Jesus lays aside His garments to wash the feet of His disciples. This was done to model the principle that if one is to be a leader, he or she must be a servant.

In the Old Testament, Isaiah prophesied that all believers would become priests in service to God (NAS):

> But you will be called the priests of the LORD; You will be spoken of *as* ministers of our God. You will eat the wealth of nations, And in their riches you will boast (Isa. 61:6)

This has been fulfilled in the New Testament as believers are now called in 1 Pet 2:5; 9 a royal priesthood:

...you also, as living stones, are being built up as a spiritual house for a holy priesthood, to offer up spiritual sacrifices acceptable to God through Jesus Christ (1 Pet. 2:5)

But you are A CHOSEN RACE, A royal PRIESTHOOD, A HOLY NATION, A PEOPLE FOR God's OWN POSSESSION, so that you may proclaim the excellencies of Him who has called you out of darkness into His marvelous light; (1 Pet. 2:9)

This passage concurs with the truth that the ministry belongs now to believers who should properly be considered ministers as they exercise the gift-mix that God has placed within them. All are now able to offer up sacrifices of service to God (Rom. 5:2; 12:1; Eph. 3:12; Heb. 10:22). Kenneth Gangel points out that it is tradition and not the Scriptures that has made a distinction between laity (λαος) and clergy. This false division is a function of ecclesiastical paradigms that were directly confronted through the Reformation. Both the laity and the clergy are ministers and one in the fellowship of Christ's community, the church, and are equally able to offer Him the sacrifice of worship and service (Gangel and Wilhoit 1993, 41-44).

There is much imagery in Scriptures that deals with what the nature of ministry is for the minister. Some of the more notable metaphors include (Ryken, Wilhoit, and Loggman 1998, 558):

- Construction of the Body (1 Cor. 3:10-15).
- Constructing a building (1 Cor. 3:10-15).
- Planting and nurturing (1 Cor. 3:5-9).
- Shepherding a flock (Jn. 10; 21:15-18).
- Functioning in priesthood (1 Pet. 2:5,9).

The Scriptures also contain descriptions of the nature of ministry as it relates to a minister. Some of these descriptions include (Monser 1983, 425; Ryken 1998, 558):

- Investing one's self in love and devotion to God (Deut. 6:5).
- Glorifying God (1 Cor. 12:5).
- Self-sacrifice (2 Tm. 1:8).

- Advancing God's Kingdom (2 Cor. 3:7).
- Being a witness to the nature of God and His message (Acts 1:8).

- Using one's God-given gifts to bring God profit (Mt. 25:14-30; Lk. 19:11-27; Rom 12:6-8).

- Being a servant (Jn. 13:1-15; Phil 2:5-10).

- Being ambassadors (1 Cor. 5:20; Eph 6:2).

- Preachers of His Word (Rom. 10:14; 1 Tm 2:7).

- Sowers of His Word (Ps. 126:6; Mt. 13:3-8).

These images and metaphors for ministry describe the essence of what New Testament service or ministry is. They, therefore, describe the role of the minister, which the Scriptures show to be every New Testament believer.

APPENDIX D

The Covergence Model Curriculum

The Dimension of Curriculum in theological training is so highly variable that it is impossible to propose one standard model for the varied settings in which it could be delivered. The Convergence Model does propose certain standards for curriculum development that are outlined in Chapter 11, but none of these proposals necessarily dictate the composition of the curriculum or the classes that actualize its intent.

This appendix contains a proposed curriculum that should be viewed as one of the possibilities that emerge from The Convergence Model. It must be remembered that the Dimension of Curriculum is only one of the five dimensions that must be considered when designing or revamping theological education. With eight factors to consider for each dimension, the actual classes offered are only one-fortieth of the picture. The curriculum dimension resides in dynamic equilibrium with all of the other dimensions and their factors.

The Convergence Model Curriculum

The Convergence Model and its purpose, mission, core values and methodologies result in a general shape to renewal-oriented training. The following is one possible outcome of its application for a specific context of training. There are ten core classes that make up the 100 level certificate curriculum, which serve as the first-year classes for the Associates and Bachelors Degrees. There are notes attached to some of the classes that indicate the possibility of testing out by formal examination. Delivery style is noted for some as well, which will be conducted in a retreat setting or in a modular manner over a one-week period. They include:

101	Understanding the Old Testament	(Can test out)
102	Understanding the New Testament	(Can test out)
103	The Life of Christ	
104	Romans	
105	Parables and Metaphors	
106	Interpreting the Scriptures	
107	Discovering Your Gifts	(Retreat Setting)
108	Discovering Your Destiny	(Retreat Setting)
109	Experiencing God	
110	Need-oriented Evangelism	(Modular)

The second-year 200 Level classes are the second year of both the Associates degree and the Bachelors Degree programs. This year delivers all of the required general studies core classes for the Associates Degree (eighteen semester hours) and half of the general studies core for the Bachelors degree. Some of the notes translate the intent of the general studies core class as it would be called in a liberal arts setting. There is a three semester hour associates degree integration project designed into the work to ensure application of what has been learned to this point. Other notes once again relate to the deliver style in which the class will be offered:

201	Spirit, Soul, and Body	(Psychology)	
202	Western Civilizations I	(History)	(Video - Self)
203	Western Civilizations II	(History)	(Video - Self)
204	History of Christian Thought	(Philosophy)	

205	Cultural Contextualization	(Anthropology)
206	Contemporary Cultures and Issues	(Sociology)
207	The Spirit Himself	
208	Servant Leadership	
209	Spiritual Disciplines	
210	Christian Marriage and Family	
220	Associates Level Integration Project	

The third and fourth year classes are Bachelors Degree classes designed to be seamless into the various masters degree programs. The remaining eighteen semester hours of general studies core classes build on the eighteen semester hours offered at the 200-level. Nine semester hours are left open at the 300 level and three semester hours at the 400 level (twelve semester hours total) to allow for portfolio and life experience credit to be awarded according to accreditation standards and the Council on Adult and Experiential Learning (CAEL) (i.e. TRACS 2000, 43, 44). These credits are also open for classes that may be based on conferences with special guest experts who may come to the school and teach in an area of their expertise. Classes offered at the 300 level and 400 level include:

300 Level Classes:

301	Theological Writing and Research	(Grammar and Comp)
302	Dynamic Communication	(Speech)
303	God's Design in Nature	(Biology)
304	Math and Stewardship	(Math)
305	Music and the Church	(Music)
306	Art and the Church	(Art)
307	Mentoring	
308	Elective/Conference/Portfolio	
309	Elective/Conference/Portfolio	
310	Elective/Conference/Portfolio	

400 Level Classes:

401	Introduction to Biblical Hebrew
402	Introduction to Biblical Greek
403	Renewal Theology
404	Natural Church Development
405	Small Group Dynamics
406	Team Ministry
407	Effective Teaching and Preaching
408	Holistic Spiritual Life
409	Cross Cultural Evangelism (Missions Trip)
410	Portfolio/Conference/Elective
420	Bachelors Integrative Project

These classes will be delivered in a semester format with three semesters offered each school year, ten weeks per semester. The development of course descriptions, the triad of knowing, doing, and being goals, relation to values, and outcomes for each class, and syllabi must be developed and yet be developed and are outside the scope of this dissertation.

Graduate and Post-graduate Programs

The graduate and post-graduate programs at the school are offered to further facilitate the spiritual and moral formation of individuals in the interdenominational renewal community. The graduate and post-graduate curriculum is designed to address development for work in specific areas of ministry and is seamless with the bachelors level work. The masters level programs at the school include:

- Masters Degree in Ministry (Two-year, 72 semester hours)
- Masters Degree in Urban Ministry (One-year, 36 semester hours)
- Masters Degree in Missiology (One-year, 36 semester hours)

The entrance requirements consist of a Bachelors level degree for any of these programs. The applicant needs to be an active participation in ministry in a local church as well as sponsorship by a local church pastor with his recommendation for study. All of the masters level classes share a common core of eighteen semester hours, consisting of four leadership classes and two class equivalent masters level integration project semester hours:

501	Leadership: Vision and Planning
502	Leadership: Organization and Administration
503	Leadership: Team Ministry Strategies
504	Leadership: Personal Life and Health
505	Masters level Integration Project
506	Masters level Integration Project

The Masters in Ministry emphasizes the practical skills necessary for pastoral ministry and is designed on the basis of a two-year equivalent offering of seventy-two semester hours that expand on the classes offered in the bachelors level studies. These classes are designed to be seamless with the terminal degree offered in ministry, which is the school's only doctoral level program, the Doctor of Ministry program. The seventy-two semester hour program consists of the eighteen specified core semester hours at the masters level and eighteen other three semester hour classes which include:

510	Sermon and Teaching Preparation
511	Methods of Preaching and Teaching
512	Leading Evangelism in the Local Church
513	Leading Cross-cultural Missions in the Local Church
514	Leading Renewal in the Local Church
515	Pastoral Counseling
516	Small Group Theory
517	Small Group Dynamics
518	Church Planting Strategies
519	Church Ethics and Law
520	Church Finance and Administration
521	Apologetics - Defending the Faith
522	History of the Church
523	Renewal Church History

524	Systematic Renewal Theology
525	Pneumatics I - Spirit-filled Life and Living
526	Pneumatics II - Fruit, Gifts, and Power of the Spirit
527	Pastor's Holistic Life and Health

These courses are highly focused offerings that all have an experimental (doing) emphasis involved with much practical work for the class.

The Masters Degree in Urban Ministry is designed for ministers who are called to work in an urban context. This degree is important for the renewal community because it reflects the trend toward urbanization on a global basis. This program is a one-year equivalency and shares the same eighteen core leadership and masters level integration project requirements with the other masters level programs. These are also six other classes offered in specialized urban ministry, which consist of:

540	Dimensions of Urban Ministry
541	Theology of the City and Critical Issues
542	Understanding and Transforming Urban Systems
543	Urban Sociology and Witness
544	Strategic Planning and Grant Writing for Urban Ministry
545	Teaching and Preaching in an Urban Setting

The ministry integration project for this masters program will involve an applied ministry project in an urban local church setting. All instructors for this program will have the academic, experience, and urban ministry context consistent with the classes taught.

The Masters Degree in Missiology is designed for ministers who are called to work in cross-cultural missions. This degree is important for the renewal community because of a lack of missions training mechanisms available. This program is a one-year equivalency and shares the same eighteen core leadership and masters level integration project requirements with the other masters level program. These are also six other classes offered in specialized missiology areas, which consist of:

560	World Christian Perspectives
561	Principle of Contextualization (Cultural Anthropology)
562	World Religions and Belief Systems
563	Christianity with Power
564	Field Practicum (In-residence missons work)
565	Field Practicum (In-residence missions work)

The participants in this program will do the eighteen core semester hours and the four specialized courses while in residence at the school. The field practicum work will be done in partnership with an experienced missionary on site in the mission field and involve missions and linguistic studies under the mentoring of the mission-ary professional. Church recommendation, sponsorship, and demonstrated sources of support are prerequisites for this program.

The Doctor of Ministry Program within The Convergence Model consists of a sixty semester hour program offered as a termi-nal degree for ministers with substantial experience in ministry or a related field. The program is designed to be seamless with the Masters Degree in Ministry. The Doctor of Ministry Degree consists of four distinct parts that include Foundational Studies (eight classes, twenty-four semester hours), Core Studies (five classes, fifteen semester hours), Elective Studies (five classes, fifteen semester hours), and Dissertation (two class equivalent, six semester hours). Individuals entering the Doctor of Ministry program must have been in active ministry for at least seven years prior to the start of classes. They must have a masters degree in a field related to ministry of at least forty-eight semester hours. If the candidate enters with a Master of Divinity degree or its equivalent consisting of at least seventy-two semester hours of study, the Foundational Studies courses in the Doctor of Ministry program are waved, reducing the program to thirty-six semester hours of core, elective, and dissertation credits. The curriculum for the Doctor of Ministry Program at the school consists of:

Foundational Studies: (24 semester hours)

701	Conflict Resolution Strategies
702	Discipleship Strategies

703	Master Equipping Strategies
704	Church Systems Design
705	Elective, Transfer, C.P.E.
706	Elective, Transfer, C.P.E.
707	Ministry Portfolio/Elective/Transfer
708	Ministry Portfolio/Elective/Transfer

Core Studies: (15 semester hours)

711	Doctor of Ministry Orientation
712	Transformational Leadership
713	Dynamics of Mentoring
714	Minister's Health and Life
715	Renewal and Transformation in Ministry

Elective Studies: (15 semester hours) - Will vary each year with guest experts, transfer credits from other Doctor of Ministry programs, or with approved C.P.E. credits transferred in from outside the program (C.P.E. is "Clinical Pastoral Education;" TBA is "to be announced").

721	TBA - Guest, Transfer, C.P.E.
722	TBA - Guest, Transfer, C.P.E.
723	TBA - Guest, Transfer, C.P.E.
724	TBA - Guest, Transfer, C.P.E.
725	TBA - Guest, Transfer, C.P.E.

Dissertation (6 semester hours)

731	Doctoral Dissertation
732	Doctoral Dissertation

As with the certificate and undergraduate programs, these masters and doctoral level classes will be delivered in a three semester per year format with each semester composed of ten weeks. The Doctor of Ministry classes will be offered in modular format for one week, with a Foundational Studies, Core Studies, and Elective Studies class offered each semester. The development of course descriptions, the triad of knowing, doing, and being goals, relation to values, and outcomes for each class, and syllabi are yet be developed and are outside the scope of this dissertation. This curriculum and the courses that result form the core of The Convergence Model as a part of the continuum of five dimensions of theological education.

APPENDIX E

Glossary of Terms

The following glossary lists common terms used in this book that deal with theological education. It is meant to give a precise definition to some of the terms that have been defined to describe the nuances of The Convergence Model as well as to provide a source to define terms for dialogue.

GLOSSARY OF TERMS

Andragogy. Education or training aimed at adult learners. In theological training, andragogy is a teaching method adapted especially for adult learners.

Athens. A reference to theological training that is characterized by formation of the being of an individual (i.e. their mind, character, morality). It is called "Athens" because it is the model used by the Greeks in the "cultivation of the soul" of individual citizens through exposure to knowledge and experiences that would allow for the shaping of the soul, or *paideia.*

Berlin. A reference to theological training that is characterized by intellectual pursuit or reason in order to shape the individual. It is called "Berlin" because this model for theological training, emphasizing reason and scientific process for knowing what is true, was popularized at the University of Berlin in 1810 when theology was included in the curriculum as a professional course of study at the university.

Calvinism. A set of beliefs and assumptions made popular by John Calvin, that includes beliefs such as election (God chooses who will be saved) and double predestination (God chooses who will go to heaven and hell and a determinism in everyday life).

Chaordic. The ability to be flexible and adaptable, even when change is on the edge of chaos.

Church. For the purposes of this dissertation, the Church will be understood to be the beloved and universal community of God's children, who, being knit together in the bonds of fellowship and love, is the visible expression of the Body of Christ. It has a decidedly organic and biotic definition, properly balancing the concept of organism and organization.

Clergy/laity paradigm. A concept common in the church that creates a distinction between clergy and laity in the church as to their rank, privilege, or position of service. Clergy is taken from the word "*kleros*", which means "reader", since the ministers were often the only ones who could "read" the Scriptures. Laity is from "*laos*" which means "common". The ability to read and further education produced a distinction between clergy and laity in the church, allowing a professional clergy to develop who handled the work of the ministry in the church. This paradigm is a product of tradition, whereas the Scriptures draw no such distinction.

Cognitive. Pertaining to factual knowledge. Knowledge that is abstract, existing in the realm of abstract fact.

Confessional. A religious body or group that holds strictly to a set of beliefs, which are often written in the form of a "confession" or statement of belief.

Contextualization. Adaptation to the specific needs of an individual, group, context, culture, or society in order to make something meaningful to them in a way that they can better understand. Contextualization has been adopted as one of The Pittsburgh Model's core methodologies, ensuring that the model is adapted to meet the specific needs of the interdenominational renewal community in Pittsburgh through the model's design.

Core Shaping Factors. A set of five core values and three core methodologies used in the design of The Convergence Model.

The Convergence Model. The model for interdenominational renewal-oriented theological training developed for Pittsburgh in this dissertation project.

Developmental Model. A means of delivering theological training that emphasizes a balanced blend of cognitive, experimental, and affective (feeling or emotion-based) knowledge leading to spiritual and moral formation, and characterized by active student participation in the process.

Distinctive. A belief or assumption that is the mark of a religious group, often serving as a defining mark of that group. This often develops into a set of differences that collectively represent a group's core assumptions, known as its "distinctives."

Dynamic Communication. The ability of theological training to adapt its styles and modes of communication to communicate with its recipients. This enables the training to best communicate in a relevant and effective manner. It is one of the core methodologies used in the design of The Convergence Model.

Ekklesia. A Greek word use in the New Testament, often translated "Church." The word has been borrowed in this dissertation to capture the picture of the Church as a biotic-organic thing as opposed to an organization. It represents the holistic conception of the Church as the living Body of Christ, which is the context for and recipient of the product of theological training. This concept calls for partnership between the local church and institutions offering theological training. *Ekklesia* represents one of the core values used in designing The Pittsburgh Model.

Enculturate. To expose someone to the set of beliefs and assumptions of a particular group or culture with the hope of transmitting them to that individual.

Enlightenment Christianity. Assumptions and beliefs held by Christian individuals or groups that originate in enlightenment thought, such as a bias against the supernatural, materialistic or mechanistic worldview, and emphasis on rationalism and reason over revelation.

Five-fold Ministry. The five ministry offices in the church described in Eph 4:11-13: apostle, prophet, evangelist, pastor, and teacher. All of these offices are said to be designed to "equip the saints for the work of the ministry" and should be addressed in the process of theological training.

Formation. Growth and maturity of the spiritual and moral component of an individual. This process cannot be directly caused, but is the result of knowledge being applied to real-life situations and reflection, producing growth and maturity in the inner person. It is ultimately the work of the Holy Spirit.

Global Factors. Factors in theological training that affect the design of training delivery such as its target (full time and lay ministers), accreditation and degree orientation.

Incarnational. Referring to the paradigm of the incarnation in the Scriptures as represented in the act of divinity taking on human flesh. This refers to the physical demonstration of a spiritual truth by an individual who lives out that truth, giving the truth "flesh" through his or her actions.

Integral worldview. A term use to describe the postmodern worldview that is often a syncretistic mix of many philosophies, cultures, and religions that are knit together to form reality and truth.

Interdenominational. A religious body or group that welcomes fellowship and association with all Christian denominations and does not align with any particular one of them. This is opposed to denominational groups that are aligned with a central denomination and many times restrict fellowship to those in their particular denomination.

Koinonia. A Greek word often translated "fellowship." It is used in this dissertation to represent the symbiotic relationship between the believer and other believers as well as the believer, the Church, and theological training. It is the biblical healing community of the church and its fellowship that is the context of theological training. This same kind of fellowship must be present in theological training and is a core value that was used to design the Convergence Model.

Materialism. A philosophy that emphasizes material creation as what is real and valuable, many times to the exclusion of the supernatural.

Minister. For the purposes of this dissertation, ministers are considered to be anyone who is serving God according to his or her individual gift-mix and according to the destiny-mix God has designed for them. There is no distinction drawn between clergy and laity, since this is not a biblical concept, but originates in church tradition.

Paideia. A term borrowed from the Greek used to mean the spiritual and moral formation of a person's being. The term was originally used in Greek culture to describe the process by which individuals were exposed to knowledge and experiences that would "cultivate the soul" and form them to be good citizens in society. For the purposes of The Convergence Model, it refers to the process of theological training that forms a person's mind, moral life, attitudes, and character. It is the central purpose of The Convergence Model, which emphasizes the spiritual and moral formation of individuals to do the work of ministry, and is one of the models' core values.

Paradigm. A set of rules and regulations (written and unwritten) that does two things: (1) it establishes or defines boundaries; and (2) it tells you how to behave inside the boundaries in order to be successful (Barker 1992, 32).

Paradigm enhancer. A person who attempts to improve an existing paradigm by incremental adjustment of its rules and regulations.

Paradigm paralysis. The inability to conceive of new ways of doing things because of familiarity with the rules or regulations of an existing paradigm. This is sometimes referred to as inability to "think outside the box."

Paradigm pioneer. An individual who begins to implement a new paradigm with a group or organization, experiencing the first success in applying a new paradigm to solve a problem.

Paradigm shift. A change in paradigms for problem solving within an organization or group.

Pedagogy. Education or training aimed at children.

Pericope. A particular passage of Scripture, often under investigation or the focus of study.

Pneumatics. A term that is constructed from the Greek root *pneuma*, often translated "spirit." It captures the beliefs, assumptions, essence, and distinctives of Spirit-filled living embodied in the renewal movement, such as the Baptism in the Holy Spirit, sapiential relationship with God in the new birth, and the operation of the gifts and fruit of the Holy Spirit. Since its target is the interdenominational renewal community, it is one of the core shaping values used to design The Convergence Model.

Postmodern Worldview. The set of beliefs and assumptions that represent the core distinctives of the generation that followed the baby-boomer generation, generally born after 1960. Some of these distinctives include relativism, renewed interest in the supernatural, emphasis on community and virtual reality with multiple possibilities and validity. Postmodern thought is not always linear, but rather mosaic in nature and embraces chaotic change.

Praxis. Referring to practical application of knowledge. A core methodology for the Pittsburgh Model that emphasizes the application of knowledge from theological training to an individual's context of ministry in real life situations.

Rationalism. A philosophy that asserts that reason is the best way to determine what is true, often to the exclusion of faith and the supernatural.

Renewal. Associated with the Pentecostal, Charismatic, or neo-Pentecostal (third wave) movements. A term used to encapsulate these movements and their distinctives.

Renewal-oriented. Associated with the renewal movements or their distinctives. A term used to locate a religious body or group in reference to the renewal.

Romanticism. A philosophy that emphasizes the goodness of man and his ability to improve the world by his own human efforts.

Sapiential. Personally experienced or real to an individual. Something that individuals have personally experienced for themselves and therefore have direct knowledge of by their own experience.

Septuagint. The Greek translation of the Hebrew Old Testament.

Specific Factors. Factors that influence the delivery of theological training such as beliefs, assumptions, *ethos*, and delivery methods.

Syncretism. The tendency to combine different philosophies and beliefs to form a personal set of beliefs, borrowed from a variety of sources.

Theologia. A sapiential and personal divine self-disclosure through God's inspired Word. This is one of the core values used to design The Convergence Model, which emphasizes the verbal plenary inspiration of the Scriptures and their use and place in providing personal revelation that leads to formation of an individual's being.

Theological Training. The process of spiritual and moral formation that takes place in the fellowship with God and the Christian community by which cognitive knowledge and wisdom are given and their direct application facilitated, resulting in increasing discipleship and maturity.

Verbal plenary inspiration. The belief that the Scriptures are inspired (directly given) by God to man on a word by word (verbal) and entire (plenary) basis. This view of biblical inspiration does not imply a dictation theory (God literally controls the mind and pen of the author) for the origin of the Scripture. Rather, this term implies that God led the individual writer to use the words that were used in the Scriptures and saw to it that all of the Scriptures in the Bible are intended to be there.

Wissenschaftliche. A thought process common to German theological education that focuses on rigorous scientific method and research to uncover truth. It was championed at the University of Berlin in 1810 when theology was added to the university's subjects of study.

Worldview. The set of beliefs and assumptions held by an individual or group that have been shaped by culture, society, religion, and tradition.

Printed in the United States
95217LV00002B/5/A

9 781591 602866